INTERPRETING THE
PENTATEUCH

HANDBOOKS FOR OLD TESTAMENT EXEGESIS

INTERPRETING THE
PENTATEUCH

An Exegetical Handbook

Peter T. Vogt

David M. Howard Jr.
SERIES EDITOR

Kregel
Academic & Professional

Interpreting the Pentateuch: An Exegetical Handbook

© 2009 by Peter T. Vogt

Published by Kregel Publications, a division of Kregel, Inc., P.O. Box 2607, Grand Rapids, MI 49501.

The Hebrew font used in this book is New JerusalemU and is available from www.linguistsoftware.com/lgku.htm, +1-425-775-1130.

ISBN 978-0-8254-2762-6

Printed in the United States of America

09 10 11 12 13 / 5 4 3 2 1

To my children,
Joshua, Charis, and Eliana,
in the hope that each of you will learn to love and serve
the God revealed in the pages of the Torah
with all your heart,
with all your soul,
and with all your strength.

CONTENTS IN BRIEF

CONTENTS

SERIES PREFACE

AN APPRECIATION FOR THE RICH diversity of literary genres in Scripture is one of the positive features of evangelical scholarship in recent decades. No longer are the same principles or methods of interpretation applied across the board to every text without regard for differences in genre. Such an approach can, however, lead to confusion, misunderstanding, and even wrong interpretations or applications. Careful attention to differences in genre is, then, a critical component of a correct understanding of God's Word.

The Handbooks for Old Testament Exegesis series (HOTE) offers students basic skills for exegeting and proclaiming the different genres of the Old Testament. Because there is no one-size-fits-all approach to interpreting Scripture, this series features six volumes covering the major genres in the Old Testament: narrative, law, poetry, wisdom, prophecy, and apocalyptic. The volumes are written by seasoned scholar-teachers who possess extensive knowledge of their disciplines, lucid writing abilities, and the conviction that the church and the world today desperately need to hear the message of the Old Testament. These handbooks are designed to serve a twofold purpose: to present the reader with a better understanding (principles) of the different Old Testament genres, and provide strategies (methods) for preaching and teaching these genres.

These volumes are primarily intended to serve as textbooks for graduate-level exegesis courses that assume a basic knowledge of Hebrew.

There is no substitute for encountering God's Word in its original languages, even as we acknowledge the limitations of language in plumbing the depths of who God is. However, the series is also accessible to those without a working knowledge of Hebrew, in that an English translation is always given whenever Hebrew is used. Thus, seminary-trained pastors for whom Hebrew is a distant memory, upper-level college students, and even well-motivated laypeople should all find this series useful.

Each volume is built around the same six-chapter structure as follows:

1. The Nature of the Genres
2. Viewing the Whole
3. Preparing for Interpretation
4. Interpreting the Text
5. Proclaiming the Text
6. Putting It All Together

Authors are given freedom in how they title these six chapters and in how best to approach the material in each. But the familiar pattern in every volume will serve students well, allowing them to move easily from one volume to another to locate specific information. The first chapter in each handbook introduces the genre(s) covered in the volume. The second chapter covers the purpose, message, and primary themes in the individual books and canonical sections under consideration. The third chapter includes such diverse matters as historical and cultural backgrounds, critical questions, textual matters, and a brief annotated bibliography of helpful works. The fourth chapter sets forth guidelines for interpreting texts of the genre(s) under consideration. The fifth chapter details strategies for proclaiming such texts. The final chapter gives one or two hands-on examples of how to move through different stages of the interpretive process, in order to demonstrate how the principles discussed previously work out in practice. Each volume also includes a glossary of specialized terms.

The Scriptures themselves remind us in many ways about the importance of proper interpretation of God's words. Paul encouraged Timothy to "do your best to present yourself to God as one approved by him, a worker who has no need to be ashamed, rightly explaining the word of truth" (2 Tim. 2:15 NRSV). In an earlier day, Ezra the scribe, along with the Levites, taught God's Word to the postexilic community: "So they read from the book, from the law of God, with interpretation. They gave the sense, so that the people understood the reading" (Neh. 8:8 NRSV). It is my prayer, and that of the authors and publisher, that these handbooks will help a new generation of God's people to do the same.

    Soli Deo Gloria.

—DAVID M. HOWARD JR.
Series Editor

PREFACE

THIS BOOK FOCUSES ON two of my greatest academic passions: the Torah and hermeneutics. The books of the Pentateuch have been my primary focus throughout my academic career, beginning with my doctoral dissertation on Deuteronomy.[1] I have never tired of wrestling with the texts of the Pentateuch, and I find myself consistently drawn closer to God as a result of encountering him in all his grace and glory in these books.

At the same time, I have become more and more aware of the tremendous need for proper interpretation of biblical texts in the church today. I delight in teaching hermeneutics to students at Bethel Seminary; it is a blessing to be a part of God's work in transforming men and women called to leadership in the church and to help them better interpret the Word of God. Proper understanding of interpretation is necessary for, and invariably results in, greater love for God and motivation to serve him.

This book combines these two passions, in that it focuses on the proper interpretation of the Pentateuch. The two main genres found in the Pentateuch, law and narrative, often are daunting to readers. The legal material can seem dense and foreboding; many readers have little or no

---

1. A revised version of that work has been published as *Deuteronomic Theology and the Significance of Torah: A Reappraisal* (Winona Lake, IN: Eisenbrauns, 2006).

idea how to interpret the text, and they struggle with the issue of the relevance of the legal material for a contemporary audience. With narrative, readers often feel on surer ground, but the theological depth and literary artistry of the pentateuchal narratives are often overlooked. The aim of this book is to provide a more solid footing for understanding the texts of the Pentateuch and the ways in which they are relevant for contemporary audiences. Through this work, I hope to build confidence on the part of interpreters, so that they will feel better able to understand, teach, and preach from the Old Testament in whatever ministry context they serve. This, I pray, will strengthen the people of God through exposure to the whole counsel of God and encourage them to more deeply love and more effectively serve the great God revealed in the Torah.

I have attempted to reduce the amount of overly technical language in the book. Technical terms that are used and may be unfamiliar are marked in boldface type at their first occurrence in each chapter. A glossary at the end of the book provides a brief explanation of these terms.

Bible versions used are indicated with quotations of the biblical text. Where no translation is indicated, the translation is my own.

I would like to thank a number of people for their assistance in completing this book. Though the shortcomings that remain are my own, these people in a variety of ways helped eliminate many errors.

First, I thank David Howard, the series editor and my colleague and friend, for giving me this opportunity. His encouragement and patience have been a blessing to me. In addition, his careful editing of the work has strengthened it immeasurably. I am grateful, too, to Jim Weaver and all the staff at Kregel for their patience as the completion of this work was delayed significantly following the death of my mother. They exhibited tremendous professionalism and Christian compassion toward me at every turn.

I am also grateful to the many students to whom I have taught hermeneutics and the course Genesis–Ruth at Bethel Seminary. The questions, insights, and enthusiasm of my students have contributed greatly to this work. In addition, students in the various upper-level elective courses I taught on Genesis and Deuteronomy helped shape my thinking in profound ways as we wrestled with those books together. Teaching assistants Sara Wilhelm and Jan Hamilton provided invaluable assistance in countless ways. Both served cheerfully and capably no matter what tasks I asked them to do.

The broader community at Bethel Seminary also has provided intellectual stimulation, camaraderie, and spiritual nurture throughout this project. While I appreciate the contributions of everyone at Bethel, whether intentional or unwitting, I would like to especially thank colleagues Jeannine Brown and Thorsten Moritz. In different ways, they each helped shape my thinking on important aspects of hermeneutics, the New Testament, and biblical theology. I believe this work is stronger because of their influence.

Finally, I want to thank my wife, Cami. She has been a bedrock of support throughout this project and an unfailing encouragement to me at every turn. She provided ideas and insights to this project that made it stronger, while at the same time magnificently living out her calling of full-time ministry to our three children. I could not ask for a more wonderful עֵזֶר and friend than she.

Soli Deo Gloria.

ABBREVIATIONS

AB	Anchor Bible
ANET	*Ancient Near Eastern Texts Relating to the Old Testament.* Edited by James B. Pritchard. 3rd ed. Princeton: Princeton University Press, 1969.
AOTC	Apollos Old Testament Commentary
BDB	Brown, F., S. R. Driver, and C. A. Briggs. *A Hebrew and English Lexicon of the Old Testament.* Oxford: Oxford University Press, 1907.
BHS	*Biblia Hebraica Stuttgartensia.* Edited by K. Elliger and W. Rudolph. Stuttgart, 1983.
CAD	*The Assyrian Dictionary of the Oriental Institute of the University of Chicago.* Edited by Ignace J. Gelb, et. al. Chicago: Oriental Institute, 1956–.
CBQ	*Catholic Biblical Quarterly*
COS	*The Context of Scripture.* Edited by William W. Hallo. 3 vols. Leiden: Brill, 1997–2000.
DOTP	*Dictionary of the Old Testament: Pentateuch.* Edited by T. Desmond Alexander and David W. Baker. Downers Grove, IL: InterVarsity Press, 2003.
DSS	Dead Sea Scrolls

EncJud	*Encyclopaedia Judaica*. Edited by Michael Berenbaum and Fred Skolnik. 2nd ed. Detroit: Macmillan, 2007.
ESV	English Standard Version
HOTE	Handbooks for Old Testament Exegesis
JETS	*Journal of the Evangelical Theological Society*
JPS	Jewish Publication Society
JSOTSup	Journal for the Study of the Old Testament: Supplement Series
KJV	King James Version
KTU	*Die keilalphabetischen Texte aus Ugarit*. Edited by M. Dietrich, O. Loretz, and J. Sanmartín. AOAT 24/1. Neukirchen-Vluyn, 1976.
LXX	Septuagint
MS/MSS	manuscript/manuscripts
MT	Masoretic Text
NAC	New American Commentary
NET	The NET Bible
NIBC	New International Biblical Commentary
NICOT	New International Commentary on the Old Testament
NIDOTTE	*New International Dictionary of Old Testament Theology and Exegesis*. Edited by W. A. VanGemeren. 5 vols. Grand Rapids: Zondervan, 1997.
NIGTC	New International Greek Testament Commentary
NIV	New International Version
NLT	New Living Translation
NRSV	New Revised Standard Version
NSBT	New Studies in Biblical Theology
OTL	Old Testament Library
OTS	Old Testament Studies
SBLAB	Society of Biblical Literature Academia Biblica
SP	Samaritan Pentateuch
TNIV	Today's New International Version
TOTC	Tyndale Old Testament Commentaries
WBC	Word Biblical Commentary

1

THE GENRES OF THE PENTATEUCH

ALTHOUGH THE PENTATEUCH IN its current form is a unified work,[1] it nevertheless consists of a variety of literary types or **genres**. Knowing how to interpret the various genres will ensure more accurate interpretation of the various texts.

Within the Pentateuch there is law, **narrative**, poetry, songs, lists, and genealogies. Each of these genres will be interpreted in slightly different ways as a result of the communicative function of the genre. We will focus in this book on the two most prominent genres in the Pentateuch, law and narrative.[2]

Law is one of the most important genres found in the Pentateuch,

---

1. The unity of the Pentateuch (or lack thereof) has been a topic of great interest to many Old Testament scholars for the better part of the last 150 years. For a discussion of the issue, see chapter 4, as well as the more detailed discussions in John H. Sailhamer, *The Pentateuch as Narrative* (Grand Rapids: Zondervan, 1992), 1–25. See also T. Desmond Alexander, *From Paradise to the Promised Land: An Introduction to the Pentateuch*, 2nd ed. (Carlisle: Paternoster, 2002), 3–83; and R. N. Whybray, *The Making of the Pentateuch: A Methodological Study*, JSOTSup 53 (Sheffield: JSOT Press, 1987).
2. A brief introduction to narrative is provided here. A more complete discussion is found in chapter 1 of Robert Chisholm, *Interpreting the Historical Books: An Exegetical Handbook*, HOTE (Grand Rapids: Kregel, 2006).

but it is also one of the most misunderstood. Too often, readers of the Pentateuch approach law with notions of the purpose, function, and nature of law that reflect a contemporary worldview rather than the ancient worldview held by the original author and audience of the Pentateuch. Proper interpretation of any text must start with understanding the text as intended by the original author. In the case of the legal texts of the Pentateuch, that necessarily means understanding how the original author and audience understood the idea of law.

The Nature of Torah

The Hebrew word usually translated "law" is תּוֹרָה. The connotations of the word, however, are much broader than the English word *law*. Whereas the word *law* is usually associated with the actions of legislatures and brings to mind ideas of crime, punishment, courtrooms, and litigation, the Hebrew word תּוֹרָה is better translated "instruction" or "teaching." It is theologically centered instruction in the things necessary for the people of God to know in order to live a righteous life.[3]

Moreover, the word תּוֹרָה is used to refer to the Pentateuch as a whole, including the narrative sections. The entire Old Testament is sometimes referred to as the Tanak, which is an acronym formed from the Hebrew names of the sections of the book: תּוֹרָה (*Torah*, "instruction, law"), נְבִיאִים (*Nebi'im*, "prophets"), and כְּתוּבִים (*Kethubim*, "writings"). For the ancient Israelite, then, the whole of the Pentateuch—including the narrative sections—was considered "instruction" or "teaching" as to how to live a life pleasing to God.

Most surprising, perhaps, from a contemporary point of view, is the fact that this instruction or guidance in how to live life includes the legal material. Readers of the Old Testament often erroneously believe that the laws of the Pentateuch were meant to be understood in a legalistic sense and that strict adherence to the letter of the law was the way in which the ancient Israelite earned salvation. But if this is so, what are we to make of texts like Psalm 119:111–12?

> Your testimonies are my heritage forever,
> for they are the joy of my heart.

---

3. For more on this idea of Torah as instruction, see Peter Enns, "Law of God," *NIDOTTE*, 4:893–900.

I incline my heart to perform your statutes forever,
to the end. (ESV)

The terms עֵדוּת ("testimony") and חֹק ("statute") are used elsewhere
to refer to specific stipulations in the legal material of the Pentateuch, as,
for example, in Deuteronomy 4:45: "These are the testimonies (עֵדֹת), the
statutes (חֻקִּים), and the rules, which Moses spoke to the people of Israel"
(ESV). The psalmist is expressing his[4] delight in the terms of the law. The
psalmist elsewhere says, "How I delight in your commands! How I love
them!" (Ps. 119:47 NLT) and "Truly, I love your commands more than
gold, even the finest gold" (Ps. 119:127 NLT). Clearly, to the author of
Psalm 119, at least, <u>the law and its stipulations were not an onerous burden
but a delightful gift from God</u>.[5] This suggests that the common understanding of the law as a heavy legalistic burden should be reconsidered.

We should note, further, that the Torah was given to the people of
Israel *after* they had been delivered from Egypt. Indeed, in the initial encounter between **Yahweh** and Moses, God says,

> "I am the God of your father, the God of Abraham, the God of
> Isaac and the God of Jacob." . . . The LORD said, "I have indeed
> seen the misery of my people in Egypt. I have heard them crying
> out because of their slave drivers, and I am concerned about their
> suffering. So I have come down to rescue them from the hand of
> the Egyptians. . . . And now the cry of the Israelites has reached
> me, and I have seen the way the Egyptians are oppressing them.
> So now, go. I am sending you to Pharaoh to bring my people the
> Israelites out of Egypt." (Exod. 3:6–10 TNIV)

In expressing his intention to deliver the people of Israel from the
bondage of slavery, God repeatedly refers to them as *his* people, which
suggests that a relationship already exists between Yahweh and the people
of Israel. This is seen further when God notes the relationship between
the Israelites he intends to save and the patriarchal ancestors, whom he

---

4. Since all available cultural and textual evidence suggests that the authors of biblical books were
men, I will refer to them as such.
5. This attitude is not limited to the author of Psalm 119 or the book of Psalms more generally, of
course. Rather, this same perspective permeates the whole of the Old Testament. See, for example,
Leviticus 18:5; Deuteronomy 4:1, 40; 6:1–3; 28:1–14; Psalm 1:1–3.

had chosen for relationship with him. What is most telling at this point is that God's decision to save the Israelites from Egypt was *not* based on their adherence to the law, since the law had not yet been given. Instead, he chose to save them because of who they were, namely, the people of Israel, descendants of Abraham, Isaac, and Jacob.

When the law was given later at Sinai, it was given not as the means of establishing a relationship with God (since the Israelites were already in relationship with Yahweh), but rather as a means of living out relationship with a holy God, who would be in the midst of his people. In light of this, it is easier to see how the stipulations of the Torah could be seen as a delight to the psalmist. Rather than being a burden of legalistic requirements necessary to earn relationship with God, the Torah was a gracious gift from God, who, out of love for his people, sought to tell them what they needed to know in order to live their lives as the people of Yahweh. In this way, the Torah should be compared to a doctor's prescription, rather than a job description.[6] That is, it was not the means by which a reward is earned, such as when a paycheck is received for work performed under the terms of one's employment contract. It was, instead, something that was done because it was necessary for proper living (from the perspective of God, who, by virtue of being the Creator, knows that which is best and right for his people). In the Torah, we find God's "prescription" for how to live a life in relationship to him.

While we will examine the purpose or function of the law in more detail below, it may be helpful at this point to note one of the most important elements of Yahweh's "prescription" for his people. The Israelites were called to a unique role in the world. They alone were called to be the people of Yahweh, which, in turn, meant that they were called ultimately to be a blessing to the nations (Gen. 12:1–3). But the witness of the Israelites to Yahweh would be compromised if they simply adopted the worldview and practices of the nations around them. One vital function of the Torah was to ensure that the unique identity of the Israelites as the people of Yahweh (which, in turn, is for the blessing of the nations) was maintained.

This may be seen in Exodus 19:1–6. There, just prior to the giving of the law, God tells Moses to remind the Israelites of his past actions

---

6. See Daniel P. Fuller, *The Unity of the Bible: Unfolding God's Plan for Humanity* (Grand Rapids: Zondervan, 1992), 352.

on their behalf. But he also goes on to call the people to fidelity to him, so that they might continue to be the "treasured possession" (סְגֻלָּה) of Yahweh among all the peoples of the earth. They are also called to be a "kingdom of priests" and a "holy nation." The idea of being a "holy" nation is that the Israelites were to be separate from the nations around them. They were to be set apart because Yahweh had chosen the Israelites to be his people. Being a kingdom of priests, on the other hand, implies that the Israelites existed to serve the nations in some sense. A priest functioned as a mediator between God/the gods and human beings. Since Israel as a whole was envisioned as being a "kingdom of priests," the people for whom it would act as mediator were the Gentiles (non-Israelites). In other words, Israel was to serve as mediator for the rest of humanity.

We see this further in Deuteronomy, Moses' final speeches to the people, in which he articulates—with great vigor—the fundamental things they need to know in order to live out their lives as the people of Yahweh in the midst of Gentiles. Deuteronomy 4:5–8 says,

> See, I have taught you statutes and rules, as the LORD my God commanded me, that you should do them in the land that you are entering to take possession of it. Keep them and do them, for that will be your wisdom and your understanding in the sight of the peoples, who, when they hear all these statutes, will say, "Surely this great nation is a wise and understanding people." For what great nation is there that has a god so near to it as the LORD our God is to us, whenever we call upon him? And what great nation is there, that has statutes and rules so righteous as all this law that I set before you today? (ESV)

It is clear that Moses conceives of Israel as living out its national life on the world's stage, and the obedience (or lack thereof) of the Israelites will prompt questions and admiration on the part of the nations. Thus, part of the need for Torah keeping is to be a witness to the world. Further evidence of this perspective is found in Deuteronomy 28:9–10, where Israel's obedience to Torah is again described as being observed by the nations.

One of the most important functions of the law, then, was to allow the Israelites to live a life that was different from the people around them.

Christopher Wright notes that "the law was given to Israel to enable Israel to live as a model, as a light to the nations, such that, in the prophetic vision, the law would 'go forth' to the nations, or the nations would 'come up' to learn it from the LORD through Israel."[7] This aspect of the purpose of the law further undermines the view that Torah keeping was intended to be a means to earning salvation.

The Law After Moses

We have briefly examined how the law was intended to be understood (and presumably was so understood) by the original audience. But readers of the Pentateuch since the time of Moses are not in exactly the same situation as that of the original audience being addressed by Moses.[8] As a result, later readers have to determine how to interpret and apply the legal material in their situation. For later generations of Israelites, living as the people of God under his reign in the land he promised them, this was not a terribly difficult task. Though living at a later time period, their situation was in many ways similar to that of the original audience, so the Torah could be applied in much the same way as done by the original audience. After all, they too were living in the land promised to Abraham, in the midst of the nations, and their very existence as the "treasured possession" and "kingdom of priests" of Yahweh, coupled with Torah obedience, was to serve as a witness to the nations around them.

With the coming of Christ, however, the situation became much more complex. Jesus very self-consciously redefined the nature of the people of God around himself, such that there is no longer any ethnic component to the identity of the people of God. Rather, the kingdom envisioned by Jesus (consistent with the vision of the Old Testament before him) was one in which the people of God—that is, all people of any ethnicity who identified themselves with the Messiah and trusted in his righteousness— would live out a life of devotion to God evidenced by righteous living and concern for their neighbors. This would result in the blessing of all the nations, as promised in the call of Abram (Gen. 12:1–3). Though this was very much the calling of Israel as demonstrated in the Old Testament, the makeup of the people of God would no longer consist primarily of those

---

7. Christopher J. H. Wright, *Old Testament Ethics for the People of God* (Downers Grove, IL: InterVarsity Press, 2004), 320.

8. The authorship of the Pentateuch is discussed in chapter 4.

who were the physical descendants of Jacob. Rather, it would include all those who seek to identify themselves with Jesus.[9]

This redefinition of the people of God necessarily affects the understanding of the law. Since part of the law's purpose, as we have seen, was to protect the unique identity of the Israelites as the chosen people of God, the transformation of the people of God by Jesus necessitated changes in how the law was to be understood and applied.

Moreover, Jesus' own attitude to the law is ambiguous. While a thorough treatment of Jesus' perspective on the law is beyond the scope of this book, it is necessary to understand something of his perspective, as this accounts to a great degree for the variety of perspectives among Christians as to how to interpret and apply the law.

Overall, Jesus demonstrates a respect for the Torah. As required by the Torah (see Num. 15:38–41), he apparently wore tassels on his robe (Matt. 9:20). In addition, he attended the major feasts in Jerusalem, as commanded in Exodus 23:14–17 and Deuteronomy 16:16. Moreover, there is no clear indication of his having violated the Sabbath in any way described by the Torah itself (that is not clearly the case with respect to the oral traditions of the Jews, but this oral tradition was not the same as the written Torah).[10]

In his explicit statements about the law, he speaks in some instances of the eternal nature of the law, noting in Matthew 5:18 that "until heaven and earth disappear, not the smallest letter, not the least stroke of a pen, will by any means disappear from the Law until everything is accomplished" (NIV). Just prior to this verse, he indicates that his mission is fulfillment of the law, not its abolition (Matt. 5:17). He even goes so far as to chastise his fellow Jews for their failure to keep the law (John 7:19), and he speaks of the righteousness of the Pharisees (Matt. 5:20), who were Torah-keepers and then some.

On the other hand, at points Jesus' approach to the law is less positive. In Mark 7:14–23 he abolishes the distinction between clean and unclean foods, despite the fact that these categories are clearly established in the Torah in Leviticus 11 and Deuteronomy 14:1–21. Further, crucial

---

9. Though a complete discussion of the nature of Jesus' ministry is well beyond the scope of this work, we will examine the nature of Jesus' redefinition of the people of God in more detail in chapter 2.

10. Douglas J. Moo, "Law," in *Dictionary of Jesus and the Gospels*, ed. Joel B. Green, Scot McKnight, and I. Howard Marshall (Downers Grove, IL: InterVarsity Press, 1992), 451–52.

elements of Torah keeping, such as sacrifice and other ritual aspects of the faith, circumcision, the temple, and priesthood, are all conspicuous by their relative absence in the teaching of Jesus.

Perhaps not surprisingly, the ambiguous nature of Jesus' attitude and expectations about the law has resulted in a variety of perspectives as to how the follower of Christ is to approach the legal material of the Old Testament. We will now turn our attention to various ways in which Christians have sought to understand their obligations to living out the terms of the law.

Historical Approaches to the Law

Patristic Interpretation of Law

Like contemporary Christians, thinkers in the **patristic** era wrestled with the relationship between the Christian and the legal material of the Old Testament. This is evident in the text of the New Testament itself, where, for example, Paul seeks to counter the "Judaizers" and help Christians understand their responsibilities under the law, which had been fulfilled in Christ (Gal. 6:12–15; Phil. 3:1–14). Unfortunately, though not unexpectedly, the Pauline Epistles are rarely explicit on the exact nature of the responsibilities of the Christian to adhere to the terms of the Torah, not least because Paul at points seems to be responding to popular (mis-) conceptions of the law.[11] This lack of specificity led to continued attempts to refine the understanding of the law and its applicability to Christians.

Marcion. One approach to the law is represented by the second-century writer Marcion of Sinope. Based largely on his understanding of the book of Galatians (which he saw as central to understanding the relationship between Christians and the law), Marcion rejected all things Jewish. In fact, he felt that the God of the Old Testament was not the same God revealed as Father of Jesus Christ; and, since the New Testament reveals a different God, the teachings of Jesus are opposed to the teachings of the Old Testament. Accordingly, Marcion rejected the whole of the Old Testament, including the legal material of the Pentateuch. (He also rejected parts of the New Testament on the grounds that they were too

---

11. See Thomas R. Schreiner, *The Law and Its Fulfillment: A Pauline Theology of Law* (Grand Rapids: Baker, 1993); and James D. G. Dunn, ed., *Paul and the Mosaic Law* (Grand Rapids: Eerdmans, 2001).

deeply "infected" by Judaism and Jewish concerns.) Thus, for Marcion, the law of the Old Testament held *no* relevance for the Christian, since it was the revelation of a different god. To adhere to the Torah, in effect, would be to show loyalty to a false god.

Marcion's attacks on Judaism and the Old Testament forced the leaders and thinkers of the early church to respond. Tertullian, for example, maintained that Marcion was wrong to reject the Old Testament and its revelation of God, since the prophets anticipated the coming of Christ and his ministry. Moreover, the abolition of the law and elevation of the gospel were ordained by the creator God revealed in the Old Testament.[12] In Tertullian's view, the law was given by God for the early instruction of his people but was later abolished by God when Christ came to fulfill his redemptive purposes. Despite this abolition, God still confirms certain moral aspects of the law for human society where necessary.[13]

The wholesale rejection of the Old Testament, including the law, was itself rejected by the early church.[14] In countering Marcion (as well as other heretical views of the time), the church maintained that the corpus of Scripture included the whole of the Old Testament. In this way, the rejectionist approach to the law was repudiated. But, while there was agreement that the Old Testament law was relevant for Christians, there was still no consensus on the nature of that relevance.

The Alexandrian School.[15] Interpreters in Alexandria sought to highlight the positive features of New Testament perspectives on Old Testament law by adopting (with some modification) an **allegorical** approach to interpretation favored by Alexandrian Jews. The best-known representatives of this school are Clement of Alexandria and Origen.

Clement maintained that the Old Testament law was given by God for training and "preparatory instruction."[16] The law was given to prepare

---

12. Richard N. Longenecker, "Three Ways of Understanding Relations Between the Testaments: Historically and Today," in *Tradition and Interpretation in the New Testament: Essays in Honor of E. Earle Ellis for His Sixtieth Birthday*, ed. G. F. Hawthorne and O. Betz (Grand Rapids: Eerdmans, 1987), 24.

13. Ibid.

14. Wright, *Old Testament Ethics*, 388.

15. Many scholars question whether it is proper to refer to an Alexandrian "school" per se. While there are drawbacks to using such terminology, it is nevertheless helpful to refer to tendencies in interpretation in this way, as has become customary.

16. Clement of Alexandria, "Who Is the Rich Man That Shall Be Saved?" in *Ante-Nicene Fathers*, vol. 2, *Fathers of the Second Century: Hermas, Tatian, Athenagoras, Theophilus, and Clement of Alexandria* (Entire), ed. Alexander Roberts and James Donaldson (Peabody, MA: Hendrickson, 1994), 593.

God's people for the "supreme" lawgiving of Jesus. Through that revelation, Christians were freed from bondage to the terms of the law itself and instead were called to believe and obey the Father's will. Clement, then, saw the law as relevant for the Christian but not in the sense of being obligatory in all its details. Like those who followed him, Clement maintained that the text of Scripture could be seen on different levels. The first was the literal level, which Clement held was the starting point and suitable for the majority of Christians.[17] More important for the mature Christian, however, was the spiritual sense. For Clement, "the literal sense indicated what was said or done, while the allegorical showed what should be believed. The allegorical approach . . . was adopted for apologetical and theological purposes."[18]

The Alexandrian school (especially Clement's successor as head of the **catechetical** school, Origen) notably separated the law into two parts, the ceremonial and the moral. The first was understood as having been fulfilled in Christ, whereas the second was retained and even amplified by Christ.[19] This division of the law (with the addition of a third category of civil law; see below) has been an extremely influential position in Christian approaches to the law to the present day. It is noteworthy that in this approach, the Alexandrian interpreters sought to emphasize the continuity between the two Testaments.

The Antiochene School. An alternative to the allegorical approach of the Alexandrian school was that of the Antiochene school. Whereas the Alexandrian school emphasized the spiritual sense of Scripture and sought to emphasize continuity between the Old and New Testaments, the Antiochene school emphasized the literal sense of the text and also saw in the ministry of Christ a dramatic shift in God's interaction with his people. This necessarily resulted in a change to the way in which the relevance of the law for the Christian was understood.

One of the major figures associated with the Antiochene school was John Chrysostom. He maintained that the advent of Christ marked a new dynamic for the world. He saw the law as a means of grace for the Old Testament believer (thus denying a dichotomy between law and grace) but a means of grace that was superseded when Christ came. In Chrysostom's

---

17. David S. Dockery, *Biblical Interpretation Then and Now: Contemporary Hermeneutics in the Light of the Early Church* (Grand Rapids: Baker, 1992), 83.
18. Ibid.
19. Wright, *Old Testament Ethics*, 389.

view, adhering to the law would be subjecting oneself to bondage. Given the reality of Christ and his ministry, the Old Testament was understood as having no authority—even in the moral sense—for the Christian. Chrysostom even maintained that Christians could reject things allowed by the Old Testament (such as slavery) because of the new dynamic that Jesus' life and ministry inaugurated.[20]

As one might expect, the interpreters of the Antiochene school represented a variety of perspectives.[21] Despite the differences among the various representatives of the Antiochene school, it nonetheless represented a consistent stream of thought in seeing the law as less relevant for the Christian. As we have seen, some felt the Mosaic law had no relevance at all for the Christian, due to the new era inaugurated by Christ. Others, while seeing some value in the law, nevertheless felt that the Christian for various reasons was not required to adhere to it.

It is interesting to note that subsequent thinking on the relevance of the law for the Christian can, in large measure, be traced to these early approaches.[22] Though the church officially and forcefully rejected Marcion's approach,[23] the "ghost of Marcion has haunted the hermeneutical house down through the ages, making its appearance in the antinomian tendencies of the radical wing of the Reformation, the ahistorical existentialism of Bultmann and kindred spirits, and (for very different theological reasons) in modern Dispensationalism."[24] The Alexandrian tendency toward seeing the Old Testament as pointing to Christ and in seeing the law as a meaningful guide for Christians may be seen in some **Reformed** traditions, even though they reject the allegorical approach to exegesis. Finally, the Antiochene stress on the primacy of the New Testament in light of the ministry of Christ, coupled with the resulting lack of emphasis on the relevance of Old Testament law, finds an echo in the work of Martin Luther, as well as in contemporary Mennonite thinking.

---

20. Ibid.; see also Longenecker, "Three Ways," 27–28.
21. Diodore of Tarsus, for example, saw value in the Old Testament, assuming it was properly interpreted through a literal reading of the text. Theodore of Mopsuestia argued for a strong contrast between law and gospel, seeing two covenants, one Mosaic and the other founded in Christ. See Wright, *Old Testament Ethics*, 390.
22. See Longenecker, "Three Ways."
23. Marcion was excommunicated in A.D. 144, and his views were vigorously attacked by a number of church leaders, most notably Irenaus and Tertullian.
24. Wright, *Old Testament Ethics*, 390.

Medieval Interpretation of Law

In the medieval era, many of the approaches of the patristic era continued. The allegorizing approach of the Alexandrian school emerged as the more dominant approach,[25] though political realities ensured that absolute hegemony was not maintained by the Alexandrian school.[26] In the later medieval era, Thomas Aquinas emerged as one of the most important contributors to understanding the relationship between the Christian and the law.

Thomas advocated a more systematic, scientific approach to the interpretation of the Bible. This led to the triumph of the more literal approach to biblical interpretation. The allegorizing approach associated with the Alexandrian school was largely replaced by a more literal approach to the biblical text, though the Alexandrian emphasis on allegory was not entirely supplanted.

In terms of law, Thomas expanded the idea put forth by Origen and envisioned a tripartite division of the law, seeing moral laws, ceremonial laws, and a third category, judicial laws. Thomas saw the moral laws as binding on the Christian, as they were an addition to the "natural law" that governs all human beings.[27] The ceremonial law, on the other hand, was fulfilled in Christ and his ministry, and therefore is not binding on the Christian per se. He notes, however, that the ceremonial law lasts "forever in respect of the reality which those ceremonies foreshadowed."[28] That is, since the Old Testament ceremonial laws were designed to foreshadow and anticipate Christ's coming, they are binding not in their specifics but in terms of their fulfillment in Christ. Moreover, Thomas maintained that it would be a mortal sin to try to observe the ceremonial laws, since they assume that Christ had not yet been born. The Christian who observes the ceremonial laws, in effect, would be denying the birth of Christ.[29] The

---

25. The dominance of the Alexandrian school was at least partly due to the fact that some of the major figures of the Antiochene school, most notably Nestorius, a student of Theodore, were condemned as heretics.

26. For more on the nature and origin of the political machinations of the Alexandrian and Antiochene schools, see Justo L. González, *The Story of Christianity*, vol. 1, *The Early Church to the Dawn of the Reformation* (New York: Harper Collins, 1984), 252–57.

27. Thomas Aquinas, *The Basic Writings of Saint Thomas Aquinas*, ed. Anton C. Pegis (New York: Random House, 1944), 2:819. The natural law may be understood simply as the moral will of God expressed in creation.

28. Ibid., 913.

29. Ibid., 916.

third category, judicial laws, consists of those laws that regulate justice among human beings. The judicial laws may be observed as a practical matter because they provide wise counsel for living, not because they are part of the old covenant, which was fulfilled in Christ.[30]

Clearly, the ancient interpreters through the medieval era sought to understand how Christ's ministry affected the relationship of the Christian to the Old Testament law. The struggle to understand that relationship did not end in the medieval era, however, but continues to the present day. We now turn our attention to the Reformation and how major figures of that era dealt with the law.

The Reformation and the Interpretation of Law

The Lutheran Approach. The early writings of Martin Luther demonstrate the influence of the more allegorical approach of the Alexandrian school. His rather dramatic rediscovery of the significance of the New Testament gospel, which he understood as freeing people from the condemnation of sin through justification by faith, altered his approach to law.

For Luther, God is revealed in Scripture through law and gospel. He saw law and gospel not as contradictory but rather understood them to function together in important ways. The law "holds a mirror before us; we peer into it and perceive that we are devoid of righteousness and life. And this image impels us to cry: 'Oh, come, Lord Jesus Christ, help us and give us grace to enable us to fulfill the Law's demands.'"[31] The law teaches the believer that he or she is mired in sin and in desperate need of salvation. This leads to repentance and an embrace of the good news of the gospel. Without the weight of the law convicting sinners of their sin, the joy of the gospel would not be as readily appreciated.

In terms of the Old Testament law more specifically,[32] Luther saw two uses for it. The first was a civil one, in which the law served to restrain

---

30. Ibid., 923.

31. Martin Luther, *Luther's Works*, vol. 22, *Sermons on the Gospel of St. John Chapters 1–4*, ed. Jaroslav Pelikan (St. Louis: Concordia, 1957), 144.

32. For Luther, *law* was not simply a term for the Pentateuch, the legal material in it, or the Old Testament generally; neither was law found only in the Old Testament. Rather, *law* refers in many ways to what effect the particular text has on a person, whether it is condemning or freeing. Thus the book of James was considered to be "law" by Luther, even though it is in the New Testament.

sin among the people of Israel. The second use, which was primary for Luther, was to convict the sinner of the need for repentance and to lead to an embrace of the gospel. It is unclear whether or not Luther embraced the so-called third use of the law, in which the law is seen as a moral guide for Christians to live their lives. Luther seems to have rejected the idea that the Christian was obligated to adhere to the terms of the law. On the other hand, in his teachings on how the Christian is to live, he made frequent use of the law, particularly the **Decalogue**. He insisted, however, that the authority of even the Decalogue is due to the fact that it is grounded in natural law, not because it was the authoritative law given to the Israelites.[33]

Though it is customary to think of a strict dichotomy between law and gospel in Luther's (and Lutheran) thinking, the relationship is actually more complex than that. The terror that the law induces is transformed when the gospel is received, such that the law becomes a delight. Luther notes, "Formerly I found that I had no delight in the Law. But now I discover that the Law is precious and good, that it was given to me for my life; and now it is pleasing to me. Formerly it told me what to do; now I am beginning to conform to its requests, so that now I praise, laud, and serve God. This I do through Christ, because I believe in Him."[34] But despite this joy in the law, it remains relevant to the Christian, not primarily as a source of guidance for how to live, but rather as a means of recognizing one's failures and need for the gospel.

The Reformed Approach. John Calvin took a very different approach. He saw the so-called third use of the law as its primary function. Because he emphasized the essential continuity between the Old and New Testaments, seeing just one covenant of grace uniting the two Testaments, and because he took as an essential starting point Jesus' statement on the continuing validity of the law in Matthew 5:17, Calvin was more favorably disposed to seeing a positive function for the law in the life of the Christian. Indeed, he argued that the law "is the best instrument for enabling [believers] daily to learn with greater truth and certainty what that will of the Lord is which they aspire to follow, and to confirm them in this knowledge."[35] He further noted that the law "has the force of exhortation, not to bind their

---

33. Wright, *Old Testament Ethics*, 392.
34. Luther, *Works*, 144.
35. John Calvin, *Institutes of the Christian Religion*, trans. Henry Beveridge (Grand Rapids: Eerdmans, 1975), 2:309.

consciences with a curse, but by urging them, from time to time, to shake off sluggishness and chastise imperfection."[36]

Calvin and those Reformed thinkers following him envisioned a tripartite division of the law, similar to the approach of Thomas Aquinas. The three categories they envisioned were the civil, ceremonial, and moral laws. Civil laws are those that were given to govern the nation of Israel, while ceremonial laws are those laws that regulated worship for ancient Israel and foreshadowed Christ and his ministry. The moral laws are those that derive from the character of God. In this view, then, the civil and ceremonial laws do not apply directly to the Christian, though they are of great relevance and interest to the Christian. They are, in the words of the Westminster Confession of Faith (a Reformed statement of faith), "of great use to [Christians], as well as to others; in that, as a rule of life, informing them of the will of God and their duty, [the law] directs and binds them to walk accordingly; discovering also the sinful pollutions of their nature, hearts, and lives. . . . [Civil and ceremonial laws are] likewise of use to the regenerate, to restrain their corruptions."[37] The moral law, on the other hand, is directly binding on the Christian, since it derives from the very character of God.

The Christian, then, is obligated to obey the moral law because it derives from the will of God and does not change with variation in culture, worldview, or setting. The civil and ceremonial laws were superseded in Christ in terms of their being a binding legal authority for the Christian, but they are viewed as very relevant for instruction in living a life pleasing to God. The law also serves to convict the believer of sin and is therefore useful in that regard as well.

A subset of Reformed thinking is the **theonomist** or **Christian reconstructionist** movement. This approach to the law agrees that the ceremonial laws were fulfilled in Christ but maintains that Reformed thinkers are mistaken in seeing the civil laws as also superseded in Christ. Theonomists argue that the civil laws, as well as the moral laws, are obligatory for all people in all times. This includes even the application of the death penalty for crimes such as blasphemy, adultery, homosexuality, and incorrigibility of children.[38] For the theonomist, the Old Testament

---

36. Ibid., 2:310.
37. "Of the Law of God," in *Westminster Confession of Faith* (1647), chap. 21.
38. Greg L. Bahnsen, *Theonomy in Christian Ethics*, 2nd ed. (Phillipsburg, NJ: Presbyterian and Reformed, 1984), 466–68. See also Bahnsen's, "The Theonomic Reformed Approach to Law and

law is relevant for the Christian and is largely directly applicable to the contemporary believer.

Other Contemporary Approaches to the Interpretation of Law

Dispensationalism. At the other end of the spectrum from Christian reconstructionism is the approach of dispensationalism. This approach arose in the nineteenth century through the work of John Nelson Darby, who came to see God's interaction with human beings as being different at various times, or dispensations. Though the number of dispensations envisioned is not uniformly agreed upon, the most significant of the dispensations are the dispensation of law and the dispensation of grace. In this view, the dispensation of law marked God's means of interacting with Israel. Consequently, Israel's law, including the so-called moral laws, was intended for the nation of Israel. The dispensation of grace, on the other hand, was inaugurated through Christ and will continue until his return. It represents a wholly different way in which God relates to his people. Since the law was given as part of the earlier dispensation and was specifically for Israel alone (and will become relevant again when Christ returns to establish his earthly millennial reign among the converted Jewish people), the law is not relevant for the Christian.

It is clear that Jesus himself incorporates some of the pentateuchal laws into his teachings. But some dispensationalists argue that the relevance of these laws for the Christian is found in the fact that they have been incorporated into the "law of Christ," not because they are part of the Old Testament law, since that was for Israel alone.[39] Indeed, some have argued that though the principles are the same in the case of laws from the Old

---

Gospel," in *Five Views on Law and Gospel*, ed. Wayne G. Strickland (Grand Rapids: Zondervan, 1993).

39. See, for example, Charles C. Ryrie, "The End of the Law," *Bibliotheca Sacra* 124 (1967): 239–47. As is the case with other theological systems, there is variety among dispensationalists. Progressive dispensationalists, for example, differ with classical dispensationalists in the extent to which Israel and the church should be seen as representing two different manifestations of God's purposes and plans. The progressive dispensationalist approach to the law (understood primarily as the Mosaic covenant), however, is largely in keeping with the classical dispensationalist view. For more on progressive dispensationalism generally, see Robert L. Saucy, *The Case for Progressive Dispensationalism: The Interface Between Dispensational and Non-Dispensational Theology* (Grand Rapids: Zondervan, 1993). A progressive dispensationalist view of the Mosaic law and the Christian is presented by Craig A. Blaising, "The Fulfillment of the Biblical Covenants Through Jesus Christ," in *Progressive Dispensationalism*, ed. Craig A. Blaising and Darrell L. Bock (Wheaton: Victor, 1993), 194–99.

Testament that have been incorporated into the "law of Christ," this does not mean that they are, in fact, the same laws. Rather, the commands of God have been modified according to the people being addressed.[40]

According to this view, the Old Testament law is generally useful as an example to believers in the new dispensation, for comfort and hope, as a prophetic view of Christ, and to understand the character of God.[41] But it is *not* to be seen as the means by which the believer is to live his or her life and is not considered to be directly applicable to the Christian.

Roman Catholicism. Another contemporary approach to understanding the relevance of the law for the Christian is that taken by the Roman Catholic Church. According to official Catholic teaching,[42] the Old Testament law was meant to prepare the people for the coming of Christ.[43] The ministry of Christ inaugurates the "Law of the Gospel," which is understood as the fulfillment and perfection of the "Old Law."[44]

Following Thomas Aquinas, Catholic teaching today recognizes a tripartite division of the law into civil, ceremonial, and moral categories. The moral law, understood both as natural law and the Decalogue (which is understood as an expression of natural law), remains applicable to the Christian. The *Catechism of the Catholic Church* notes that the Ten Commandments "are fundamentally immutable, and they oblige always and everywhere. No one can dispense from them. The Ten Commandments are engraved by God in the human heart."[45]

Though the rest of the stipulations of the Torah are not directly applicable to Christians, the Old Testament, including its laws, is still of benefit and relevance to them. In describing the history of God's interaction with human beings prior to Christ, the Old Testament provides for understanding salvation history in a way that is of great benefit to the Christian.[46]

---

40. Norman L. Geisler, "Dispensationalism and Ethics," *Transformation* 6, no. 1 (1989): 10.
41. Ibid., 10–11.
42. That is, according to the *Catechism of the Catholic Church with Modifications from the Editio Typica* (New York: Doubleday, 1994). While there are differing views on this issue among the various groups within Catholicism, we will be focusing here on the perspective set forth in the official teaching of the church.
43. Ibid., 529.
44. Ibid., 531.
45. Ibid., 559. See also Peter J. Kreeft, *Catholic Christianity* (San Francisco: Ignatius, 2001), 202.
46. Peter S. Williamson, "Catholic Principles for Interpreting Scripture," *CBQ* 65, no. 3 (2003): 339. For a more thorough treatment of Catholic interpretation of the Old Testament, see the relevant sections in Peter S. Williamson, *Catholic Principles for Interpreting Scripture: A Study of The Pontifical Biblical Commission's "The Interpretation of the Bible in the Church,"* Subsidia Biblica, no. 22 (Rome: Pontifical Biblical Institute, 2001).

Judaism. Though we have focused here on Christian approaches to law, we should note that contemporary Jews also seek to interpret and apply the law, though their approaches to the law and its application differ from Christian ones.[47]

Jewish tradition sees 613 commandments in the law and has divided those commandments in one of four ways. Some interpreters have simply divided the commandments into two categories: positive precepts and prohibitions. Others have identified three categories: positive precepts, prohibitions, and laws involving the community rather than the individual. A third approach sees all laws as falling under one of the Ten Commandments. Finally, some have taken the two broad categories (positive command and prohibition) and subdivided them into smaller logical groupings.[48] The most widely accepted grouping, developed by the medieval rabbi Maimonides, has thirty-four categories.

For Jews, adherence to Torah consists in obeying not only the laws in the Pentateuch but also traditional elements of the oral law (interpretation of the written law and logical deductions from it produced by rabbis throughout the centuries) and custom.[49] Though each is considered equally authoritative, the written law takes precedence over the oral Torah if there is any conflict between the two.

These sources of authority together are known as *halakhah*, which is derived from הָלַךְ ("go, walk"), and refers to a way of living.[50] Today Jews seek to live out the *halakhah* by applying its principles to contemporary situations.[51]

A Paradigmatic Approach to Law

Problems with Traditional Approaches to Law

We have seen that there have been various approaches to explain the

---

47. As was the case with dispensationalists and Catholics, the Jewish people are diverse in their views. I am here describing approaches that are true for most Jews, though the various branches of Judaism differ in the extent to which they seek to live according to the *halakhah*.

48. *EncJud*, s.v. "Commandments, the 613."

49. *EncJud*, s.v. "Halakhah."

50. Jacob Neusner, *An Introduction to Judaism: A Textbook and Reader* (Louisville: Westminster/John Knox, 1991), 64.

51. Joel Roth, *The Halakhic Process: A Systematic Analysis* (New York: Jewish Theological Seminary Press, 1986), presents a useful guide to the methodology for determining how the *halakhah* may be lived out today. For a more general introduction to Judaism, see Nicholas de Lange, *An Introduction to Judaism* (Cambridge: Cambridge University Press, 2000), and Neusner, *Introduction to Judaism.*

relationship between the Christian and the law.[52] Many of these have in common a division of the law into two or three categories. The most common approach is to see the law as divided into civil, ceremonial, and moral laws, and, as we have seen, it is usually argued that only the moral law is obligatory for the Christian today, the other categories having been fulfilled in Christ.

However, there are problems with this view. First, the categories of civil, ceremonial, and moral laws are not found anywhere in Scripture. There is no hint in the text that Moses saw any such distinctions in the law he was promulgating or that the original audience would have understood the law to be divided in this way. Consider, for example, Leviticus 19. Verse 18 says, "Do not seek revenge or bear a grudge against anyone among your people, but love your neighbor as yourself. I am the LORD" (TNIV). There is general agreement that this would be a moral law, not limited in its scope to ancient Israel, and therefore that it is applicable to the Christian. The very next verse, however, says, "Do not mate different kinds of animals. Do not plant your field with two kinds of seed. Do not wear clothing woven of two kinds of material" (TNIV). These regulations are usually understood as being ceremonial law, given to the Israelites to help differentiate them from the nations around them. As ceremonial law, it is not seen as obligatory for the Christian. But there is nothing in the text to suggest that the author thought the one law was universal and the other of temporary applicability for the people of God. Indeed, the two verses are joined together rhetorically, as verse 18 ends with God emphatically noting, "I am Yahweh," while verse 19 continues the thought with the exhortation to "keep my decrees." The argument here is that the people are to love each other because they are the people of Yahweh, the creator of all people in his image. Moreover, they were to obey his commands for the same reason. It is an arbitrary distinction to say that verse 18 applies universally while verse 19 does not, since the basis for obedience according to the text is the same.

Second, the categories of civil, ceremonial, and moral are not as clear-cut as some would suggest. Leviticus 19:19 demands that categories be maintained by proper boundaries such that fields are not planted with two kinds of crops and clothing is made of only a single type of material. But

---

52. For a concise presentation of various contemporary approaches to law and its relevance for today, see Wayne G. Strickland, ed., *Five Views on Law and Gospel* (Grand Rapids: Zondervan, 1996).

the likely purpose behind these laws regulating boundaries is to highlight the idea that holy things must be kept separate from common or profane things. This further stresses that there is an order to the universe, God is unique in his place, and human beings must recognize their place in the created order as well. So the laws regulating separation may be understood, at least in part, as an object lesson designed to demonstrate the holiness of God and the separation between fallen creatures and the holy Creator.[53] With this understanding, how are we to classify laws like those in Leviticus 19:19? The motivating principle behind the law is to acknowledge the holiness of God and to highlight the fact that human beings are in a separate category from God. Acknowledging one's rightful place with respect to God is a moral issue, obligatory for all people at all times; and so these laws, though dealing with issues that are apparently not directly relevant to the contemporary believer, cannot simply be dismissed as inapplicable.

A related point may be made about the way in which the Israelites conceived of their lives. In the ancient Near East, and in Israel, all of life was seen to have religious significance. There is no evidence to suggest that people in ancient Israel or the broader cultures of the ancient Near East saw a distinction between those areas of life that were of interest to God/the gods and those that were not. Rather, God (or the gods) was interested—and involved—in *all* aspects of life. Thus, for the original audience of the legal material of the Pentateuch, issues relating to "civil" life were considered to bear as much religious significance as moral or ceremonial issues, because all of life was lived in the presence of Yahweh. It is hard, then, to draw distinctions that would have been foreign to the mind of the original author and audience of the laws.

Finally, there is a problem related to the authority of Scripture. Second Timothy 3:16 notes that *all* Scripture is God-breathed and is useful for teaching, rebuking, correcting, and training in righteousness. If two-thirds of the putative categories of law can be dismissed as being inapplicable for Christians, we are suggesting that those texts are not particularly useful for training in righteousness. We should bear in mind that when Paul wrote these words to Timothy, he had in mind the Old Testament, not primarily those texts that were later incorporated into the New Testament. Moreover, some of Paul's letters deal with the issue of how the Christian is

---

53. Gordon J. Wenham, *The Book of Leviticus*, NICOT (Grand Rapids: Eerdmans, 1979), 269–70. For more on the worldview of the ancient Israelites as reflected in the laws of the Pentateuch, see Mary Douglas, *Purity and Danger* (London: Routledge, 1966).

to approach the law of the Old Testament. Nowhere in the New Testament is the solution offered that the law can be categorized and two of the three categories dismissed as inapplicable to the Christian.[54]

An Alternative: A Paradigmatic Approach

In light of these concerns, it is increasingly recognized among Old Testament scholars that these divisions in the law are simply untenable. So, an alternative understanding must be sought.

A helpful way to conceive of law in light of the concerns noted with the more traditional approaches to the law is a paradigmatic approach. As we noted above, the purpose of the legal material was to instruct the people as to how they were to live in light of their calling as the people of Yahweh who live with a holy God in their midst. As the people of God, the Israelites were chosen by Yahweh to be an example to the rest of humanity as to how to live life in relationship with God.

To put it another way, Israel was to be a **paradigm** for how people were to live. In the study of language, a paradigm is a useful tool that helps the student understand how the language works. A verb paradigm, such as the imperfect of קָטַל ("he killed"), for example, helps us to understand the forms that the strong Hebrew verb will take in the imperfect. When the paradigm is mastered, we can write the correct forms of any strong verb in the imperfect, even if we don't know the meaning of the word. Similarly, seeing Israel as a paradigm helps us understand how to live life in relationship with God. Like the verb paradigm, Israel is called to be a known quantity, the knowledge of which helps determine what is correct in unknown situations. This is part of what it means for Israel to be a nation of priests, for priests serve as mediators between God and human beings.[55]

A paradigmatic approach to law helps us avoid the problems of the more traditional approaches to law outlined above. Rather than categorizing laws in an attempt to determine whether the Christian must keep them, a paradigmatic approach seeks to understand how the law functioned for ancient Israel in its mission as witness to the rest of humanity concerning humans' proper relationship with God. Once that has been

---

54. In Matthew 23:23, Jesus refers to "weightier" matters of law in contrast to those presumably considered less weighty. But the point he is making is that all laws, both weighty and otherwise, must be kept.
55. Wright, *Old Testament Ethics*, 64–65.

accomplished, we can look for ways in which the paradigm applies to our situation, even though we live in vastly different circumstances in terms of salvation history, worldview, culture, technology, etc. As Wright notes, "By seeing how [the ancient Israelites] addressed, within *their* cultural and historical context, problems and issues common to humanity in principle or practice, we are helped to address (if not always to solve) the ethical challenges *we* face in our different contexts."[56] The question in a paradigmatic approach is not "Is the law applicable to the Christian?" but, rather, "*How* is the law applicable to the Christian?" In this way, the "usefulness" of all of Scripture is maintained, as is the integrity of the original author's intention regarding the unity and relevance of the law.

We also should note at this point that this approach helps us to recover the whole of the Pentateuch as Torah, in its broadest sense. The legal material of the Pentateuch helps us understand what behavior was acceptable to God and what was not; it is, therefore, instruction in holy living. But the legal material is not the last word on what was required of the people. Many of the laws establish the *minimum* requirement for the people. Adherence to the terms of the law protected the people from engaging in behavior (and, in some instances, attitudes) that would endanger their relationship with God. But even the strictest adherence to the law would not necessarily result in behavior that was entirely pleasing to God.[57]

For example, the Pentateuch provides regulations concerning divorce (Deut. 24:1–3). Does that mean that an Israelite man who strictly adhered to the terms of this law was totally righteous in God's sight? That seems unlikely, given the portrayal in Genesis 1–2 of the marriage relationship being a union of one man and one woman for life. This suggests that the law in Deuteronomy 24 establishes a minimum standard of behavior for the people of Yahweh. If, because of human sin (since "hating" his wife is hardly a godly attitude toward her), a man divorced his wife, there were nevertheless requirements as to how she was to be treated and how the relationship was to be understood. Adherence to the terms of this law protected the Israelites from degrading their brothers and sisters, and also served as a witness (paradigm) to a watching world.[58]

---

56. Ibid., 69.
57. Other laws present the heights of righteousness. The point is simply that strict adherence to the terms of the Torah does not in itself result in righteousness.
58. For a discussion of views of divorce and remarriage in the Old Testament, see Joe M. Sprinkle, "Old Testament Perspectives on Divorce and Remarriage," *JETS* 40, no. 4 (1997): 529–50.

But God's expectations are far greater. We discern this, not in the "floor" established by the legal material related to divorce, but in the narrative accounts of Scripture. There, we learn of God's creational intentions for the marriage relationship (Gen. 1–2). We also are introduced to history's first bigamist, Lamech, who is portrayed as self-aggrandizing and vicious (Gen. 4:19–24). The account of Jacob and his two wives shows the difficulties associated with multiple wives, as his love for Rachel and hatred for Leah affected his children as well. While the law permits and regulates bigamy in recognition of reality, the narratives of the Pentateuch show what righteousness is and is not.[59]

We can summarize the relationship between the requirements of the law and righteousness in this way: Law establishes the parameters within which righteousness can be lived out. One cannot violate the minimum standards of the law and be considered righteous. At the same time, strict adherence to the law doesn't result in righteousness either. Rather, righteousness consists of wholehearted devotion to God and his ideals for human living in relationship to him.[60] A paradigmatic approach to law helps us recover the ethical instruction of the narrative texts as well as the legal material of the Pentateuch. It also recognizes the unique calling Israel had to be a nation of priests ministering to a watching world.

It may be helpful at this point to delve more specifically into what is meant by the paradigmatic approach. Although we will be discussing guidelines for interpreting legal texts more extensively in chapter 4, it is necessary here to examine how Israel as a paradigm relates to the interpretation of the biblical text.

When we examine a biblical law, we must first determine what the text meant to the original author and audience. Part of that process involves establishing what the purpose of the law was for ancient Israel, bearing in mind the call of Israel to be a paradigm for holy living and, as

---

59. On the role of narrative in ethical instruction, see Gordon J. Wenham, *Story As Torah: Reading the Old Testament Ethically*, OTS (Edinburgh: T & T Clark, 2000). This is related to the concept of "showing" versus "telling" in speech act theory. In seeking to convey intentionality, the author can "tell" (state) something, e.g., polygamy is wrong. Alternatively, the author can "show" that the behavior is wrong, by relating accounts of consequences, rewards for the desired behavior, etc. While we usually think of "telling" as more forceful, many argue that "showing" is more powerful in shaping worldviews. For more on this, see Meir Sternberg, *The Poetics of Biblical Narrative: Ideological Literature and the Drama of Reading* (Bloomington, IN: Indiana University Press, 1985), 1–57.

60. This may be seen in Genesis 26:5, where Abraham is described as having kept the laws of Yahweh, though they were not yet given.

such, a witness to the rest of humanity. Then we can articulate a principle that underlies the law. Finally, we can identify ways in which the principle is applicable in other settings.

But the principles are always to be understood in light of the overarching idea of Israel as a paradigm. That is, this idea, which was intended to be part of the worldview of ancient Israel, is an integral part of the worldview of the original author and audience. The paradigm helps us to understand how the principles "hang together" and grounds our interpretation and application of them.

In chapter 2, we will look at the thematic elements of the Pentateuch that shed light on the worldview conveyed by the author of the text. This will help us as we seek to understand the overarching paradigm through which the individual texts are to be examined. Then, in chapter 4, we will discuss some guidelines to assist us in the proper interpretation and application of the texts in light of the paradigm that is assumed by the texts.

NARRATIVE

The second major genre found in the Pentateuch is narrative. Like law, narrative often has been misunderstood by contemporary interpreters, despite the fact that narrative is the most common literary genre in the entire Bible.[61]

The Nature of Narrative

We will begin our examination of narrative with a look at what narrative actually *is*. While this may seem to be very elementary, it is actually quite important, as misunderstandings of narratives often stem from incomplete or inaccurate conceptions of the nature of narratives.

A narrative is a selective record of a series of events that uses shared conventions to convey the author's communicative intention[62] in an engaging manner. In the case of the biblical narratives, this communicative

---

61. A fuller treatment of narrative is found in Robert Chisholm, *Interpreting the Historical Books: An Exegetical Handbook*, HOTE (Grand Rapids: Kregel, 2006), 25–88.

62. I deliberately use the term "communicative intention" to highlight the fact that in reading a text, we are seeking to understand what the author intends to communicate. Other facets of an author's intentionality may be unknown to us and cannot be a part of our analysis. For more on this, see Jeannine K. Brown, *Scripture as Communication: Introducing Biblical Hermeneutics* (Grand Rapids: Baker, 2006), 47–51.

intention is usually a theological one, and the author understands the events described as having actually taken place. It may be helpful at this point to "unpack" this definition somewhat, in order to facilitate more accurate interpretation of the genre.

Narratives Are a Selective Record of Events

We must first notice that narratives are a selective record of events. That is, not *everything* that happened is recorded in the biblical narratives. Rather, the authors chose to include those things that would help communicate what they wanted the reader to understand.

If we think of contemporary, everyday events, we can see how selectivity comes into play in presenting an event. Suppose I wanted to write an account of my commute to work on one particular day. If I wanted to exhaustively describe this fairly mundane event, I would need to convey a tremendous amount of information. I would need to describe the route I took, the road and weather conditions, which cars I passed on my way, what I was thinking while I drove, and what I was listening to on the radio. To be truly exhaustive, I also would need to include information about the mechanical performance of my car and even include the reactions of other drivers to my presence (in some instances).

It should be clear that a comprehensive account of even my short commute would quickly become unwieldy (not to mention quite uninteresting!). Moreover, I simply would not be able to write such an account, since I would not have access to all the information necessary to write it, as I could not know what other drivers were thinking.

This example illustrates that narrative accounts of any event are necessarily selective. Since it would be impossible to write an exhaustive account of my commute, I would need to be selective in what I included in my account. The same was true for the biblical authors, who were selective as they wrote their accounts. They shaped their material in order to most effectively communicate to their audience.[63] This meant that some facts, events, and dialogue were left out of the account, since they would not contribute to accomplishing the author's purpose(s). We find explicit reference to this selectivity throughout the books of Kings, for example,

---

63. Of course, the biblical authors, inspired by God, were also effectively communicating what God wanted the audience to understand.

This is more likely the case

where there is a repetition of the phrase, "As for the other events of Rehoboam's reign, and all he did, are they not written in the book of the annals of the kings of Judah?" (1 Kings 14:29 TNIV).[64] Clearly, the book of Kings is not meant to be understood as an exhaustive account of the events of the reigns of the kings, since there are fuller accounts elsewhere.

Narratives Have a Purpose

The author's purpose, then, governs the choice of what is included in the selective record of the event(s). To take up again the example of the narrative account of my commute, what I include is determined by what I want to communicate by my account. If, for example, I am complaining to my wife about the traffic I encountered on my way to work, I will focus on that aspect of the event. I will leave out information about what I was listening to on the radio, since that does not help me accomplish my purpose (even though that is a legitimate part of the account of "what happened" on my commute overall). On the other hand, if I am talking to my son, who for a time when he was younger was interested in different kinds of cars, I will describe what types of unusual cars I encountered. Again, I will leave out certain types of information since their inclusion will not help me to accomplish my communicative intention in speaking to him.

The biblical narratives are no different. As we noted above, they too are selective accounts of events. Moreover, the decision about what to include or leave out is based on what will help accomplish the authors' communicative purposes.

Consider, for example, the account in Genesis 39 of Joseph and Potiphar's wife. As with any event, an exhaustive account of this event would be impossible to write and would detract from the understanding of what the author wanted to communicate. So, for example, we don't know anything about Joseph's day-to-day routine in working for Potiphar. We are not told what, exactly, Joseph did that caught Potiphar's attention. Instead, we are simply told in Genesis 39:3, "His master saw that the LORD was with him, and that the LORD caused all that he did to succeed in his hands" (ESV). Given that narratives are necessarily selective, we can conclude from this that inclusion of more detailed information about

---

64. Other occurrences of this phrase (or "the book of the annals of the kings of Israel") are found in 1 Kings 11:41; 15:7, 23, 31; 16:5, 14, 20, 27; 22:39, 45; 2 Kings 1:18; 8:23; 10:34; 12:19; 13:8, 12; 14:15, 18, 28; 15:6, 21, 36; 16:19; 20:20; 21:17, 25; 23:28; 24:5.

what Joseph did so well was not necessary to accomplish Moses' purposes. Rather, Moses included what would most effectively communicate his intentions.

We also must bear in mind that biblical narratives usually have a theological purpose. That is, the authors were less interested in conveying details about the lives of even the biblical "heroes" than in communicating something about God and his interaction with his people. In Genesis 39, the emphasis is not on Joseph per se but on God's faithfulness in being with Joseph, in helping him to prosper, in preserving and protecting him, and in placing Joseph where he wanted him in order to accomplish his purposes in the lives of the descendants of Abraham (see, e.g., Gen. 50:20).

Understanding the author's purposes in writing a narrative helps us avoid a common error in the interpretation of narratives. Many times we approach narratives and look for a readily applicable "moral" that is relevant to our lives. But sound interpretation of the text means seeking to understand the author's intention, not simply looking for something readily applicable.

Consider, again, Genesis 39. Often, contemporary readers look at this chapter and conclude that Moses was seeking to communicate the importance of maintaining proper boundaries in order to avoid sexually dangerous or tempting situations. That is certainly relevant to an audience living in our sexually overcharged culture. But that hardly seems likely from the text, since the emphasis overall seems to be on God's faithfulness in protecting and preserving Joseph in accordance with his plan to use the descendants of Abraham to bless the nations (Gen. 12:1–3; see chapter 2, below). There is no discussion of boundaries or how Joseph maintained them. Instead, there is a great deal of emphasis on God's presence with Joseph. This suggests that the author's intention was to communicate that, not the importance of boundaries.[65]

Recognizing that the biblical authors crafted their narratives in order to accomplish their communicative purposes helps us ask the right questions of the text. Often we have questions we would like answered, but the author is not necessarily seeking to address those questions. He is, rather, seeking to address those questions that were relevant to him and his audience. Part of sound interpretation means being content with (or, at least, accepting) the fact that not all of our questions will be answered.

---

65. See chapter 6 for a detailed examination of Genesis 39.

Narratives Are Written in an Engaging Manner

The final aspect of the definition of narrative we need to note is the fact that narratives are written in an engaging manner. Narratives seek to communicate. But communication, whether ancient or contemporary, is most effective when carried out in a way that engages the reader or listener. Biblical narratives are no exception; they presented the accounts in ways that were engaging to the original audience. (Since the conventions of Hebrew narrative differ from those of English ones, the contemporary reader may not find the narratives to be as engaging as the original audience would have.)

It is important that this aspect of narrative be kept in mind when interpreting the biblical narratives. Narratives work powerfully in the lives of the reader to reinforce, challenge, and shape worldviews. This is true in contemporary societies as much as in ancient ones. We must bear in mind that the reading of the biblical narratives was not simply a diversion from the challenges of life (something to be read when there was nothing good on TV!) but rather was part of the means by which the identity of the people of God was fostered and maintained.

Part of interpreting the pentateuchal narratives is understanding and coming to appreciate the literary artistry with which the narratives are presented. While the conventions of Hebrew narrative may seem especially foreign to us, they are nevertheless powerful tools used by the author to convey his intentions to the original audience.

Features of Narrative

So how did the biblical authors shape their material to be engaging to the reader? To properly understand the text, we must be aware of the techniques and conventions the authors used to present their material. We do not, of course, have any guidelines from the ancient world as to how to write a first-class narrative. But we can discern certain features of narratives and examine what effect they had on the communication of the author's message.[66]

---

66. There are many other important features of narrative that could be discussed. The features of plot, setting, and character often are addressed in analyzing narratives. The four features listed here are emphasized because of their unique usefulness in understanding the biblical narratives. Discussion of other narrative features may be found in Shimon Bar-Efrat, *Narrative Art in the Bible*, JSOTSup 70

Scene

The first feature of narrative we will examine is the scene. A narrative is constructed through the use of scenes that represent where the action takes place, who is involved, and what actually occurs. Since narratives are selective, we can readily identify those things that are important to the author by noting what is included or left out in a particular scene.

Consider as an example the account of Moses' flight to Midian in Exodus 2:11–22. This brief account consists of two scenes. The first is found in verses 11–15a and includes as characters Moses, three Hebrews, an Egyptian, and Pharaoh, though the major characters are Moses and the Hebrew who speaks to him. This first scene is set in Egypt. The second scene (vv. 15b–22) shifts the action to Midian and consists of Moses, Reuel, his seven daughters, and the shepherds.

The importance of scene may be recognized in considering this story. Note that the author does not emphasize the journey to Midian; he simply states that Moses fled to Midian. We can confidently conclude that a narration of the journey itself was not important to accomplishing the author's purpose in relating this account. In addition, we note that Pharaoh is a minor character in this scene. He is said to have sought to kill Moses when he learned of the slaying of the Egyptian, but there is no dialogue or interaction between Moses and Pharaoh here. Once again we can conclude that inclusion of any statements Pharaoh may have uttered in ordering Moses' death do not advance the author's interests in this narrative. Identifying the elements of the scene helps us understand the author's purposes.[67]

Plot

The next feature of narrative we will consider is plot. Simply put, every narrative has a beginning, a middle, and an end. Narratives are more complex than that, however, and may also be seen as building up tension to a **climax**. Identifying this climax is helpful in understanding the author's purposes.

The climax of the narrative is the point at which the reader has questions about what will happen but no answers. After the climax, the text

---

(Sheffield: Sheffield Academic Press, 2000); Chisholm, *Interpreting the Historical Books*, chap. 1; Robert Alter, *The Art of Biblical Narrative* (New York: Basic Books, 1981).

67. For more on scene, see Bar-Efrat, *Narrative Art in the Bible*, 184–96.

resolves the tension through the provision of answers to (at least some of) the questions.

The key to analyzing tension is to ask what the **implied reader** would have been asking or thinking. The implied reader is a literary construct that describes the reader presupposed by the narrative. It generally describes the kind of reader (audience) the author has in mind when writing the text. This reader is an "ideal" one, who is able to understand and respond to the text as the author intends. This construct helps ensure that we ask the right questions of the text. Our questions and responses, as contemporary readers, will almost certainly differ from those of the original readers. By considering how the implied reader would have responded (and, by extension, what response the author was seeking), we can correct for the historical and cultural distance between the original author and audience and us as readers.[68]

It may be helpful to construct a graph of the tension in order to more readily identify the climax of the narrative. This need not be a complex chart. Consider the following graph of tension in Exodus 2:11–22. I have represented the scenes and significant actions in the narrative and placed them on a graph (see figure 1).

In this narrative, we see that Moses has now grown up in Pharaoh's household. He "went out to his people and looked on their burdens" (Exod. 2:11 ESV). Seeing an Egyptian overseer beating a Hebrew slave, Moses killed the Egyptian and buried him in the sand. Tension begins to rise at this point, as the reader does not know what will become of Moses. Though a member of Pharaoh's household, Moses is nevertheless a foreigner. Moreover, Moses seems to be deliberately identifying with the oppressed Israelites rather than the powerful Egyptians, despite his upbringing.[69] The reader is therefore unsure as to what consequences Moses might face if he is discovered.

The next day, Moses goes out once again and encounters two Hebrews fighting. Given the oppression of the Hebrews, Moses presumably desires to foster a sense of solidarity among them and thus chastises the two for fighting. Then, it is revealed that Moses' own actions have become known. Accordingly, the tension rises still further. When Pharaoh hears of Moses'

---

68. For more on the construct of the implied reader, see Brown, *Scripture as Communication*, 26–27. A fuller treatment of this issue is available in idem, *The Disciples in Narrative Perspective: The Portrayal and Function of the Matthean Disciples*, SBLAB, no. 9 (Atlanta: SBL, 2002), 123–28.

69. Douglas K. Stuart, *Exodus*, NAC (Nashville: Broadman & Holman, 2006), 95.

sin, he seeks to put him to death. This is the climax of the narrative, as it is the point at which the reader has only questions but no answers (resolution) to them. Will Pharaoh kill Moses? What would his death mean for the Hebrews?

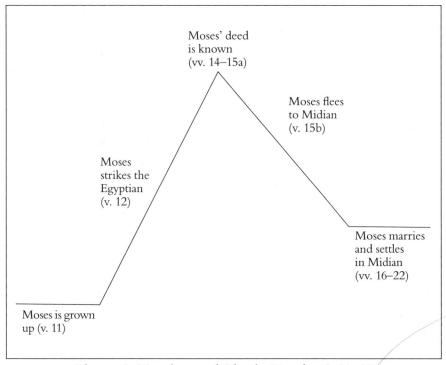

Figure 1: Tension and Plot in Exodus 2:11–12

As the graph illustrates, the tension begins to be relieved as questions are resolved. According to verse 15b, Moses flees to Midian. There is no mention of pursuit by agents of Pharaoh, and Moses settles in Midian. The tension flattens out on the graph when Moses marries Zipporah and has a child with her. The normality of life in Midian suggests that, for now at least, the danger from Pharaoh is past. For the implied reader, having children is a sign of blessing from God, so the tension is relieved to a great extent.

Notice, however, that the tension is not completely reduced to the level it was at the start of the narrative. This is because at the end Moses is, as demonstrated by the name of his child (v. 22), a sojourner in a foreign land. He is cut off from his people, the Hebrews. The implied reader likely was concerned about how this situation affected the promises to Abraham from Genesis and what would become of Moses and the descendants of Jacob.

Dialogue

Another feature of narrative is dialogue. Dialogue is frequently used to introduce or highlight the main point(s) of the passage.

As noted above, narratives are selective in what they record. Some authors choose to record speech using indirect speech. In indirect speech the author conveys the content of the speech but does not use the actual words spoken. For example, Genesis 26 gives the account of Isaac and Abimelech and the treaty of peace that is made between them. Verse 31 says, "In the morning they rose early and exchanged oaths" (ESV). The author of Genesis does not record the content of the speeches made. Rather, he simply notes that the oaths were taken.

Much more common, however, is direct speech, or dialogue, in which the writer records the actual words spoken. This reflects a deliberate choice on the part of the author, since any speech that is presented in direct speech also could have been rendered indirectly. It seems likely, then, that the author sought to convey something through the use of direct speech, or dialogue.

Direct speech can convey a number of things. An author may have chosen to use direct speech to highlight the importance of the speech or to draw attention to the character of the speaker. Presumably, in Genesis 26 the content of the oaths is not particularly important to the author. By contrast, note that in Genesis 28:20–22, the author records the content of the vow that Jacob made to Yahweh at Bethel as he was departing for Haran. Rather than simply record the vow indirectly, as in chapter 26, the author includes the words of the vow. This highlights the character of Jacob at this point, since the vow is somewhat self-serving in light of the fact that Yahweh himself had just revealed to Jacob that he would be heir to the promises made to his ancestors. Thus the rather weak tone of the vow ("if God will be with me . . . then Yahweh shall be my God") accentuates the lack of character on Jacob's part. This lack of character is effectively communicated through the use of direct speech.

Similarly, direct speech may convey important aspects of the author's intended meaning. In Genesis 50:20, Joseph reassures his brothers that he will not seek revenge against them for their earlier sins now that their father has died. He says, "You intended to harm me, but God intended it for good to accomplish what is now being done, the saving of many lives" (TNIV). By putting this statement on the lips of a major character, whom the reader has gotten to know well through the course of the previous thirteen chapters, Moses powerfully conveyed his understanding of the sovereignty of God and how he works in and through the lives of his people. Moreover, this accentuates the understanding of God's purposes that have been intimated throughout the rest of the Joseph cycle, such as the repeated emphasis on Yahweh's presence with Joseph in the midst of his trials.

Frequently, a narrative repeats dialogue or speech. While this may seem tedious to a contemporary reader, this characteristic or convention of Hebrew narrative highlights the importance of the message and, if repeated without significant alterations, the reliability of the messenger. If the dialogue does change, that may indicate that the author desires to show the unreliability of the messenger.

Perhaps the best-known example of changes to speech occurs in Genesis 3. There, the serpent confronts Eve and asks her about the commands God had given concerning which trees the humans could eat from. The original command is given in Genesis 2:16–17, which says, "You may surely eat of every tree of the garden, but of the tree of the knowledge of good and evil you shall not eat, for in the day that you eat of it you shall surely die" (ESV). In her response to the serpent, Eve says, "God said, 'You shall not eat of the fruit of the tree that is in the midst of the garden, neither shall you touch it, lest you die'" (Gen. 3:3 ESV). The differences between the two speeches are important. In her response, Eve adds to the command God had given, claiming that they were not even to touch the tree, but she also subtracts from it, since the original command demonstrates God's generosity in providing for the human beings. This suggests that Eve was already beginning to reflect the worldview of the serpent.[70] Through the careful and deliberate use of repetition, the author effectively communicates his intentions.

In examining dialogue, it is useful to look at where speech is introduced into the narrative. Given the general predominance of direct speech over indirect speech in Hebrew narratives, the introduction of direct speech into a story may be important in conveying the author's intention.

---

70. For more on the interpretive significance of Eve's addition and subtraction to the command of Yahweh, see Gordon J. Wenham, *Genesis 1–15*, WBC (Waco: Word, 1987), 73.

Often, the introduction of dialogue into a narrative will give insight into the character of the speaker or convey thematic elements important to the interpretation of the story.[71]

Point of View

The final feature of narrative that we will consider is point of view. Point of view refers to the perspective of the **implied author**, a literary construct that refers to the presentation of the empirical ("real-life") author within the text. The construct of implied author conveys a perspective that the empirical author desires to present. This perspective is shared both explicitly and implicitly in the text.

The implied author communicates point of view through the narration of the story. The empirical author chooses a certain type of narrative perspective. Although there are a variety of possible perspectives to choose from, most biblical narratives are written using an omniscient, third-person perspective.[72] That is, the implied author's perspective is represented in the story in the "voice" of the **narrator**. This narrator stands outside the story, referring to the "characters"[73] in the story as "he," "she," or "they."[74] In addition, the narrator knows everything, including those things that are beyond normal human observation. Thus, the biblical narrator knows what the characters think and feel, even when they are alone. In Genesis 38:6–10, for example, the narrator knows both the nature of Onan's sinful actions in refusing to provide an heir for his deceased brother and his motivations for refusing. Knowledge of these things comes from the narrator's omniscience.

Since the narrator is understood as literarily omniscient, his comments are authoritative. In Genesis 29:31 the narrator notes, "When the Lord

---

71. See Alter, *The Art of Biblical Narrative*, 67–79, for more on the interpretation of dialogue.

72. For more on alternative narratorial perspectives, see Bar-Efrat, *Narrative Art in the Bible*, 13–20; and M. H. Abrams, *A Glossary of Literary Terms*, 7th ed. (Fort Worth: Harcourt Brace, 1999), 231–36.

73. Though the language used to discuss the biblical narratives often is the same as that used to discuss fiction, I am not suggesting that the biblical stories should be thought of as fictional. Rather, the biblical narratives can be analyzed in terms of their literary artistry while still being accurate and true. So, the people in the biblical stories are "characters" in a literary sense (i.e., presented by an author in accordance with his intentions) but are nevertheless historical figures.

74. An alternative perspective is a first-person one, in which the implied author speaks in his own voice, saying, "I" and "we." In this perspective, the implied author is part of the story as a character and is rarely omniscient.

saw that Leah was hated, he opened her womb, but Rachel was barren"
(ESV). Because the narrator states that Leah was "hated," that must be taken
as fact. Though we perhaps could come up with plausible alternative interpretations of the situation (such as that Jacob loved both his wives but
simply loved Rachel more than Leah), the comments of the omniscient
narrator must be given the weight of authority. *I'm not sure about this,*

The narrator's comments convey the point of view of the implied author. In describing Onan's actions in refusing to father a son in the name
of his dead brother, the implied author (through the voice of the narrator)
says that "what he did was wicked in the sight of the LORD, and he put
him to death also" (Gen. 38:10 ESV). Through this comment on Onan's
behavior, the implied author communicates his (and Yahweh's) point of
view. Rather than allowing the readers to draw their own inferences about
Onan's behavior, the implied author communicates directly through this
explanation. Since God's feelings are only rarely described explicitly, it is
usually significant when they are included.[75] We are left with no doubt
that the implied author (with Yahweh) feels that Onan's behavior is evil
and therefore should not be emulated by the reader.

Dialogue also conveys point of view. Here, however, we must be
more careful. Simply because a biblical character—even a heroic one—
says something does not necessarily mean that it represents the point of
view of the implied author, even if the character and the actual (empirical)
author are the same person! Moses, for example, is the prophet of Yahweh
par excellence (Num. 12:6–8; Deut. 34:10–12) and is therefore usually a
reliable conveyor of the implied author's point of view. However, there
are times when Moses as character says or does things that would not align
with his ideals and perspective and so is therefore contrary to Moses the
implied author's point of view. Examples include his reluctance to serve
Yahweh as he was called to do (Exod. 4:13–17) and his rebellion at Meribah
(Num. 20:10–13). These are not presented as praiseworthy or actions to
be emulated. In these instances, Moses as author conveys his point of view
through narratorial comments that surround those speeches and actions of
Moses as character that are contrary to his point of view.

In evaluating whether or not a speech on the part of a character represents the implied author's point of view, we must examine comments by
the narrator surrounding the speech, as well as information we know about

---

75. Bar-Efrat, *Narrative Art in the Bible*, 19.

[handwritten marginalia: Maybe the author is exposing his own bias or prejudice or lack of understanding of the situation]

the implied author that has been communicated in the text. For example, the implied author of Numbers is one who is fervently devoted to Yahweh and is harshly critical of the complaints ("grumblings") of the Israelites. This may be discerned through the comments made by the narrator, as well as through the emphasis on the unity of the people at Sinai/**Horeb** and the contrasting dissonance of their complaints following the departure from Sinai. Consequently, we can evaluate the speeches of various characters in light of this information we know about the implied author. In the incident with the spies in Numbers 13–14, for example, the point of view of the implied author is reflected in the speeches of Joshua and Caleb, not the ten faithless spies. We know this because the attitudes of Joshua and Caleb comport to what we already have learned about the implied author.

Interestingly, the implied author's point of view can be expressed even through unsavory characters. The character of Balaam is a fascinating one in the book of Numbers. On the one hand, he seems to be a faithful messenger of Yahweh, indicating that he will speak only what Yahweh commands him to (Num. 22:18). But the overall assessment of Balaam, both within Numbers (Num. 31:16) and outside it (Deut. 23:4–5; 2 Peter 2:15; Jude 11; Rev. 2:14), is uniformly negative. Despite this negative assessment, what Balaam actually says may be understood as reflecting the implied author's (and God's!) point of view. This is not simply because he blesses rather than curses Israel, but also because the content of his blessings confirms the promises made to the patriarchs and stresses the faithfulness and sovereignty of Yahweh in keeping those promises. Once again, we know this to be in keeping with the implied author's perspective because of what we have learned about the implied author to this point. We cannot base our decision as to whether or not a speaker reflects the point of view of the implied author simply on the status of the speaker ("hero" or "villain"). Rather, we must carefully analyze the speaker's message in light of what we know about the implied author.[76]

---

76. Distinguishing between author, narrator, and implied author can at times be confusing. For simplicity, I will most often use the term *author* unless specific differentiation from other terms is needed. Be aware, however, that I am using that term as synonymous with implied author as discussed above.

2

MAJOR THEMES
OF THE PENTATEUCH

IN ITS PRESENT FORM, the Pentateuch tells a coherent and complete story. It begins, appropriately, "in the beginning" and recounts God's activity in creating all that is. In the early chapters of Genesis, we learn about the creation of human beings, their rebellion against **Yahweh**, and the dramatic effects their actions have on their relationship with Yahweh, each other, and the rest of creation. We also learn about God's actions to restore creation to its intended glory through the call of Abram, through whom all nations will be blessed (Gen. 12:1–3). From Genesis 12 onward, the Pentateuch describes the successes and failures of the descendants of Abram as they seek to live out their unique relationship with Yahweh. It also presents a portrait of a God who is faithful to his people despite their faithlessness and who is determined to accomplish his good purposes in the world he created.

In telling this important story, the Pentateuch develops certain themes that are part of the author's communicative intention. Understanding these themes helps us properly understand the message of the books. Even as we seek to better interpret the major **genres** of the Pentateuch—law and **narrative**—we must bear in mind the themes that the specific texts are developing. This helps us as we look at the details of particular texts.

specific text → themes → major genres

At the same time, we identify the themes by means of interpreting the specific texts. So, there is a dynamic relationship between the specifics of the text and the overarching, big picture.

Though there are many themes that are developed in the Pentateuch, we will concentrate here on three of the most important. We will also examine how these themes contribute to the coherence of the Pentateuch.

 Theme #1

THE SOVEREIGNTY AND SUPREMACY OF YAHWEH

Genesis

The first theme we will deal with is the sovereignty and supremacy of Yahweh. In many ways, this is the foundational theme, because the development of the other themes assumes this one.

The Pentateuch opens with an account of Creation. While as contemporary readers we often approach the creation accounts in Genesis with questions about how they relate to Darwinism and other forms of evolution, these theories were not in the minds of the **implied reader** and **implied author**. Rather, the author of Genesis interacts with ancient Near Eastern creation accounts and engages in a vigorous polemic against those understandings of the origins of creation. This same polemical stance toward ancient Near Eastern ideas and theology is found elsewhere in the Old Testament, notably in Jeremiah 10:11, which says, "You people of Israel should tell those nations this: 'These gods did not make heaven and earth. They will disappear from the earth and from under the heavens'" (NET). Similar ideas are expressed in Isaiah 44:24 and Psalm 96:5.[1]

The polemic against ancient Near Eastern theology centers on the supremacy of Yahweh, the God of Israel. Whereas many ancient Near Eastern creation accounts saw creation as the result of the activity of many gods, Genesis insists that the universe was created by one God. Moreover, Genesis 1 describes the creation of even those things understood as divine and worshipped as gods in the ancient Near Eastern world. So, for example, Genesis 1:16 describes the creation of the two "great lights," the greater to rule the day and the lesser to rule the night. It then includes the stars, almost as an afterthought. In some ancient Near Eastern creation

---

1. See chapter 3 for a discussion of the uses of ancient Near Eastern parallels in the interpretation of the Pentateuch.

accounts, the stars were understood as semidivine entities that were part of the divine, not created, realm. In the **Akkadian** epic of creation, the *Enuma Elish*, the triumphant god Marduk is described as bringing order to the universe, part of which includes establishing constellations of stars, but the stars themselves already exist and are described as likenesses of the great gods.[2] The sun and the moon are not directly named in Genesis (referred to instead simply as "great lights" [הַמְּאֹרֹת הַגְּדֹלִים]), perhaps to downplay the significance of those entities that were primary gods in some ancient Near Eastern myths.[3] According to the creation account in Genesis 1, God made everything, including everything that is worshipped by the people in the cultures around Israel.

In this way, God is elevated to a status far above that of any other ancient Near Eastern god or goddess. The portrayal of God in Genesis 1 is radically countercultural. The insistence that this God is able to speak and create everything—and to set limits even on those things (such as sun, moon, and stars) that were worshipped as gods in other ancient Near Eastern cultures—points to the sovereignty and supremacy of God.

The very fact that this God is referred to simply as אֱלֹהִים ("Elohim") throughout Genesis 1 and then named specifically as יהוה ("Yahweh") first in Genesis 2:4 may underscore the author's desire to highlight the supremacy of Yahweh. Suspense is built up on the part of the reader because this radically unique God is unnamed ("Elohim" can be a name or a generic reference to "gods"). The implied reader (familiar with ancient Near Eastern creation accounts and the anthropomorphic and amoral presentation of the gods there) may well be wondering, "Which god is this, who is able to create out of nothing and who created even those things worshipped as gods?" The answer is revealed in Genesis 2:4: Yahweh, the God of Israel, is this utterly unique God![4]

---

2. *Enuma Elish* 5:1–2.

3. Bruce K. Waltke and Cathi J. Fredricks, *Genesis: A Commentary* (Grand Rapids: Zondervan, 2001), 62–63.

4. Since the late nineteenth century, critical scholarship has tended to divide the Pentateuch into four major hypothetical sources, J, E, D, and P. In this view, usually known as the documentary hypothesis, Genesis 1 is assigned to P (representing a later and more sophisticated view of God than the earlier sources), while Genesis 2 is assigned to J (the earliest and most theologically primitive source). The use of the divine name is one criterion by which the sources are identified. More recent scholarship has challenged this understanding on a number of grounds. What is often overlooked in source-critical analyses is the possibility that the use of multiple divine names may be for rhetorical effect. By not naming Yahweh until Genesis 2:4, the author may be seeking to raise the implied reader's interest, and the revelation of this remarkable God's identity highlights

Like a myth created to explain the flood rather than a historical narrative of the flood.

The supremacy of Yahweh is further seen when comparing the biblical flood narrative with ancient Near Eastern accounts of a deluge. For example, in Atrahasis, an Akkadian epic that includes a flood story, the gods resolved to send a flood to destroy humanity because the noise made by humans disturbed their sleep. One god warned Atrahasis, who built an ark and was saved. Following the flood, the gods were surprised to discover that anyone had survived and were desperate for the sacrifices humans offered. Apparently, their decision to destroy humanity was rather shortsighted since it cut off their food supply![5]

In contrast, the reasons for the flood in Genesis are moral. The sin of human beings ultimately becomes so egregious that God executes judgment. He knows all the inclinations of humans and pronounces judgment on them. In this way, Yahweh is again portrayed as unlike the gods of the nations.

Moreover, he is sovereign in instructing Noah on the construction of the ark, preserving the animals, sending the floodwaters, and causing them to recede. Yahweh himself closes the door to the ark (Gen. 7:16). The God of Genesis is neither surprised nor terrified by the flood, which is always portrayed as an exercise of his sovereignty. In another ancient Near Eastern parallel account, the Epic of Gilgamesh, the gods are terrified by the flood and cower like dogs.[6] As in the creation account, the biblical account of the flood insists that Yahweh is qualitatively different from the gods of the ancient Near East and that he alone is supreme.

This portrayal of Yahweh's supremacy and sovereignty continues throughout the rest of Genesis. Confronted with the fact of human sin, Yahweh chooses Abram, through whom he will bless all nations (Gen. 12:1–3). Though there are many obstacles and threats to Yahweh's plan to bless all nations through Abram and his descendants (including, especially, the actions of those descendants themselves!), Yahweh protects and preserves them. Joseph's statement to his brothers highlights the development

---

the supremacy of Yahweh. For recent critiques of the documentary hypothesis, see T. Desmond Alexander, *From Paradise to the Promised Land: An Introduction to the Pentateuch*, 2nd ed. (Grand Rapids: Baker, 2002), 7–94; and Gordon J. Wenham, "Pondering the Pentateuch: The Search for a New Paradigm," in *The Face of Old Testament Studies: A Survey of Contemporary Approaches*, ed. D. W. Baker and B. T. Arnold (Grand Rapids: Baker, 1999). The documentary hypothesis is also taken up in chapter 4, below.

5. For an introduction and translation of Atrahasis, see Stephanie Dalley, *Myths from Mesopotamia: Creation, the Flood, Gilgamesh and Others* (Oxford: Oxford University Press, 1989), 1–38.

6. Epic of Gilgamesh, tablet 11.3.

of the theme of Yahweh's sovereignty and supremacy in the second part of Genesis (chaps. 12–50). Joseph notes, "As for you, you meant evil against me, but God meant it for good, to bring it about that many people should be kept alive, as they are today" (Gen. 50:20 ESV). In Genesis, the God of Israel is utterly unlike the gods of the nations, and he acts decisively in the world on behalf of people.

Exodus

The supremacy of Yahweh is further developed in Exodus, which depicts him as seeing the plight of his people and acting on their behalf. The sending of the plagues is best understood as a confrontation between Yahweh and the gods of Egypt. Of the ten plagues the Egyptians suffered, eight may be seen as a direct challenge to Egyptian gods.[7] Thus, the turning of the Nile to blood (Exod. 7:14–25) is a challenge to Khnum, the guardian of the Nile; Hapi, the spirit of the Nile; and Osiris, for whom the Nile was the bloodstream. Similarly, the plague of darkness (Exod. 10:21–29) challenges the sun god Re, as well as Atum, Aten, and Horus. The final plague, the death of the firstborn (Exod. 11:1–12:36), directly challenges Pharaoh himself, who was considered to be a deity.[8] Exodus portrays Yahweh as superior to the Egyptian gods, who cannot control events or protect themselves or their devotees from the experience of the plagues (Exod. 8:18–19).

It is significant, moreover, that Yahweh defeats the Egyptian gods within the land of Egypt (Exod. 12:12). In the ancient Near Eastern world, gods were largely understood as territorial, and their power and influence limited to some degree to the geographical area in which they "lived." All the inhabitants who lived in that area were under the dominion of these gods.[9] Given this worldview, the uniqueness of the claims made about Yahweh becomes apparent, as he exercises power and dominion in Egypt.

---

7. The plagues for which no corresponding Egyptian deity is known are the plagues of gnats and flies (Exod. 8:16–32).
8. For more on the Egyptian gods/goddesses themselves, see Barbara Watterson, *The Gods of Ancient Egypt* (New York: Facts on File, 1984). For a chart depicting the possible correspondence between the plagues and the Egyptian gods concerned, see John H. Walton, *Chronological and Background Charts of the Old Testament*, rev. ed. (Grand Rapids: Zondervan, 1994), 85.
9. See Daniel I. Block, *The Gods of the Nations: Studies in Ancient Near Eastern National Theology*, 2nd ed. (Grand Rapids: Baker, 2000), for a discussion of the ancient Near Eastern understanding of the relationship of the gods, their land, and the inhabitants of the land.

Yahweh's ability to protect the Israelites from seven of the plagues (most notably the plague of the death of the firstborn) further highlights his sovereignty and supremacy.[10]

The crossing of the Sea of Reeds[11] and the wilderness experience further develop the theme of the supremacy of Yahweh. Yahweh delivers the Israelites from Pharaoh's army through manipulation of the natural world[12] and then provides food for them in the midst of a harsh natural environment.

The description of Israel at Sinai develops the theme of Yahweh's supremacy further. There Yahweh sets forth the terms of the covenant between Israel and himself. The idea of a covenant or treaty (בְּרִית) was well known in the ancient Near Eastern world. It was the practice, for example, for two kings, as representatives of their respective nations, to enter into a treaty with one another. Usually, such a treaty was the result of a conquest or threat of conquest on the part of the more powerful king. Thus, there was an unequal relationship between the two parties. The greater power, sometimes referred to as the **suzerain** or "Great King," would dictate the terms of the treaty, which the lesser king, the **vassal**, would accept.[13] In light of this background, the account of the covenant between Yahweh and Israel highlights the supremacy of Yahweh. The account of the giving of the **Decalogue** and the subsequent instruction as to how the Israelites were to live as God's people portrays Yahweh as the "Great King."[14] He dictates the terms of the covenant with the Israelites. By virtue of who he is (that is, the unique God who created everything), he is able to tell the

---

10. In predicting the fourth plague, flies, Yahweh says that there will be division between the Israelites and the Egyptians (Exod. 8:22–23). Presumably, the previous three plagues affected all the inhabitants of Egypt, including the Israelites, while the text is explicit in noting that subsequent plagues did not.

11. This is a more accurate translation of יַם־סוּף and avoids the confusion that often results from referring to a crossing of the "Red Sea." Since Exodus makes clear that the Israelites followed a more northerly route rather than heading to the south toward the Gulf of Suez (an arm of the Red Sea), "Sea of Reeds" is a more accurate translation than "Red Sea."

12. Some have maintained that the wind that caused the parting of the Sea of Reeds was a natural occurrence. This may be so (but is ultimately unknowable); even if that is the case the text clearly indicates that the timing of the wind was the result of Yahweh's actions (Exod. 14:21).

13. Other known treaties reflect more parity between the parties, but the suzerain–vassal treaty model is more common. See John H. Walton, *Ancient Israelite Literature in Its Cultural Context: A Survey of Parallels Between Biblical and Ancient Near Eastern Texts* (Grand Rapids: Zondervan, 1989), 95–109; Kenneth A. Kitchen, *Ancient Orient and Old Testament* (Downers Grove, IL: InterVarsity Press, 1966), 90–102; and idem, *On the Reliability of the Old Testament* (Grand Rapids: Eerdmans, 2003), 283–307.

14. A term used in Hittite treaties to refer to the suzerain.

people how they are to live and what he expects of them. Moreover, the terms of the covenant are not arbitrary regulations designed to restrict the pleasure of the people. Rather, they are given for the people's good by the one who knows, by virtue of being the sovereign creator God, what is good, best, and right for them.

The final section of Exodus deals with the construction of the tabernacle. Here, again, the sovereignty and supremacy of Yahweh are highlighted, as Yahweh directs the construction of the visible symbol of his presence with his people. That the tabernacle is a grand construction further points to his supremacy. The elaborate and lavish tabernacle testifies to the awesome nature of this God.

Leviticus

Leviticus continues to develop Yahweh's supremacy through the continuation of the instructions surrounding his worship. The first seven chapters of the book concentrate on the sacrificial system. While at first glance this may not seem to have much to do with developing the theme of Yahweh's supremacy, it actually does contribute to the development of the theme.

The sacrificial system highlights Yahweh's sovereignty and supremacy because he has determined that there will be a system for dealing with human failures. This may be seen in Leviticus 17:11, which states, "For the life of the creature is in its blood, and I myself have bestowed it on you on the altar to make atonement for your lives; for it is the blood that makes atonement, by the life." This verse notes that the sacrificial system is a gracious gift from Yahweh himself, which he gives as the sovereign God. That is, he has provided a means by which human sin may be atoned for, and he establishes the parameters in which that will be accomplished. This stands in stark contrast to many ancient Near Eastern cultures. There, sacrifice was a means by which people manipulated the gods and something the gods needed (note again that ancient Near Eastern flood accounts portray the gods as starving after being deprived of sacrifice for the duration of the flood). In Leviticus the supreme God gives the sacrificial system as a gracious gift.[15]

As in Exodus, the rest of the laws in Leviticus detail how to live a life

---

15. John E. Hartley, *Leviticus*, WBC (Dallas: Word, 1992), 273–74.

that is pleasing to Yahweh. The presentation of the law demonstrates that the Israelites were to live differently from their neighbors because Yahweh is a different kind of God. So, the regulations concerning food, clothing, sowing, and so on were designed, at least in part, to highlight the singularity of the people of Yahweh and their unique God. In addition, the prohibition from imitating such things as the worship practices, beliefs, sexual habits, and food choices of the Canaanites highlights the Israelites' unique status as the people of Yahweh. But the status of the Israelites as the people of Yahweh was itself a result of his sovereignty in choosing Abraham and preserving his descendants.

Numbers

As the previous books do, the book of Numbers highlights the sovereignty and supremacy of Yahweh by describing his actions on behalf of Israel and the uniqueness of the people that he chose. In the early chapters of the book, Moses meticulously portrays the people as seeking to do everything that Yahweh commands.[16] In this way, Moses implies that Yahweh is sovereign, since the Israelites are seeking to obey him down to the most minute detail. Moreover, the census in chapter 1 further points to Yahweh's sovereignty and supremacy, as the strength of each tribe is numbered, with a total of 603,550 (Num. 1:46). Regardless of whether the Hebrew word אֶלֶף is taken as "thousand" or as a reference to clans or military units,[17] the figure demonstrates the greatly expanded size of the nation, which had entered Egypt as a group of 70 (Exod. 1:5) and is now large, organized, and confident. This is a result of Yahweh's presence and protection.

The wilderness journeys further highlight Yahweh's supremacy. As in Exodus, the book of Numbers describes Yahweh's provision of water and food for the people, even in the desolate conditions of the wilderness. Moreover, he executes judgment on the people when their "grumblings" are unwarranted (see, e.g., Num. 11:1–3). When Miriam and Aaron

---

16. This is explicit in Numbers 1:54; 2:34; 3:16, 51; 4:37, 49; 5:4; 7:10–11; 8:1–4; 9:5, 8. The frequent repetition demonstrates the importance of the idea.

17. A variety of translations are possible. Though אֶלֶף usually means "thousand" (see BDB, 48), in places it means "clan" (e.g., Judg. 6:15; Num. 1:16; 1 Sam. 10:19). The exclusion of the Levites from this census may point to the reference of a military unit, since the Levites would not fight alongside the other tribes but would bear the ark into battle. See the discussion in Philip P. Jenson, "אֶלֶף" in NIDOTTE, 1:416–18.

oppose Moses and challenge his special role and relationship with Yahweh, claiming in Numbers 12:2 that Moses has spoken "with" them as well as with Moses,[18] Yahweh defends Moses' unique status and so highlights his sovereign ability to choose his servants and determine their roles.

Perhaps the clearest attestation of Yahweh's supremacy in Numbers comes in response to the rebellion of the people at Kadesh Barnea (Num. 13–14). Despite having seen all of Yahweh's actions on behalf of his people in the exodus, the Israelites fear the inhabitants of the land and desire to return to Egypt (Num. 14:1–4). After deciding not to annihilate them for their rebellion (in order to protect his reputation among the nations), Yahweh determines that none of that generation will enter the land he has promised his people. Moreover, when the Israelites belatedly seek to obey and conquer the land, the Canaanites defeat them (Num. 14:39–45). This demonstrates that the success of the nation is entirely dependent on Yahweh, not its own courage or military prowess. In every instance where the Israelites challenge Yahweh's sovereignty and plan, Yahweh is vindicated and shown to be the utterly unique and supreme God.

What is probably the most famous narrative in the book of Numbers, the story of Balak and Balaam, further develops the theme of Yahweh's sovereignty. On the one hand, Yahweh causes a donkey to speak, and on the other hand, he prevents Balaam from speaking any words other than blessings on the Israelites. This is an obvious example of Yahweh's sovereignty. Less often noticed, however, is the content of Balaam's blessings. Each of Balaam's four oracles reaffirms some aspect of the promises made to the patriarchs. Thus the first oracle (Num. 23:7–10) reaffirms Yahweh's relationship with Israel as well as his promise of many descendants. This corresponds to the promise made in the call of Abram in Genesis 12:1–3. Similarly, the second oracle (Num. 23:18–24) confirms the covenant relationship and the promise of divine protection. The third oracle (Num. 24:3–9) envisions Israel in the land and so highlights the promise that Israel will inherit the land. The final oracle (Num. 24:15–19) deals with an Israelite king who is anticipated in the promises to the

---

18. Seeing the בְּ in the phrase גַּם־בָּנוּ דִבֶּר as meaning "with" is preferable to understanding it as "through" (as most contemporary English translations do). Since, according to Exodus 15:20, Miriam is a prophetess, it makes little sense to see her claiming that Yahweh speaks "through" her. That, after all, is the role of a prophetess. Rather, Miriam and Aaron claim that God speaks to them as he does to Moses, as seen by Yahweh's response in Numbers 12:6–8.

patriarchs (see Gen. 17:6, 16; 35:11). By portraying Balaam as only able to bless Israel, and also reaffirming the promises made to the patriarchs, Numbers highlights the ability of Yahweh to accomplish his plans and purposes for humanity and the world. In this way, Numbers once again reveals Yahweh as utterly unlike the gods of the nations around Israel and points to his supremacy.

The final chapters of Numbers highlight Yahweh's supremacy by describing the start of the conquest by the **Transjordanian** tribes (Num. 32). Just as the earlier, failed attempt to conquer the land without Yahweh pointed to the necessity of Yahweh's presence for any degree of success, the description of the beginning of the conquest here also points to the need for his presence. The Israelites will succeed only when they acknowledge and live out their dependency on the supreme and sovereign God.

Deuteronomy

Deuteronomy highlights the sovereignty and supremacy of Yahweh in many of the same ways that the other books of the Pentateuch do. The opening chapters recount the failure to obey Yahweh at Kadesh Barnea and highlight Yahweh's sovereignty in his response. Similarly, the account of the defeat of Sihon and Og (Deut. 2:26–3:22) illustrates that Israel's success comes from Yahweh.

Perhaps Deuteronomy's most distinctive contribution to the development of this theme comes in chapter 4, with its extended discussion on idolatry. Here, Moses reminds the people that they are to worship Yahweh alone, for he is unlike any of the gods of the nations. Deuteronomy 4:19 specifically cautions against worshipping any created thing he has allotted to all people.[19] The reason for this prohibition is because Yahweh created everything that exists, including all that others worship as gods. So,

---

19. This is sometimes taken to suggest that Yahweh has allotted the worship of the sun, moon, stars, etc., to other people. But this is not stated in the text. Moreover, this would be a surprising development, since later in the same chapter the author notes that there are no other gods besides Yahweh. In addition, Israel's call to be a witness to a watching world about how to live in relationship with the one true God argues against the idea that the author was suggesting that Yahweh sanctioned (through his "allotment" to people) the worship of false gods. It is better to understand this as prohibiting the worship of anything that is created, as that would be to emphasize creation over the Creator. See Christopher J. H. Wright, *Deuteronomy*, NIBC (Peabody, MA: Hendrickson, 1996), 51–52; and my book, *Deuteronomic Theology and the Significance of Torah: A Reappraisal* (Winona Lake, IN: Eisenbrauns, 2006), 131–32.

worshipping idols or anything in the natural world is to worship creation rather than the Creator. Yahweh, as the unique God, establishes the nature of proper worship.

The prohibition of making an image of Yahweh (Deut. 4:16–17) further illustrates Yahweh's supremacy. As the one supreme God, Yahweh established how he would be represented. Yahweh determined to allow human beings to function as his image on earth (Gen. 1:26–27). Making an image of Yahweh would serve to represent him in an unauthorized way. Yahweh demanded that the Israelites worship and represent him in a way that acknowledged his uniqueness.

It is also significant that Deuteronomy 4:39 is explicit in claiming that Yahweh is the one true God, noting, "Know therefore today, and lay it to your heart, that the LORD is God in heaven above and on the earth beneath; there is no other" (ESV). While this has been taken as expressing *monolatry* (belief that only one god should be worshipped, though others exist) rather than *monotheism* (the belief that there is only one God), this is hard to sustain in light of the argument of the chapter as a whole[20] and the entirety of the Pentateuch.

As we might expect in a book that recontextualizes an earlier message for a new audience, Deuteronomy, like Exodus–Numbers, also develops the theme of Yahweh's supremacy in relation to the giving of Torah. Deuteronomy portrays Yahweh as the one who provides instruction in proper living by virtue of his being sovereign. The emphasis in the book of Deuteronomy on the unique community that the Israelites, as the specially chosen people of Yahweh, were to establish highlights once again Yahweh's supremacy. The Israelites were to live differently and have a different kind of community because they were in relationship with a different kind of God. All this points to the supremacy of Yahweh.

THE SERIOUSNESS OF SIN

The next theme we will consider is the seriousness of sin. Like the previous theme, this theme is developed in many ways throughout the books of the Pentateuch, so we will only sketch its development here.

---

20. Moshe Weinfeld, *Deuteronomy 1–11: A New Translation with Introduction and Commentary*, AB (New York: Doubleday, 1991), 212.

Genesis

The theme first emerges, of course, in Genesis. Following the description of the idyllic life in the garden, Genesis 3 recounts the temptation of the human beings and their subsequent rebellion against Yahweh.

Scholars have long debated the nature of "original sin" (throughout the centuries pride, sensuality, and selfishness have all been posited as being at the core of original sin[21]). Often, however, the biblical data have been overlooked. In describing the encounter between the woman and the serpent, Genesis 3:5 notes that the serpent claims that eating of the fruit will make the humans "like God, knowing good and evil" (ESV). The next verse notes that the woman chose to eat in part because it was "to be desired to make one wise" (ESV).

We must note the significance of this. According to Genesis 1–2, human beings were created in the image of God and, as such, were given the remarkable privilege of representing Yahweh on earth, as stewards of his good creation. According to Genesis (and in marked contrast to other ancient Near Eastern creation accounts) human beings were elevated to a position of prominence in creation, being representatives ("image bearers") of the creator God in creation.[22] Despite being granted the privilege of representing God and being stewards of his creation, human beings sought to become "like God." The irony is that they already were the most "like God" of any creature, and in striving to attain greater likeness to God they experienced a disruption in their relationship with him.

As a result of their failure to be content with their God-ordained, privileged position in creation, the first humans suffered a dramatic transformation in their relationship with God, each other, and their environment. Whereas before they had known fellowship with God (suggested by their knowing the sound of Yahweh walking in the garden in the cool of the day, Gen. 3:8), they now feared him. More catastrophic is the implication

---

21. See Millard E. Erickson, *Christian Theology* (Grand Rapids: Baker, 1983), 577–80; and Wayne Grudem, *Systematic Theology: An Introduction to Biblical Doctrine* (Downers Grove, IL: InterVarsity Press, 1994), 492–93.

22. For more on the meaning and implications of being created in the image of God, see Waltke and Fredricks, *Genesis*, 65–66; and Gordon J. Wenham, *Genesis 1–15*, WBC (Waco: Word, 1987), 29–32. This elevation of human beings may be further seen in Psalm 8, which describes human beings as being "a little lower than אֱלֹהִים." While אֱלֹהִים here is often translated "heavenly beings" or "angels," it is probably better translated as "God," as many ancient versions have done. See the discussion in Peter C. Craigie, *Psalms 1–50*, WBC (Waco: Word, 1983), 108.

(confirmed in Gen. 3:22–24) that the humans would be removed from the garden and, consequently, from the immediate presence of God. In addition, prior to their rebellion they had functioned harmoniously as a team (see Adam's exuberant expression of joy at recognizing a companion that was complementary to him, Gen. 2:23). After the Fall, there is division and an attempt to assign blame (Gen. 3:12). Even creation itself is affected, as thorns and thistles now mar the landscape, making it difficult to harvest the food needed for life. Finally, we learn that death is now a part of life. According to Genesis 3:19, at the end of a toil-filled life outside of the garden, death awaits the human beings.

The sin of human beings is then carried on by subsequent generations. Adam and Eve have children, who, like their parents, act in ways contrary to God's intention and design. Moreover, the nature of the sin appears to become worse over time: Cain murders his own brother as a result of his hurt pride (Gen. 4:1–16), and Lamech, the seventh generation after Cain, murders in response to slights (Gen. 4:23–24).

The seriousness of sin is most apparent in the flood narrative. In contrast to the ancient Near Eastern epics, which include accounts of deluges as means by which the gods seek to rid the world of overly noisy human beings, Genesis depicts the flood as a consequence of human sin. Yahweh determines to destroy the earth by water when he sees that "every intention of the thoughts of [human hearts] was only evil continually" (Gen. 6:5 ESV). Interestingly, this statement comes after a description of the intermarriage between angelic beings and humans, perhaps another attempt at transgressing the divine-human barrier.[23]

The flood narrative points to the fact that human sin matters to God. It has a pernicious effect on all of creation and therefore must be dealt with. The fact that *all* life (except for the remnant preserved on the ark), not just human life, is destroyed demonstrates how seriously God takes sin. It is incompatible with his nature and contrary to his intentions for creation.

Sadly, sin is not eradicated in the deluge. It persists even with Noah, a man whose righteousness was such that he was spared the flood (see Gen. 6:9). Noah gets drunk and demonstrates a loss of self-control (Gen. 9:20–21). Likewise, Ham fails to protect the dignity of his father by talking about his actions to his brothers (Gen. 9:22). Human beings later seek to

---

23. The phrase בְּנֵי הָאֱלֹהִים. ("sons of God") has traditionally been understood as referring to angelic beings. For more on this interpretation, see Wenham, *Genesis 1–15*, 138–47.

elevate themselves by building a tower to heaven (Gen. 11:1–9), which may be yet another attempt to transgress the divine-human boundary.

Throughout the patriarchal history in Genesis (chaps. 12–50), the ravages of sin may be seen. The patriarchs sin frequently, even as they are chosen by Yahweh to be the instrument of blessing to the nations (Gen. 12:1–3). Like all other human beings, the patriarchs are full of pride, envy, lust, and anger, and at points they substitute their judgment for God's (e.g., Sarai's plan to have Hagar bear children for Abram and herself), and they show a remarkable lack of faith in God (e.g., Abram's fear of Pharaoh in Gen. 12:10–20). The account of the destruction of Sodom and Gomorrah further illustrates the seriousness of sin, as the cities are destroyed because of the pervasiveness of sin and the utter depravity of those committing the sin (Gen. 18–19).

Exodus

The seriousness of sin is further seen in Exodus. Yahweh deals severely with the sinful oppression of the Israelites by Pharaoh and the idolatry of the Egyptians. This helps underscore the fact that Yahweh cares about the sinful actions of *all* humans, not just the Israelites.

The legal material in Exodus 20:22–23:33 (sometimes referred to as the "Book of the Covenant" because of the reference in Exod. 24:7) highlights the seriousness of sin primarily through the penalties incurred for various offenses. Serious transgressions—including actions showing disloyalty to Yahweh as well as murder, kidnapping, disloyalty to parents—all are punishable by death. That an offender may forfeit his or her life accentuates the seriousness of the sins of the people.

Perhaps the most significant episode in Exodus highlighting the seriousness of sin is the construction of the golden calf (Exod. 32). In response to this blatant violation of the command against iconic worship, Yahweh threatens to destroy the people and start over with Moses (Exod. 32:10). Though that fate is averted through the intercession of Moses, the fact that the people were in such jeopardy as a result of their sin demonstrates just how serious sin is to God. Sin endangers the very existence of the nation itself.

Leviticus

Like Exodus, Leviticus develops the theme of sin's seriousness primarily through the legal stipulations. The first seven chapters of Leviticus

describe the offerings and sacrifices that were required to deal with sins
committed by the Israelites. This detailed program highlights how seriously God takes sin.

What is not so readily appreciated is that, with few exceptions (e.g.,
Lev. 6:1–7), all the sacrifices and offerings described in Leviticus 1–7 are
for *unintentional* sins. Thus, Leviticus 4:2, introducing the sin offerings,
says, "Speak to the people of Israel, saying, If anyone sins unintentionally
in any of the LORD's commandments about things not to be done, and
does any one of them . . ." (ESV). Even those offenses committed inadver-
tently matter to God and must be dealt with accordingly.[24]

Later sections of the book illustrate the message of the first seven chapters. In Leviticus 10, Aaron's sons Nadab and Abihu are killed when they
offer "unauthorized" fire to Yahweh. Though the exact nature of their
transgression is not spelled out,[25] the fact that they are consumed by fire
highlights the seriousness of their sin, as does the fact that their father
Aaron "held his peace" (v. 3 ESV). Whether their error was simply a failure
to strictly follow the ritual procedures established by Yahweh or something more serious, their actions resulted in their destruction. All sin matters to God.

The well-known system of cleanness/uncleanness in Leviticus further highlights the seriousness of sin. In thinking about the relationship between cleanness/uncleanness and sin, we must first note that
cleanness is *not* the same as cleanliness. Cleanliness refers to the extent
something is free from dirt or germs. Cleanness, on the other hand,
refers to how well something adheres to a world order established by
Yahweh. So, for example, animals that conform to a perceived standard
of "normalcy" are considered "clean," whereas animals that don't are
considered to be "unclean." In the ancient Israelite worldview, sea-
dwelling creatures have scales and swim (Deut. 14:9–10). Thus, those
creatures that fit this understanding of normalcy are considered to be

---

24. Though not discussed directly, intentional sins were atoned for through the burnt offering (see
   Jacob Milgrom, *Leviticus 1–16*, AB [New York: Doubleday, 1991], 175; and Gordon J. Wenham,
   The Book of Leviticus, NICOT [Grand Rapids: Eerdmans, 1979], 57–58). By not addressing intentional sins directly, however, the author forces the reader to wrestle with the question and to come
   to the conclusion that all sin is forgivable only because of the grace of Yahweh. Leviticus 17:11
   ("For the life of the creature is in its blood, and I myself have bestowed it on you on the altar to
   make atonement for your lives; for it is the blood that makes atonement, by the life.") makes clear
   that the entire sacrificial system is a manifestation of grace.
25. See the discussion in Hartley, *Leviticus*, 132–33, for possible understandings of the nature of the
   violation here.

clean (fish, primarily). Those that don't, such as shellfish, are considered "unclean."[26]

Unclean things caused pollution of the sanctuary, since they reflected disorder in God's good creation. As a result, Leviticus calls for avoiding the unclean things and for purification not just of the individual but also of the sanctuary. Sin and uncleanness were understood as causing "spiritual pollution" that must be dealt with. In this way, the laws of clean and unclean in Leviticus highlight the seriousness of sin. The world regulated by Leviticus, with all the unclean elements in it and opportunities for contamination, stands in marked contrast to the pre-Fall, idyllic world described in Genesis 1–2. The difference between these two worlds is the reality of human sin. At times in the normal course of life, the average Israelite inevitably would become ceremonially unclean (normal bodily discharges, such as a woman's menstrual period, rendered a person unclean). In most instances, no guilt was associated with that uncleanness, but the purity system and the remedy for uncleanness served as a reminder that the post-Fall world was marred and disfigured by human sin.

Numbers

In Numbers, the idea of the seriousness of sin is developed through elaboration of the laws given earlier (such as the imposition of the death penalty on the Sabbath breaker in Num. 15:32–36), as well as through the narration of specific events that describe the consequences of human sin.

We could examine many events in connection with the theme of the seriousness of sin; we will examine just two here. Each is important in the development of this theme.

Numbers 13–14 narrates the rebellion of the Israelites. After leaving Sinai, the people journeyed to the threshold of the Promised Land. The spies who were sent in reported back to the people that the land flowed with milk and honey but that the inhabitants were giants. The people

---

26. The underlying assumptions of the system of clean and unclean (as well as the sacrificial system as a whole) have been evaluated from a variety of perspectives. Some of the most helpful insights have come from anthropologists, who have discerned a number of important aspects of the Israelite system. See especially Mary Douglas, *Purity and Danger* (London: Routledge, 1966); and Philip P. Jenson, *Graded Holiness: A Key to the Priestly Conception of the World*, JSOTSup (Sheffield: Sheffield Academic Press, 1992).

listened to the ten faithless spies rather than Joshua and Caleb and indicated their desire to return to Egypt (Num. 14:1–4).

This blatant rejection of Yahweh, his leadership, and his plan led to God's judgment on the people.[27] Because of the people's failure to trust in him, Yahweh determined that he would destroy them and accomplish his plan through Moses. It was only as a result of Moses' intercession that Yahweh relented and did not destroy the people, though he did deny them entry into the land promised to Abraham.

The extreme consequences of the actions of the people highlight the seriousness of sin. All sin is serious, but this event demonstrates that questioning Yahweh's ability and willingness to care for his people is a particularly serious offense.

The second event we will examine is Moses' own rebellion. According to Numbers 20:2–13, when the people found themselves with no water, they quarreled with Moses about it. God instructed Moses to speak to the rock and provide water for the people. Once the people were assembled, however, Moses instead struck the rock twice. For this transgression, he too was denied entry into the land.

At first glance, this may seem to be an overly harsh reaction on God's part. But there are several factors that point to this being a more significant transgression than it first appears.

First, we need to note that Moses' actions take place in the presence of "the assembly" (קָהָל). This term is used to describe a sacred gathering, where the people would have expected to hear from Yahweh.[28] In that context, Moses then fails to properly glorify Yahweh. In Numbers 20:10, he says, "Hear now, you rebels: shall we bring water for you out of this rock?" (ESV). The use of "we" suggests that Moses is glorifying himself rather than Yahweh, and God's reaction in verse 12 supports this understanding.

Second, we must recognize Moses' unprecedented relationship with Yahweh. In Numbers 12:2, Miriam and Aaron challenge Moses' unique status, claiming that they too speak with Yahweh.[29] Yahweh's response demonstrates that there is something unique about the privileged way in

---

27. The irony of the people's rebellion should be noted. After all, the people had experienced Yahweh's miraculous defeat of the gods of Egypt and the destruction of the mighty Egyptian army at the Sea of Reeds. What difference would it make if the people of the land were giants, when Yahweh was with the Israelites?

28. Eugene Carpenter, "קהל," in NIDOTTE, 3:889.

29. See footnote 18 on page 69.

which he speaks to Moses. With that privilege, however, comes responsibility. For Moses to diminish Yahweh's reputation in any way is indeed
a serious offense that is magnified because of Moses' special relationship
with Yahweh. God's refusal to allow Moses to enter the land is a just response to a grave violation. It too highlights the seriousness of sin.

Deuteronomy

The final book of the Pentateuch develops the idea of the seriousness
of sin in much the same way as the earlier books. Through the presentation of the law and the consequences for transgressions of it, Deuteronomy
highlights how seriously God takes sin.

Deuteronomy's unique contribution in this regard comes in its remarkable emphasis on the need for demonstrating total loyalty to Yahweh.
This call is most famously heard in the Shema[30] of Deuteronomy 6:4–9,
which begins, "Hear, O Israel: Yahweh is our God, Yahweh alone. You
shall love Yahweh your God with all your heart, and with all your soul, and
with all your strength. And these words that I am commanding you today
shall be on your hearts. Impress them on your children." The Israelites are
called to show loyalty to Yahweh in every aspect of their lives, in public
and private, corporately and individually.

Deuteronomy clearly demonstrates that showing loyalty to Yahweh
is an urgent matter. The very survival of the nation depends on this, as is
clear from texts such as Deuteronomy 8:19–20; 32:45–47.

In Deuteronomy, every moment presents an opportunity to show either loyalty to Yahweh (and, consequently, to choose life) or disloyalty to
him (and choose death).[31] There is no middle ground.

This emphasis on the need for total loyalty stresses the seriousness
of sin. Failure to show total loyalty to Yahweh would result in expulsion
from the land, because in their disloyalty the people would not be acting
as the people of Yahweh. This would have an impact on the nations, as
Deuteronomy conceives of the Israelites as living out their relationship

---

30. The term *Shema* refers to portions of the Pentateuch that are recited twice daily by many Jews. It
    derives its name from the Hebrew imperative שְׁמַע ("hear!") that begins Deuteronomy 6:4, and it
    includes Deuteronomy 11:13–21 and Numbers 15:37–41.
31. This idea is developed extensively in J. Gordon McConville and J. Gary Millar, *Time and Place in
    Deuteronomy*, JSOTSup 179 (Sheffield: Sheffield Academic Press, 1994); and J. Gary Millar, *Now
    Choose Life: Theology and Ethics in Deuteronomy*, NSBT (Grand Rapids: Eerdmans, 1999).

to Yahweh before a watching world (Deut. 4:6; 28:10). Total loyalty to Yahweh, expressed through adherence to his Torah, was how Israel would ensure its success in the land and in being the people of Yahweh.

Theme #3

THE GRACE OF YAHWEH

Many Christians see grace as a New Testament concept. The Old Testament, it is often thought, is about law, and salvation occurs mainly through strict (and legalistic) adherence to the stipulations of the law. The New Testament, on the other hand, emphasizes grace, and salvation is by grace through faith.

Though this understanding of the natures of the two Testaments dominates much discussion of the Bible, it is nevertheless flawed. The Old Testament emphasizes grace from the earliest pages of Genesis. Moreover, the Torah is *not* about salvation, as we noted in chapter 1. In this section, we will examine the ways in which the Pentateuch develops the theme of the grace of Yahweh.

Genesis

Genesis points to God's grace primarily through showing his gracious actions in response to and on behalf of his people. His grace may be seen in his response to the rebellion of Adam and Eve in the garden. In responding to this very serious transgression, God certainly could have destroyed his creatures and started anew. The fact that God instead chose to allow the wayward creatures to live is a manifestation of his grace.

Not only does God graciously allow the human beings to continue to live and reproduce—as seen in the description of sin's consequences for the woman, where Genesis 3:16 notes that pain in childbearing will be greatly increased—but immediately after pronouncing judgment on them, God also provides clothing for them. Furthermore, the human beings are not explicitly cursed. The serpent and ground are cursed (vv. 14, 17), but human beings are not. To curse means to cut off from blessings, and God does not do this to Adam and Eve, much though they deserved it.

Curse vs. Blessing

In Genesis 4 God protects Cain, despite his murder of Abel. Moreover, God preserves the righteous Noah, his family, and representatives of every species of animals in the ark. Genesis 6:8 expressly notes that God preserved

Noah because Noah "found grace/favor [חֵן] in the eyes of Yahweh." As
the ark floats in the midst of an again-watery earth, God "remembers"
(זָכַר) Noah (8:1) and sends the wind to dispel the floodwaters. This remembering (best understood as careful consideration, rather than recalling
something forgotten[32]), coupled with God's providing the plans for the
ark, causing the animals to come to it, and closing the doors of the ark, all
point to the grace of Yahweh.

Perhaps the greatest manifestation of grace in Genesis comes in the
call of Abram (Gen. 12:1–3). In response to human sin and the destructive
effects it has on creation, God calls Abram and promises to establish him
as a mighty nation. It is significant to note again that this is explicitly said
to be for the purpose of blessing the nations. Genesis 12:2–3 states twice
that Abram's blessing will result in a blessing of the nations. For God to
seek the blessing of creatures who continue to reject his lordship and rebel
against him at every turn points to his tremendous—one might even say
"amazing"—grace.

Throughout the rest of Genesis, the patriarchs are shown to be frail
creatures, prone (like all humans) to sin. Remarkably, despite this igno-
minious cast of characters, Yahweh reiterates his promise to bless the descendants of Abraham in order to bless all nations and restore creation to
its intended glory.

In Genesis, Yahweh's grace is bound up extensively with his sovereignty. As we have seen, Genesis 50:20 highlights Yahweh's sovereignty, as
Joseph notes that God was able to turn the evil inclinations of his brothers
into good, so that the people were preserved alive. By exercising his sovereignty, God graciously blesses his people and preserves them. Moreover,
this grace extends, not just to the Israelites, but also to the Egyptians,
who benefit from Joseph's wise, godly leadership, and the rest of the nations, who obtain grain from Egypt during a time of severe famine (Gen.
41:57).

Exodus

The book of Exodus also portrays Israel's God as one of grace and
mercy. The book opens with an account of how greatly the nation had
increased in number during their time in Egypt. That the people were able

---

32. See Leslie C. Allen, "זכר," in *NIDOTTE*, 1:1100–1101.

to "be fruitful and multiply" even in the hardship of slavery further testifies to the grace of Yahweh.

We also see in Exodus that Yahweh is not a disinterested God, watching events from afar while remaining unconcerned about what happens in his creation. He cares deeply about the oppression of the Israelites by Pharaoh and in his grace calls Moses to lead them from that suffering. That Moses, a murderer, is chosen to deliver the people further points to God's grace.

We can even see the encounter between Pharaoh and Yahweh as a witness to Yahweh's grace (and once again see the relationship between Yahweh's sovereignty and grace). As we noted above, the plagues that befell the Egyptians were a challenge to the gods of Egypt, and the encounter between Yahweh and Pharaoh is rightly seen as a testimony to the utter uniqueness and supremacy of Yahweh. But we also must recognize that this confrontation is an act of grace on the part of Yahweh. If it is true that Yahweh is the one true God and that the gods worshipped by the people of other cultures are false gods, then the most loving, grace-filled thing God could do is help them recognize their sin. So, the demonstration of Yahweh's supremacy is an act of love in that it helps the Egyptians to see that they are worshipping false gods.

Even the problematic "hardening" of Pharaoh's heart is an act of grace. Exodus 10:1 suggests that the purpose of hardening Pharaoh's heart is so that the Egyptians will properly recognize and acknowledge Yahweh. Moreover, Yahweh's grace is seen in the ways in which he "softens" Pharaoh's heart: by giving him many chances, by allowing him to hear from his own magicians that Moses' power exceeds theirs (Exod. 8:19), and by the unrelenting testimony to Yahweh that he hears.

Exodus continues with the narration of the giving of the Torah at Sinai and the establishment of a covenant between Yahweh and Israel. This is not something God needed to do but something he did because of his love for his creatures.

In addition, the giving of the Torah is a gracious act by God. Prior to the Fall, human beings presumably knew what God expected of them, since they lived in close communion with him (see, e.g., Gen. 3:8). The rejection of Yahweh in the Fall represents a tragic and significant disruption in the relationship between human beings and Yahweh. Rather than leaving humans to simply "muddle through" and try to figure out what God wanted of them and how they could live a life pleasing to him, Yahweh graciously revealed his intentions and desires in the Torah. Even prior to the giving of the Torah at Sinai, God revealed his intentions, as demonstrated by Genesis 26:5: "All this will come to pass because Abraham obeyed me and kept my charge, my commandments, my statutes, and my laws" (NET). Abraham clearly did not have the "commandments, statutes, and laws" given at Sinai, and yet God evidently revealed his expectations to him in a way that he was able to both understand them and carry them out. Torah, then, is not a legalistic burden but rather a gift from God. He tells his people how to live because he loves them and cares about what is best for them, not because he wants to deny them pleasure.

When the people violate the terms of the Decalogue and construct a golden calf as part of their worship of Yahweh (Exod. 32), God responds graciously. Though he certainly would have been justified in destroying the people and starting again (as he threatens to do), he instead relents and allows the people to live (Exod. 32:14).

Finally, Exodus includes a description of the construction of the tabernacle. Prior to the experience at Sinai, God consistently had to "come down" to the earth (cf. Gen. 11:5; 18:1; Exod. 3:2). At Sinai, however, a new era is inaugurated. By commanding the construction of the tabernacle, Yahweh demonstrates that he is going to remain with his people.[33] The Israelites will experience his protection and, more importantly, close relationship with him. Significantly, Yahweh chooses to remain with the people on his own initiative rather than in response to the petition of the people.

Finally, Exodus testifies to Yahweh's grace through the revelation of God's name. In response to Moses' petition, Yahweh reveals his glory to Moses: "Yahweh descended in the cloud and stood with him there and proclaimed Yahweh by name. Yahweh passed by before him and proclaimed: 'Yahweh, he is Yahweh, the compassionate and gracious God, slow to anger, and abounding in loyal love and faithfulness, keeping loyal love for thousands, lifting away iniquity and rebellion and sin. But he by no means leaves the guilty unpunished, responding to the sin of fathers by dealing with children and children's children, to the third and fourth generation'" (Exod. 34:5–7). Grace is obviously a major facet of Yahweh's self-understanding of who he is.

---

33. To be sure, the book of Exodus, as well as the Pentateuch as a whole, recognizes that Yahweh is not limited to the tabernacle. See Exodus 20:22–23, Deuteronomy 4:36, and the discussion in Vogt, *Deuteronomic Theology*, 113–59.

Leviticus

It is often difficult for contemporary readers to appreciate how the sometimes sleep-inducing description of sacrifices in Leviticus 1–7 helps develop the idea of God's grace. But, properly understood, the sacrificial system, like the Torah as a whole, does just that.

The very fact that a mechanism for dealing with human sin exists is a manifestation of God's grace. This is seen most clearly in Leviticus 17:11, which reads, "For the life of the creature is in its blood, and I myself have bestowed it on you on the altar to make atonement for your lives; for it is the blood that makes atonement, by the life." In this verse, particularly through the emphatic use of the personal pronoun in the phrase וַאֲנִי נְתַתִּיו ("I *myself* have bestowed it on you"[34]), the sacrificial system may be seen as a gift from God, for Yahweh did not have to provide a means of atonement for sin. Moreover, sacrifice is not magical. Rather, it atones for sin because Yahweh has determined that it does so. This turns our usual understanding of sacrifice on its head. It is not that humans bring something to God that he has need of. Rather, in the sacrificial system, he graciously provides for the needs of his people and allows blood to atone for sin.[35]

In addition, the purity laws of Leviticus, designed to reflect the division of humanity into priests, Israelites, and Gentiles, further highlight the grace of God. The purity regulations are, at least in part, culturally appropriate object lessons intended to remind the Israelites of the order that exists in the world and their role in it. Since Israel exists to be a blessing to the nations, all reminders of that role highlight Yahweh's graciousness. Moreover, as a nation made up of fallen human beings, Israel *needs* reminders of its identity and what kind of people the Israelites are to be. The purity laws, however obliquely, serve as reminders of the status of the Israelites and, in turn, help develop the idea of the grace of Yahweh.

Numbers

Numbers further develops the theme of grace through the account of Yahweh's interactions with his people and through the legal material. In the first ten chapters of Numbers, the people are unified in their devotion

---

34. On translating נתן here as "bestow," see Milgrom, *Leviticus 1–16*, 707.
35. Jay Sklar, *Sin, Impurity, Sacrifice, Atonement: The Priestly Conceptions* (Sheffield: Sheffield Phoenix, 2005), 164–65.

to Yahweh and seek to do all that Yahweh commands. The opening verse of the book reminds the reader of Israel's deliverance and is coupled with the numbering of the people in the rest of chapter 1. This people are free and numerous because of Yahweh's gracious, caring actions.

Yahweh's grace is further seen in his responses to the frequent grumblings of the people (indeed, if the book were named based on its content, it might be better called the "book of Grumblings"!). Though many of the complaints lack merit and the people experience judgment for their sin, Yahweh nevertheless stays with the people, protects them, and, most importantly, retains them as his chosen people. As was the case so often in the earlier books, God would certainly be justified in destroying the people and starting over.

Even in response to the people's rebellion and rejection of Yahweh at Kadesh Barnea (Num. 14), Yahweh demonstrates grace. In response to Moses' intercession, he relents and allows the people to live. More than that, he determines that the next generation (who were too young to have participated in the rebellion themselves, according to Num. 14:31) will be allowed to enter the land and inherit the promises made to the patriarchs. That is, they will continue to be the people of Yahweh, through whom all nations on earth will be blessed.

The theme is developed in more subtle ways as well. After the people's rebellion and judgment in Numbers 14, a description of sacrifices immediately follows. At first glance, this seems to be a fairly disjointed way to proceed with the narrative.[36] But the opening verses of chapter 15 give a clue as to why this is: Numbers 15:1–3 says, "The LORD spoke to Moses, saying, 'Speak to the people of Israel and say to them, When you come into the land you are to inhabit, which I am giving you, and you offer to the LORD from the herd or from the flock a food offering or a burnt offering or a sacrifice, to fulfill a vow or as a freewill offering or at your appointed feasts, to make a pleasing aroma to the LORD . . .'" (ESV). Immediately following the description of the judgment of the people, the text offers hope by demonstrating that the people will in fact enter the land and by indicating that Yahweh will accept the sacrifices of his people.

Finally, the book of Numbers ends with the people gathered on the plains of Moab, the "back door" to the Promised Land. But this is not the

---

36. Indeed, some see no real unity to the book of Numbers, seeing it instead as a fairly loose collection of narratives. See the discussion in R. Dennis Cole, *Numbers*, NAC (Nashville: Broadman & Holman, 2000), 36–43.

same group that had gathered earlier at Kadesh Barnea, since that rebellious generation was forbidden to enter the land and died out. Rather, it is the next generation that is gathered on the plains of Moab and stands ready to enter the land. The fact that the census of the new generation (Num. 26) results in a very similar number to the earlier census points to the fact that Yahweh has blessed the new generation, as he had the earlier one. Moreover, the book ends on a note of hope that the new generation will fare better than did the previous one. This hope can be seen only as a result of the grace of Yahweh. Were it not for his grace, there would be no people to take the land and carry out his plans.

Deuteronomy

The final book of the Pentateuch develops the theme of Yahweh's grace in much the same way as the earlier books do. The impassioned speeches of Moses in Deuteronomy may be seen as manifestations of grace, since Moses, the prophet of God par excellence, reveals to the people what they need to know in order to survive and thrive in the land and foster the unique kind of community to which they are called.

As was the case with the legal material in the earlier books, the instructions in Deuteronomy demonstrate Yahweh's grace. To the generation gathered on the plains of Moab, the instructions as to how to live help them know what is expected of the unique people of God as they enter the land. As with the earlier generation, Yahweh doesn't leave the people to figure out for themselves how they are to live; rather, he graciously tells them through Moses.

Like Exodus, Deuteronomy is explicit about the character of Yahweh. Explaining why he chose the Israelites, Deuteronomy 7:7–8 says, "It is not because you were more numerous than all the other peoples that the LORD favored and chose you—for in fact you were the least numerous of all peoples. Rather it is because of his love for you and his faithfulness to the promise he solemnly vowed to your ancestors that the LORD brought you out with great power, redeeming you from the place of slavery, from the power of Pharaoh king of Egypt" (NET).

INTEGRATIVE CONCEPT: "RESTORATION PROJECT"

It may be helpful at this point to consider how these themes relate to one another. As we have seen, the concepts of Yahweh's grace and sovereignty are closely linked. Similarly, there is a link between grace and sin, for there would be no need for grace if human beings were not sinful creatures.

All these themes may be seen as contributing to an overarching concept, or what is sometimes called a **metanarrative**. This is closely related to the idea of worldview. A worldview is a way of seeing life, ourselves, and our experiences. It is a way of ordering the disparate events and ideas we experience in life. Our worldview shapes our understanding of events and helps us to see coherence in them.[37] A worldview seeks to address fundamental questions such as: Who are we as a community? What are our basic needs? What is the solution to our problems? Given who we are, how are we to live? How do we put into practice the solutions to our problems?[38] A metanarrative expresses or reflects the worldview by communicating the perspective as an overarching story.

The Old Testament (and the entire Bible) offers a normative metanarrative that addresses these questions. By understanding this metanarrative, we can better integrate the various themes developed in particular books and passages and understand how various texts contribute to the whole. While a thorough examination of the Old Testament/biblical metanarrative is well beyond the scope of this book, it will be helpful to at least sketch its contours.

The Old Testament metanarrative begins with the story of Creation. Creation is a reflection of Yahweh's intentions and is good (Gen. 1:31). Human beings were created deliberately and with great care. Male and female humans complement one another in deep and profound ways, such that the woman, unlike any other creature, can be described as a suitable companion to the man. Both male and female were created in the image of God and called into relationship with him.

Despite this exalted position, the first humans rebelled against God and sought to achieve a status of equality with God (Gen. 3:6). This rebellion caused a cataclysmic disruption in the created order, with the result that Adam and Eve experienced enmity with each other, with their

---

37. Jeannine K. Brown, *Scripture as Communication: Introducing Biblical Hermeneutics* (Grand Rapids: Baker, 2006), 29–31. See also Albert Wolters, "Metanarrative," in *Dictionary for Theological Interpretation of the Bible*, ed. Kevin Vanhoozer (Grand Rapids: Baker, 2005), 506–7.

38. N. T. Wright, *Christian Origins and the Question of God*, vol. 1, *The New Testament and the People of God* (Minneapolis: Fortress, 1992), 122–24. See also the discussion in Vogt, *Deuteronomic Theology*, 15–19.

environment, and with God. They were cast out of Yahweh's presence in the garden. Whereas prior to their rebellion there was harmony in creation, following the Fall there was (is!) violence, discord, rebellion, and hatred.

In response to this situation, God acted. He called Abraham to be the "father of many nations," and more specifically to be the head of a new family/nation through whom all nations on earth would be blessed. Genesis 12:1–3 marks the start of Yahweh's great "restoration project," through which he is working to restore creation to its intended glory. Through Abraham's descendants, all nations will be blessed and ultimately all creation will be restored.

God thus establishes the "people of God," that is, Israel. This people of God shares a common ancestor in Jacob. Though the line begins with Abraham (Gen. 12:1–3), the line of Abraham-Isaac-Jacob is the people chosen to be the means through which Yahweh will bless all humanity (Gen. 17:19; 26:3–5; 28:13–15). Other "branches" of the line (such as Ishmael and Esau) are blessed because they are descendants of Abraham (Gen. 21:12–13; 25:23; 36), but it is specifically those descendants of Abraham who are *also* descendants of Jacob who are considered to be God's treasured possession (Exod. 19:5).

In calling and establishing a people for himself, God gave the Israelites the gift of Torah, which helped them to live out their relationship with him. Proper adherence to Torah was part of their witness to the world. In addition, God gave the Israelites the tabernacle/temple. These symbols of Yahweh's presence were entrusted to the Israelites, but like Israel itself, they were to benefit all people in all nations.

God also established his people as a readily identifiable entity. Israel is a people (with a common ancestor), and it is also a **theocratic** state.[39] It has institutions of government (Deut. 16:18–18:22), laws (Exod. 20; Deut. 5), and religious practices and expression (e.g., Lev. 1–7) that all mark it as a functioning state.

Israel was chosen to bless the nations (Gen. 12:1–3). So, it was expected that people from "the nations" would see Israel's example, hear of Yahweh's sovereign greatness, and enter into relationship with him

---

39. The use of the word *state* to refer to ancient Israel is, in many ways, anachronistic, as the state as usually conceived is a modern development. "Nations" in this period were primarily people groups with unique identities and polities. Nevertheless, it is a useful way of referring to national political entities and will be used despite the anachronism.

(Deut. 4:6; Isa. 60:3, 11; 66:18–23). Those Gentiles wanting to do so had to identify themselves to some extent with Israel, not least because Israel was the custodian of the symbols of Yahweh's presence: Torah and tabernacle/temple. Acceptable sacrifices to Yahweh could be given only at the tabernacle/temple, wherever that might be (Deut. 12:5–7). Thus, some Gentiles who wanted to enter into relationship with Yahweh would reside with the Israelites and live as they did (Lev. 24:16; Num. 9:14; 15:15, 30).[40] Presumably these Gentiles were incorporated into Israel and, through intermarriage and over time, became Israelites. Ruth is an example of this (note that Ruth, though a Moabite, becomes great-grandmother to David, the paradigmatic Israelite king; Ruth 4:18–22).

Other Gentiles presumably would associate themselves with Israel, not through taking up residence with them in the midst of the Israelites in their land, but through imitating Israel's example of holy living in relationship with Yahweh. (This is probably the idea behind Jonah's mission to the Ninevites.) This would be accomplished through Torah adherence, either literally or through the instruction provided to all prior to the Torah's proclamation at Sinai (similar to Abraham's adherence to the Torah's standards and expectations before the Mosaic law in Gen. 26:5). Some Gentiles who wanted to follow Yahweh, then, would become "functionally" Israelite. They didn't become ethnically Israelite, but they lived as the Israelites were supposed to. Moreover, access to Yahweh in a temporal sense was mediated by the Israelites through the temple and sacrifices (hence the designation "kingdom of priests" in Exod. 19:6).

So, we can speak of the "people of God" in two senses: on the one hand, it refers to the "chosen people," ethnic Israelites. On the other hand, it can refer to those people who—regardless of ethnicity—entered into relationship with and put their trust in the one true God. Being an ethnic Israelite did not guarantee inclusion among the people of God in the second sense; indeed, many Israelites failed to properly trust Yahweh. In this way, a person like Rahab (a Canaanite) could become part of the people of God, even though she was not ethnically Israelite (Josh. 2:8–14). The same is true for Ruth (Ruth 1:16–18). Similarly, Achan (an ethnic Israelite) could be "cut off" from the people of God (in both senses) because he failed to properly trust and honor Yahweh (Josh. 7:22–25).

---

40. The Torah is remarkably inclusive of the "sojourner" (גֵּר). Few laws provide for distinctions between the native-born and the foreigner dwelling among the Israelites. See, e.g., Deuteronomy 14:21; 23:20.

The relationship between Israel, the nations, and the people of God is depicted in figure 2.

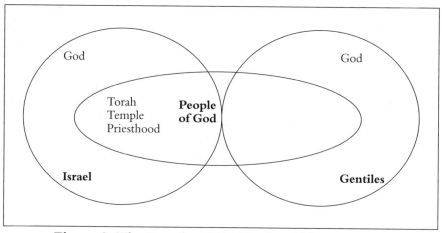

Figure 2: The People of God in the Old Testament

As a nation comprised of sinful people, Israel was not able to live out its calling perfectly. This is recognized even in the Torah, as Deuteronomy 30:6 notes that obedience will come from the action of God (referred to there as the "circumcision of the heart"), not through the people's own efforts. The impossibility of proper obedience as a means of living out loyalty to Yahweh demands a radical solution. As intimated throughout the Old Testament, God himself will enable obedience, accomplished through a radical, divine intervention in human history.

Jesus is that radical intervention. He is the fulfillment of many things "Israelite": Torah, temple, priest, and king. Indeed, he fulfills the identity and mission of Israel itself, for he is the perfectly obedient Israelite, and his example becomes the one to follow (John 14:15). He is the perfect mediator between *all* humans and God (Heb. 8:1). In short, Jesus may be seen as the embodiment and fulfillment of faithful Israel; everything that Israel was to have been and done, Jesus was and did. Accordingly, any human beings who want to be part of the "people of God" need only to identify/ associate themselves with Israel's Messiah. This is true for ethnic Jews and Gentiles alike.

Jesus' life and ministry thus redefines what it means to be the people of God in both senses described above. Whereas earlier, a readily identifiable, ethnically related people and state was to serve as the **paradigm** of how to live in relationship with Yahweh, that is no longer the case today. No political entity was established to serve as the manifestation of God's people after Jesus. Israel maintained the symbols of Yahweh's presence and was itself a symbol of that presence, but Jesus *is* God with his people (Matt. 1:23; John 1:14). He advances the restoration project that will ultimately be completed when he returns to create the new heavens and the new earth.[41]

Jesus also redefines the second sense of the term "people of God." He becomes the new paradigm to imitate. He also objectively accomplishes salvation and ensures that his righteousness is credited to any who unite with him (Rom. 3:21–25). Moreover, the fulfillment of Torah, temple, priest, and king means that it is no longer necessary for the followers of God to associate themselves with the nation of Israel. They need to associate/identify with Israel's Messiah. The redefinition of the identity of God's people may be seen in figure 3.

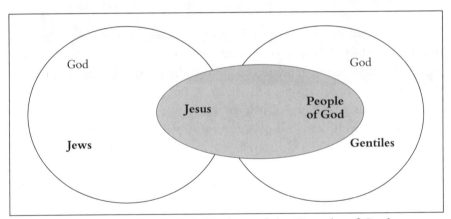

Figure 3: Jesus' Redefinition of the People of God

We can now see how understanding the metanarrative of the Old Testament helps us to see the ways in which the key themes in the Pentateuch relate to one another. Because of human sin, God acted decisively in history to restore creation to its intended glory. This is a

---

41. It is not accidental that the book of Revelation describes the new heavens and the new earth in terms reminiscent of the Garden of Eden. The restored creation is understood as a return, in many ways, to the idyllic situation of pre-Fall creation. On the relationship between Revelation and the creation account, see Richard Bauckham, *The Theology of the Book of Revelation,* New Testament Theology (Cambridge: Cambridge University Press, 1993), 133–36.

manifestation of his grace, for he acted out of his love, not out of a sense of obligation. Knowledge of the metanarrative helps us begin to understand *why* God acts in the ways he does and why sin matters so much. In short, it provides a framework for interpretation.

This framework will be useful as we continue to explore the methods for interpreting law and narrative. As we examine particular ways of interpreting these genres, we will seek to integrate our conclusions about particular texts with the metanarrative. There is a dynamic relationship between the metanarrative and the texts from which we derive it. The parts help us understand the overarching metanarrative, while at the same time the metanarrative provides direction for integration of the various parts. This interactive dynamic provides a check for our interpretations and ensures that we properly understand the God-breathed intention of the biblical text.

3

GETTING STARTED

We have now examined the **genres** of the Pentateuch, identified three major theological themes developed in it, and seen how these themes contribute to the **metanarrative** of Scripture. We will focus now on some important preliminary aspects of interpretation.

TEXT CRITICISM OF THE PENTATEUCH

Before we begin interpreting a text, we must first identify what the text is. Text criticism is the science and art of evaluating different manuscripts in order to determine what the original text likely said. In the case of the Old Testament, this usually consists of identifying variant readings of the primary Hebrew text, the ***Biblia Hebraica Stuttgartensia (BHS)***, and comparing it with other witnesses, such as the **Samaritan Pentateuch** (SP), the **Dead Sea Scrolls** (DSS), and the **Septuagint (LXX)**.

As we consider the variant witnesses, we should bear in mind that most Old Testament scholars consider the **Masoretic Text** (MT)—the text on which *BHS* is based—to be an authoritative text of the Hebrew Old Testament.[1] Among the DSS, over 50 percent of the biblical texts

---

1. Emanuel Tov, *Textual Criticism of the Hebrew Bible*, 2nd ed. (Minneapolis: Fortress, 2001), 177–79.

discovered may be described as "proto-Masoretic."[2] That is, they closely resemble the text of the MT in terms of spelling, **orthography**, and even paragraph divisions. This suggests that the text of the MT became fixed at a fairly early period.[3]

Nevertheless, there are differences between the MT and the other versions. At some points, the MT may preserve the original text; at others the variants may reflect the original reading. The interpreter must weigh the available evidence to determine which text is original and, therefore, to be used in interpretation and proclamation.

Principles of Text Criticism

In evaluating the evidence to determine the original reading, bear in mind the following key principles.

The MT Is Not Always the Original

Though it is an extremely reliable version and is widely viewed as authoritative, the MT is not perfect. The interpreter must be aware of this fact and be prepared to follow the reading of another version if the evidence suggests that it is more likely to be original.

Rely on Internal Evidence

A proposed alternative reading must make sense in the context of the passage being interpreted. Thus, lexical, syntactical, literary, and theological factors must be weighed in determining which reading is correct. External factors such as the witness of other ancient manuscripts and versions may be considered, but primary emphasis should be on internal evidence.

The Reading That Explains the Others Is Probably Original

Some interpreters maintain that the shorter and/or more difficult reading is usually the original. However, the more difficult reading could

---

2. Walter C. Kaiser Jr., *The Old Testament Documents: Are They Reliable and Relevant?* (Downers Grove, IL: InterVarsity Press, 2001), 49.

3. Peter J. Williams, "Textual Criticism," in *DOTP*, 836.

have been introduced by scribal error.[4] A more reliable principle is to prefer the reading that explains the others. This means being sensitive to the internal factors described above, as well as having a solid understanding of orthography and spelling.

Text Criticism in Action

Deuteronomy 32:8

Let's take as an example Deuteronomy 32:8, particularly the second half of that verse. The MT (represented in *BHS*) reads:

$$\text{יַצֵּב גְּבֻלֹת עַמִּים לְמִסְפַּר בְּנֵי יִשְׂרָאֵל}$$

("He [Yahweh] established the borders of the people according to the numbers of the sons of Israel"). However, there is a textual note indicating that the LXX, DSS,[5] and three other versions[6] read either בְּנֵי אֵל ("sons of God") or בְּנֵי אֱלִים ("sons of gods") instead of בְּנֵי יִשְׂרָאֵל.

Which is the correct reading? Bearing in mind the principles introduced above, we must first acknowledge that it is possible that the MT is not the original reading. We then need to examine the internal evidence in favor of each option.

The MT reading suggests that God ("Most High") allocated territory to the nations based on the number of Israelites. In one sense, this presents a logical problem, as the Israelites presumably did not exist when the territorial allocations were made, though it is certainly consistent with the theology of Deuteronomy (and the Pentateuch as a whole) to conclude that God knew how many Israelites there would ultimately be. But this does seem an unlikely fit with the context of the chapter, in which Israel's election is shown to be grounded in the **primeval history**, when God created all that is. The focus appears to be on the allocation of territory to the nations, while noting the unique relationship between Israel and **Yahweh**.

---

4. Robert B. Chisholm Jr., *Interpreting the Historical Books: An Exegetical Handbook*, HOTE (Grand Rapids: Kregel, 2006), 149. See also Bruce K. Waltke, "Textual Criticism of the Old Testament and Its Relation to Exegesis and Theology," *NIDOTTE*, 1:63–64.
5. J. Gordon McConville, *Deuteronomy*, AOTC (Downers Grove, IL: InterVarsity Press, 2002), 448, identifies the specific manuscripts as *4QDeut*[j] and *4QDeut*[q].
6. They are Symmachus (a Greek version), Old Latin, and the Syrohexapla (a Syriac translation of the LXX in Origen's Hexapla).

McConville notes that "the reading 'sons of God' . . . matches the theme of a primeval election of Israel."[7] Thus, the variant reading seems a more likely fit with the overall theme of the chapter.

In addition, the reading בְּנֵי אֵלִים ("sons of God/gods") helps set up the contrast between what God allocated to the heavenly host, and the fact that he kept Israel for himself as his inheritance. This is seen through the repetition of forms of נחל ("possess, possession, inheritance") in verses 8–9. The reading בְּנֵי יִשְׂרָאֵל would obscure this contrast. Internal evidence thus favors the variant rendition.

Moreover, one can easily see why the **Masoretes** would alter the reading from בְּנֵי אֵלִים to בְּנֵי יִשְׂרָאֵל, as the former could suggest that the gods of the nations were, in fact, real.[8] It is less clear why the translators of the LXX, for example, would switch *to* that, if the MT reflects the original. In this instance, the variant reading can explain the MT, but not the other way around. The third principle thus further supports seeing the original reading as בְּנֵי אֵלִים.

In light of these considerations, the most likely original reading of Deuteronomy 32:8 is בְּנֵי אֵלִים ("sons of God"), not בְּנֵי יִשְׂרָאֵל ("sons of Israel"). Making well-founded text-critical decisions is vital in understanding the author's communicative intention.

Exodus 20:17

The next example we will consider is Exodus 20:17. The MT of the text reads:

לֹא תַחְמֹד בֵּית רֵעֶךָ לֹא־תַחְמֹד אֵשֶׁת רֵעֶךָ
וְעַבְדּוֹ וַאֲמָתוֹ וְשׁוֹרוֹ וַחֲמֹרוֹ וְכֹל אֲשֶׁר לְרֵעֶךָ

("You shall not covet your neighbor's house; you shall not covet your neighbor's wife, or his male servant, or his female servant, or his ox, or his donkey, or anything that is your neighbor's" [Exod 20:17 ESV]). Here, a textual note indicates that SP reads the same as the MT but adds to it.

In this case, the SP adds material (shown in italics below) from Exodus

---

7. McConville, *Deuteronomy*, 453–54.
8. This is not a necessary conclusion to draw, as בְּנֵי אֵלִים is used in Psalms 29:1 and 89:6 [Heb. 7] to refer to angels ("the heavenly host"). McConville, *Deuteronomy*, 454, further notes that the "gods" of Canaan were "de-divinized, and became simply heavenly beings attending Yahweh."

20:25 and Deuteronomy 11:29–30 and 27:2–3 after our verse, creating a tenth commandment that demands worship of Yahweh on Mount Gerizim (the first two commandments are combined into one to allow for this tenth commandment).[9] The text thus reads:

> You shall not covet your neighbor's house. You shall not covet your neighbor's wife, his field, his male or female servants, his ox, his donkey, or anything else that is your neighbor's. *And when Yahweh your God brings you to the land of the Canaanites that you are entering to possess, you must erect for yourselves great stones, and you must whitewash them with whitewash, and write on them all the words of this Torah. And when you cross over the Jordan you must erect these stones that I am commanding you today on Mount Gerizim. And you must build there an altar to Yahweh your God, an altar of stones. You must not wield iron tools on them; with whole stones you must build the altar of Yahweh your God. And you must offer up on it burnt offerings to Yahweh your God. You must sacrifice peace offerings and eat there and rejoice before Yahweh your God at that mountain beyond the Jordan in the West, in the land of the Canaanites who dwell in the Arabah opposite Gilgal, beside the oak of Moreh opposite Shechem.* (Exod. 20:14 SP,[10] my translation)

Again we must determine the correct reading. Though we may be tempted to simply accept the MT as original, we need to examine the evidence to determine whether that is in fact the case.

The decision is not as straightforward as it may first appear. The SP reading is generally consistent internally, as the additional text is plausibly still the words of Yahweh to the people. Throughout the **Decalogue**, Yahweh refers to himself in the third person, as in the variant reading. Moreover, the **narrative** continues exactly as in the MT in the next verse, providing further support for seeing the variant text as part of Yahweh's speech. Finally, neither reading conclusively explains the other. If Gerizim is original, the Masoretes may have removed it to solidify the place of Jerusalem as the authorized center of Yahweh worship in the text. Similarly, the Samaritans may have added Gerizim to advance their theological interests.

---

9. Kaiser, *Old Testament Documents*, 44–45.

10. Abraham Tal, ed., *The Samaritan Pentateuch: Edited According to the MS 6 (C) of the Shekhem Synagogue* (Tel Aviv: Tel Aviv University, 1994). Italicized type indicates material unique to SP.

Here is an instance where external considerations ultimately are decisive. The fact that no other manuscripts (MSS) have the additional material here raises suspicion that this may be an idiosyncratic addition to the original text. More importantly, the addition of the reference to Mount Gerizim supports the Samaritan claim that Mount Gerizim, not Jerusalem, is the proper place of Yahweh worship. Thus the additional text supports the sectarian claims of the Samaritans. The fact that the word "Gerizim" does not appear in Exodus in any major version except the one in which its inclusion would advance a theological claim suggests that it is added in the SP. On balance, the evidence points to the MT as the original, and the SP as adding to it to advance the sectarian interests of the Samaritans.[11]

Text Criticism and Biblical Authority

For some, the need for text criticism causes concerns about the reliability and authority of the biblical text. If copying errors exist in the MSS, can we be certain that we are interpreting the God-inspired text?

While the size of the textual apparatus of *BHS* might suggest problems with the texts, very few true problems with the text of the Old Testament actually exist. Fully 90 percent of the text of the Old Testament is not in question; text criticism focuses on the 10 percent of the text about which there is some question. Indeed, one expert maintains that "text critical work is boring because the differences are inconsequential."[12] Stuart notes that

> it would not be correct to suggest that the various ancient versions of the Bible are in hopeless disagreement with one another, or that the percentage of textual corruption is so high as to render questionable large blocks of Scripture. Rather, it is fair to say that the verses, chapters, and books of the Bible would read largely the same, and would leave the same impression with the reader, even if one adopted virtually every possible *alternative* reading to those now serving as the basis for current English translations. In fact, absolutely nothing essential to the major doctrines of the Bible

---

11. For more on the Decalogue in the SP, see Robert T. Anderson and Terry Giles, *Tradition Kept: The Literature of the Samaritans* (Peabody, MA: Hendrickson, 2005), 34–42.

12. Waltke, "Textual Criticism," 65.

<u>would be affected by any responsible decision in the area of textual</u> <u>criticism.</u>[13]

If this is the case, why should we concern ourselves with textual criticism? Though major doctrines are unaffected by the textual decisions we make, we are better able to understand the nuances of the author's intention when we rightly discern the original reading. Text criticism contributes to better, more complete interpretation.

ANCIENT NEAR EASTERN PARALLELS TO BIBLICAL TEXTS

In addition to knowledge of the methods and role of text criticism, knowledge of ancient Near Eastern parallels to the biblical texts also assists in interpretation. Like all texts, the texts of the Old Testament were not written in a vacuum. <u>The authors of the Old Testament had worldviews</u> <u>that influenced what they wrote. The worldviews they held developed in</u> <u>important ways as a result of contact with the</u> surrounding cultural environment, just as, for example, Americans have a distinctive worldview that is shaped by a shared "Western" culture.

The worldview of the ancient Israelites had much in common with the tenets of the broader ancient Near Eastern worldview. At the same time, Israelite culture rejected some tenets and modified others. Other ancient texts show the interpreter of the Old Testament how different cultures understood their world and provide a better understanding of the unique emphases and perspectives in the Old Testament.[14]

We also should note that it is likely that the author and audience of the Pentateuch were familiar with the ideas and contours of parallel texts and had these ideas in mind when writing or reading the texts.[15] The perspectives represented in parallel texts were part of the cultural backdrop of

---

13. Douglas Stuart, "Inerrancy and Textual Criticism," in *Inerrancy and Common Sense*, ed. Roger R. Nicole and J. Ramsey Michaels (Grand Rapids: Baker, 1980), 98.

14. For an introduction to comparative study, see John H. Walton, *Ancient Near Eastern Thought and the Old Testament: Introducing the Conceptual World of the Hebrew Bible* (Grand Rapids: Baker, 2006), 15–40.

15. Note that, according to Joshua 24:2, 14, Abram's father, Terah (and so, presumably, Abram himself), worshiped the Mesopotamian gods of their native land. They were almost certainly familiar with the accounts of the gods and the literature of their people. That knowledge may have shaped the transmission of the accounts that later became part of the Pentateuch.

the Israelites, much as contemporary Americans are familiar with aspects of Western culture. For example, a recent sports article opened with the sentence, "With everything on the stat sheets just about even, the Eastern Conference finals have come down to Jedi mind tricks."[16] The reference to "Jedi mind tricks" comes from the *Star Wars* trilogy. The author clearly is not referring to a specific moment in a *Star Wars* movie but rather is describing psychological tricks to gain advantage over a weaker party. The phrase has become part of the presuppositional knowledge of Western popular culture, and we can understand the author's intention without explanation.[17] Similarly, we can speak of the Holocaust or the fall of the Berlin Wall as historical events, and most adult listeners understand the events and their significance.[18]

This shared presuppositional knowledge allows the author of the Pentateuch to allude to the ideas of ancient Near Eastern texts and culture without explicitly citing or quoting them. In fact, many see in Genesis a polemic against the ancient Near Eastern understandings of creation. Such a sentiment is expressed explicitly elsewhere in Scripture. Jeremiah 10:11, which is likely a deliberate polemical echo of Genesis 1, says, "You people of Israel should tell those nations this: 'These gods did not make heaven and earth. They will disappear from the earth and from under the heavens'" (NET). Similar ideas are expressed in Isaiah 44:24 and Psalm 96:5. By drawing on the reader's knowledge of ancient Near Eastern gods and conceptions of creation, Genesis makes the same point implicitly yet powerfully.

Overview of Ancient Near Eastern Worldview

A complete description of the worldview of the ancient Near East is well beyond the scope of this book. The difficulty is compounded when we consider that the ancient Near East was not homogenous in its thinking. That is, Philistines and Canaanites had much in common, to be sure, but it would be incorrect to say that all peoples of the ancient Near

---

16. Julian Benbow, "Series Is Really Heating Up; Auburn Hills Was a Pressure Cooker," *Boston Globe*, May 28, 2008, D6.

17. See Jay D. Atlas, "Presupposition," in *The Handbook of Pragmatics*, ed. Laurence R. Horn and Gregory Ward (Malden, MA: Blackwell, 2004), 29–52. See also Louis Cummings, *Pragmatics: A Multidisciplinary Perspective* (Mahwah, NJ: Lawrence Erlbaum Associates, 2005), 29–35, and the more general discussion of pragmatic theory there.

18. For more on this aspect of textual communication, see Jeannine K. Brown, *Scripture as Communication: Introducing Biblical Hermeneutics* (Grand Rapids: Baker, 2007), 100–119.

East thought the same about any given subject. In making a comparison in contemporary terms, it would be wrong to say that because the United States and Italy are both Western nations, the people of both nations hold a common view on every issue.

Keeping that warning firmly in mind, we can nevertheless look at a few aspects of an ancient Near Eastern worldview that are important for understanding the Old Testament and its perspective.

The Gods Were Very Real

In every ancient Near Eastern society, the people acknowledged and worshipped many gods. Many nations had a primary or patron deity they believed to be superior to the other gods, but they recognized the existence of other deities as well.[19]

The gods in ancient Near Eastern societies were different from what we think of when we think of gods, and certainly when we think of God. They were far from perfect, being subject to infighting, jealousy among themselves, malice, and envy. Moreover, no single god was considered to be all-powerful.

Since there were many gods, many felt that one needed to appease them all, even if there was one particular god to whom the person felt personal loyalty. So, a worshipper might offer sacrifices to many gods, in order to avoid the wrath of one that might be angry with the worshipper.

It is easy to see the importance of this aspect of ancient Near Eastern culture when approaching the Pentateuch. We already have noted the ways the Pentateuch argues for the uniqueness of Yahweh. Deuteronomy 4:39 states that there is no god besides Yahweh. Moreover, Exodus 34:6–8 says, "The LORD passed by before him and proclaimed: 'The LORD, the LORD, the compassionate and gracious God, slow to anger, and abounding in loyal love and faithfulness, keeping loyal love for thousands, forgiving iniquity and transgression and sin. But he by no means leaves the guilty unpunished, responding to the transgression of fathers by dealing with children and children's children, to the third and fourth generation.' Moses quickly bowed to the ground and worshiped" (NET). To the Israelites Yahweh was real, but he was unlike the gods of the ancient Near Eastern world.

---

19. For a helpful discussion of ancient Near Eastern understanding of the relationship between the gods and the people, see Daniel I. Block, *The Gods of the Nations: Studies in Ancient Near Eastern National Theology*, 2nd ed. (Grand Rapids: Baker, 2000).

All of Life Had Religious Significance

A second aspect of life in the ancient Near East generally was the view that all of life had some religious significance. That is, there was no conception of a distinction between the sacred and the secular. There simply was no such thing as "secular" life. The gods provided, or they did not. Misfortune was seen as judgment of the gods. The way in which one lived life had religious significance; nothing was beyond the realm of the religious.

In many ways, the Old Testament largely accepts this aspect of the ancient Near Eastern cultural perspective. There simply is no place in the perspective of the Old Testament for a division between the sacred and the secular.[20] All of life was lived out in the presence of Yahweh. He chose Israel for relationship, and the way in which that relationship was lived out by each person and the nation was significant. The Torah makes this clear through the covenant obligations that encompass everything from major issues such as preservation of life (Exod. 20:13) and social justice (Deut. 14:27–15:18)[21] to seemingly minor issues such as permissible clothing (Lev. 19:19).

Corporate Identity Was Paramount

The final important aspect of ancient Near Eastern society concerns the nature of identity. In the ancient Near East, the individual was not nearly as important as the group. People thought of themselves as members of a family, clan, tribe, and nation.

This emphasis on the group is important when it comes to interpreting the texts of the Old Testament. Westerners are used to thinking of themselves as individuals. The Bill of Rights in the Constitution of the United States, for example, primarily emphasizes the rights that individuals, not groups, have in our society. We also tend to think of ourselves in very individualistic terms; we are not especially concerned with group identity.

When we evaluate the texts of the Old Testament, we must remember that they are addressed to people who thought largely in terms of group identity. The law of levirate marriage in Deuteronomy 25:5–10 often strikes contemporary North American readers as bizarre and even offensive, since

---

20. See my book, *Deuteronomic Theology and the Significance of Torah: A Reappraisal* (Winona Lake, IN: Eisenbrauns, 2006), 89–97.
21. Deuteronomy's perspective on social justice is examined in my article, "Social Justice and the Vision of Deuteronomy," *JETS* 51, no. 1 (2008): 35–44.

a decision about whom to marry is an intensely personal and individual decision in our culture. But it makes sense when viewed from the perspective of people for whom preservation of tribal integrity and property rights were more important than individual freedom to choose a spouse.[22] In many instances, the benefit to the group outweighs consideration of individual gain.[23] That is not to say that individual responsibility and the value of individuals are *never* important (as can be seen in texts such as Jer. 31:29–30 and Ezek. 18); rather, we must simply bear in mind that the biblical texts are the product of a culture that places great emphasis on corporate identity.

Related to this is the idea of ethnic connections. According to the genealogies in Genesis and the patriarchal narratives, the Hebrews represented one minor branch of the larger Semitic world. They were related to the Edomites (descendants of Esau) and were more distant relatives of the Moabites and Ammonites (who descended from Lot). Awareness of these kinship relationships contributes to understanding many Old Testament texts and a society that placed primacy on them. For example, this understanding of kinship relations explains why Deuteronomy 23:3–8 permanently excludes Moabites and Ammonites from the sacred assembly while permitting Egyptians to enter in the third generation. From a contemporary perspective, the offense of the Egyptians toward the Israelites was far worse than the refusal of the Moabites and Ammonites to allow the Israelites passage through their land and to sell them food and water. But from an ancient Israelite perspective, Moabites and Ammonites were "family," and therefore the Israelites expected more of these nations.

Legal Texts

The discovery and analysis of legal material from other ancient Near Eastern cultures greatly enhanced our understanding of the biblical laws.[24]

---

22. Luciano C. Chianeque and Samuel Ngewa, "Deuteronomy," in *Africa Bible Commentary*, ed. Tokunboh Adeyemo (Grand Rapids: Zondervan, 2006), 243, discuss the implications of this law for more communal, tribal societies in contemporary Africa.

23. For more on the communal nature of ancient Israelite society, see Victor H. Matthews and Don C. Benjamin, *Social World of Ancient Israel 1250–587 BCE* (Peabody, MA: Hendrickson, 1993), and the discussion on broader ancient Near Eastern tendencies in Wolfram von Soden, *The Ancient Orient: An Introduction to the Study of the Ancient Near East* (Grand Rapids: Eerdmans, 1994), 72–74.

24. In this section, we will examine just two codes, the Code of Hammurabi and the Middle Assyrian Laws. There are many more codes from the ancient Near Eastern world. Translations of some of them may be found in *ANET* and *COS*.

Some of these texts are remarkably similar to biblical laws. There are also some important and striking differences.

The ancient Near Eastern law codes provided for the well-being of society. The Code of Hammurabi, for example, states that Hammurabi was appointed

> to make justice prevail in the land, to abolish the wicked and the evil, to prevent the strong from oppressing the weak, to rise like the sun-god Shamash over all humankind, to illuminate the land. . . . When the god Marduk commanded me to provide just ways for the people of the land (in order to attain) appropriate behavior, I established truth and justice as the declaration of the land, I enhanced the well-being of the people.[25]

The epilogue further indicates the purpose of the laws. There, Hammurabi notes,

> I am Hammurabi, noble king. I have not been careless or negligent toward humankind, granted to my care by the god Enlil, and with whose shepherding the god Marduk charged me. I have sought for them peaceful places, I removed serious difficulties, I spread light over them. . . . I enhanced the well-being of the land, I made the people of all settlements lie in safe pastures, I did not tolerate anyone intimidating them. . . . In order that the mighty not wrong the weak, to provide just ways for the waif and the widow, I have inscribed my precious pronouncements upon my stela and set it up before the statue of me, the king of justice.[26]

Similarly, biblical laws foster the well-being of society. Deuteronomy 4:5–6 says, "See, I have taught you decrees and laws as the LORD my God commanded me, so that you may follow them in the land you are entering to take possession of it. Observe them carefully, for this will show your wisdom and understanding to the nations" (TNIV). Deuteronomy consistently emphasizes blessing if the people obey the commandments (see Deut. 28, where the blessings for obedience and the curses for disobedience appear).

---

25. Martha Roth, "The Laws of Hamurabi," COS, 2:336–37.
26. Ibid., 351.

Moreover, the pervasive stress on social justice throughout the Torah (e.g., Exod. 21:1–23:9; Lev. 19:9–18; 24:17–22; 25:47–55; Deut. 15; 16:18–20; 17:18–20; 19; 24:1–4) demonstrates that a just and harmonious society, centered on and grounded in relationship with Yahweh, is a major goal of Torah adherence.

Clearly, the legal codes of ancient Near Eastern and Israelite societies shared similar objectives. We will see, however, that the foundations of the respective societies were very different from each other, as were some specific aspects of the laws themselves.

Code of Hammurabi

The Code of Hammurabi is a legal code dating to about 1792–1750 B.C. It is named for the king who codified and promulgated it. Though it is perhaps the longest and best known of the Mesopotamian law codes, it is similar to other legal codes.

In fostering a just and well-ordered society, the Code of Hammurabi addresses many common elements of an ancient Near Eastern agrarian society. Thus, we find in the code both criminal laws and laws governing claims (torts) between two parties. Guidelines for court procedures are present, in addition to laws regulating conscription for military service, interest rates, slavery, property and inheritance rights, marriage and divorce, and even regulations on fees for services rendered by veterinarians! Almost all these laws have counterparts in the recorded biblical law codes in the Pentateuch.

An examination of parallel laws will illustrate some similarities. The Code of Hammurabi §3 says, "If a man comes forward to give false testimony in a case but cannot bring evidence for his accusation, if that case involves a capital offense, that man shall be killed."[27] This is very similar to Deuteronomy 19:16–19, which says, "If a malicious witness arises to accuse a person of wrongdoing, then both parties to the dispute shall appear before the LORD, before the priests and the judges who are in office in those days. The judges shall inquire diligently, and if the witness is a false witness and has accused his brother falsely, then you shall do to him as he had meant to do to his brother" (ESV).

---

27. All translations of the Code of Hammurabi are from Roth, "Hammurabi," COS, 2:335–53, unless otherwise indicated.

Like other ancient Near Eastern law codes, the Code of Hammurabi distinguishes between people of various social classes. Thus, the laws of §§196–223 provide different punishments for offenses, depending on the social status of the victim. For example, according to §§197–199, if an *awilu*,[28] a member of the upper class, breaks the bone of another *awilu*, his bone is to be broken. However, if the *awilu* breaks the bone of a commoner, he pays a fine of sixty shekels of silver. If the victim is a slave, the fine is less. Even within the *awilu* class, the status of the victim governs punishment.[29]

Here, the biblical laws differ significantly from the Code of Hammurabi. Exodus 21:20–21 describes a case in which a master strikes a slave: "Anyone who beats their male or female slave with a rod must be punished if the slave dies as a direct result, but they are not to be punished if the slave recovers after a day or two, since the slave is their property" (TNIV). Though the punishment that would be imposed if the slave died immediately is not specified, it almost certainly would be death (cf. Exod. 21:12).[30] No distinction is made on the basis of the victim's status. In fact, the biblical laws never impose different punishments based on the status of the victim, even when the victims are foreigners or slaves.[31]

Middle Assyrian Laws

The Middle Assyrian Laws (MAL) are another code sometimes compared to biblical law. The MAL originated in the time of the Assyrian king Tiglath-pileser I, who reigned from 1114 to 1076 B.C.

---

28. The term *awilu* is often used generically to refer to a man, but it also can indicate social status. Though the exact sense is unknown, it clearly refers to a free man who belongs to the upper class. For more, see *ANET*, 166n. 39, as well as the discussion in the standard resource for Assyriology, the *Chicago Assyrian Dictionary* (*CAD*), 1.2.48–57.

29. Section 202 notes that should an *awilu* strike the cheek of a fellow *awilu* whose status is higher than his own, he is to be flogged sixty times in public. If the victim is an *awilu* of the same status, the offender pays a fine.

30. Douglas K. Stuart, *Exodus*, NAC (Nashville: Broadman & Holman, 2006), 490.

31. The one law sometimes raised as an example of differing punishments depending on the victim's status is Exodus 21:32, where an owner whose ox gores someone else's servant pays a fine in addition to losing the ox to stoning. But the owner is not killed, as is the case if his ox fatally gores a free person (vv. 28–31). However, it is not explicit that the goring described in verse 32 is fatal; the money may be compensation for the temporary loss of the slave's service (cf. vv. 18–19). But even if the law envisions a fatal goring, Stuart (*Exodus*, 497–98) notes that in this type of scenario, the servant's master may bear some culpability. It is this mitigating factor, not the status of the victim, that accounts for the different punishment.

Like the Code of Hammurabi, the MAL seek to establish an orderly society. They are particularly noteworthy for the extent to which retribution is permitted or expected. While all ancient Near Eastern legal codes provide for some measure of retribution, the MAL stand out in this regard. For example, law A§55 says that if a married man rapes an unmarried woman living in her father's house, "the father of the maiden shall take the wife of the fornicator of the maiden and hand her over to be raped; he shall not return her to her husband, but he shall take (and keep?) her."[32] Law A§9 says that if in the course of attacking a woman a man should kiss her, "they shall draw his lower lip across the blade of an ax and cut it off."[33]

Another feature of the MAL that we should note here is the provision for commutation of punishment by human authorities. MAL A§15 holds that if a man finds his wife in the act of committing adultery and the couple is found guilty by the king or judges, the offended husband can choose to put his wife and her lover to death, to cut off the wife's nose and the man's testicles, or to release both of them. Interestingly, both are to be treated in the same way. That is, the offended husband can't show leniency to his wife but not the lover, or vice versa.

As with the Code of Hammurabi, the MAL differ in important ways from the biblical materials. The famous principle of "an eye for an eye" (Exod. 21:23–24; Lev. 24:19–20; Deut. 19:21) demands proportionality and justice in responding to offense (and almost certainly through communal, not individual, action), though it is often misunderstood as demanding personal retribution. Laws such as the establishment of the cities of refuge (Num. 35) presuppose and regulate personal retribution but do not require or encourage it. Similarly, the biblical laws do not provide for commutation by human victims, for reasons discussed below.

Ancient Near Eastern Laws and Worldview

The differences between the ancient Near Eastern laws and their biblical counterparts are understandable in light of the different worldviews of the societies. First, the ancient Near Eastern legal codes are not

---

32. Martha Roth, "The Middle Assyrian Laws (Tablet A)," *COS*, 2:359.
33. Ibid., 354.

grounded in the character or morality of the gods. The invocation of the gods in the prologue of the Code of Hammurabi, for example, is largely referential. It claims that the gods chose Hammurabi to rule but does not claim that the laws in the subsequent code were grounded in the morality of the gods themselves. Rather, the king is the one who promotes justice.[34] Essentially, nothing in the Mesopotamian worldview would allow for categorizing actions as "right" or "wrong." At most, something could be described simply as "pleasing" or "displeasing" to one or the other of the gods.[35]

In light of this, it is impossible to describe ancient Near Eastern ethics from a theological standpoint. Rather, the perspective of the ancient Near Eastern law codes is aptly described as "secular."[36] These codes presuppose a system of societal order, but this order is not based on the character of the gods, who often failed to adhere to the standards envisioned. This is in part a result of the closed-system worldview presupposed by the legal codes (see below).

Because of this, there was room for commutation of punishments and the judgment of human beings. As we noted, the MAL provide for the offended husband to decide his wife's (and her lover's) fate. No such provision exists in the biblical law codes; adulterers, for example, are to be executed when caught and convicted (Lev. 20:10). The absolute nature of the biblical codes derives from the fact that, from the biblical perspective, God is the offended party. Consequently, he is the only one who could conceivably alter the punishment of the offender.

Narrative Texts

In addition to ancient Near Eastern legal texts that are similar to biblical texts, we also find narrative texts similar to accounts found in the Pentateuch. We will briefly examine three of these.[37]

---

34. Paul Heger, "Source of Law in the Biblical and Mesopotamian Law Collections," *Biblica* 86, no. 3 (2005): 326–27. Indeed, the portrayals of the gods in the ancient Near Eastern cosmologies do not provide much of a basis for seeing the morality of the gods as a foundation for human conduct, since they are consistently depicted as capricious, vengeful, jealous, and manipulative.

35. John H. Walton, *Ancient Israelite Literature in Its Cultural Context: A Survey of Parallels Between Biblical and Ancient Near Eastern Texts* (Grand Rapids: Zondervan, 1989), 87–88.

36. Heger, "Source," 326.

37. These three texts have particularly strong parallels to the biblical texts and are especially useful in seeing the tendencies of ancient Near Eastern texts. They are frequently used in comparative studies.

Atrahasis

The text of Atrahasis[38] dates to about the seventeenth century B.C., though the story may have originated earlier than that.[39] In many respects, Atrahasis reflects the typical worldview of Mesopotamian cultures in terms of its anthropology, cosmology, and sociology.

The story of Atrahasis describes the origin of humanity, relationships between the gods, and a cataclysmic flood. According to the story, creation was divided among the three chief gods: Anu, Enki/Ea, and Enlil. Anu lived and reigned in the heavens, while Enki/Ea lived in and reigned over the subterranean waters. Enlil apparently lived on the earth. A cohort of lesser gods was tasked with digging the life-giving canals, and they toiled at this for forty[40] years until they finally rebelled. In response to their pleas, Ea decided to allow the creation of human beings. These creatures were formed through a mixing of clay and the blood of a slain god. They then served in place of the lower deities. As human beings became numerous, they also became noisy and disturbed the sleep of the gods, particularly Enlil. So, after successfully reducing the population somewhat through plagues and famine, the gods sent a flood to completely destroy humanity. Enki, who perhaps was more favorably disposed to humans since he was isolated from their noise in his watery dwelling,[41] warned a man named Atrahasis. In seven days, he built a boat and saved himself, animals, and birds.[42]

We can readily see similarities in Atrahasis to the biblical accounts of Creation and the flood. Both Atrahasis and Genesis deal with the origin of human beings and their relationship to God/the gods. Both include stories of a cataclysmic flood in which divine intervention spares some human beings and animals. We will examine some important differences below.

---

38. See the translation in Stephanie Dalley, *Myths from Mesopotamia: Creation, the Flood, Gilgamesh and Others* (Oxford: Oxford University Press, 1989), 1–38 (with introduction and notes); and an excerpt dealing with the flood in Benjamin R. Foster, "Atra-Ḫasis," COS, 1:450–53.

39. W. G. Lambert and A. R. Millard, *Atra-Ḫasis: The Babylonian Story of the Flood* (Oxford: Clarendon, 1969), 23–24. Some evidence suggests that the story was put together in its present form no earlier than the eighteenth or nineteenth centuries B.C., and that it is based on an earlier Sumerian version.

40. Dalley, *Myths from Mesopotamia*, 10, sees the gods as toiling for 3,600 years, but Lambert and Millard, *Atra-Ḫasis*, 45, and Foster, COS, 1:450, understand the time frame to be forty years.

41. Lambert and Millard, *Atra-Ḫasis*, 9.

42. Presumably, other human beings also were spared, but damage to the text renders certainty on this point impossible.

Enuma Elish

A second ancient Near Eastern text that provides helpful comparisons to the biblical accounts is the **Akkadian Epic of Creation**, also known as the *Enuma Elish*. The *Enuma Elish* is widely believed to have been composed from Sumerian and Amorite stories during the time of Nebuchadnezzar I (about 1126–1105 B.C.) to celebrate the accomplishments of the Babylonian kings and the chief god in the Babylonian pantheon, Marduk. Existing manuscripts of the *Enuma Elish* all date to the first millennium B.C.

The account begins with reference to Apsu and Tiamat, two gods respectively representing "sweet" water and saltwater, who existed "when on high no name was given to heaven."[43] They mate, and their offspring are born. They in turn reproduce, resulting in a growing cadre of gods. The boisterous young gods are too much for Apsu, who determines to kill them. Upon learning of the plan, Ea casts a spell on Apsu, who is then killed himself.

Though she had originally opposed her husband's plans to destroy their children, Tiamat resolves to carry out Apsu's plans following his murder. The young gods unsuccessfully seek a leader until Marduk agrees to stand against Tiamat, on the condition that the other gods will make him head of the pantheon. They agree, and Marduk subsequently defeats Tiamat.

Following the defeat of Tiamat, the other gods cede some of their power to Marduk, who then lays out the cosmos. Using Tiamat's corpse, he creates the heavens and earth. He then establishes seasons, days, and nights. Finally, he is proclaimed king of the gods.

As king, Marduk sets the gods who had been allied with Tiamat to work building Babylon, a holy city and dwelling place for himself. He later determines to create human beings to relieve the now-slave gods of their toil. He slays Kingu, Tiamat's second husband, and uses his blood to form human beings, who are then assigned the task of completing the construction of Babylon. The epic ends with an extended exaltation of Marduk, proclaiming his fifty names.

As with Atrahasis, *Enuma Elish* has many parallels to Genesis. Both texts deal with the origin of the cosmos and the relationship of God/the gods to it. In addition, both describe the creation of humans and their

---

43. Benjamin R. Foster, "Epic of Creation (*Enūma Elish*)," COS, 1:391.

relationship with the divine realm. Finally, both Genesis and *Enuma Elish* make claims regarding the status of their chief gods. The many and important differences will be discussed below.

Gilgamesh Epic

The final parallel text we will consider is the Gilgamesh Epic. This epic is probably the best known and most striking of the ancient Near Eastern parallels to the Old Testament. It recounts the exploits of a hero, Gilgamesh, widely held to have been a historical figure who reigned as king of Uruk (biblical Erech; modern-day Warka in southern Iraq) sometime in the middle third millennium B.C. (2800–2500 B.C.).[44]

The stories of Gilgamesh are known to have existed in Sumer; the earliest copies of the text are Sumerian, dating to the first half of the second millennium B.C.[45] The stories exist in at least three recognizable forms: Sumerian stories, an Old Babylonian version, and the standard version. The standard version is the best known. Its final form probably dates to the early part of the first millennium B.C., though it incorporates material from much earlier versions.

The main theme of the epic is Gilgamesh's quest for immortality. The story encompasses twelve tablets and traces the vicissitudes of his quest. Following the death of a companion, Gilgamesh seeks immortality. He travels to the very end of the world, where he meets Utnapishtim, the survivor of the flood who has already achieved immortality. Gilgamesh then seeks immortality in a number of ways but is eventually forced to return to his land and achieve immortality by becoming a leader of his nation and building up the next generation.[46]

The description of the flood narrative in the Gilgamesh Epic has attracted the most attention of biblical scholars, because of its obvious parallels to the Genesis flood narrative. As in Genesis, the hero of the flood in Gilgamesh receives divine warning of the impending deluge and constructs a boat. Animals are brought into the boat to be saved. Following the flood, the hero releases birds to determine if the floodwaters have sufficiently receded. He first sends out a dove, but the dove returns. He then

---

44. Dalley, *Myths from Mesopotamia*, 41.
45. It is possible, however, that certain parts of the stories are found in the Ebla tablets (ca. 2300 B.C.). See Walton, *Ancient Israelite Literature*, 22.
46. Walton, *Ancient Near Eastern Thought*, 51–52.

releases a raven, which does not return. He then offers sacrifices to the gods.

Other parallels with the biblical accounts are found in Gilgamesh as well. In Tablet XI, Gilgamesh learns of a plant that will grant him the immortality he seeks. With great joy, he takes it, but it is carried off by a serpent. Thus, in both Genesis and Gilgamesh we find plants, humans, snakes, and the issue of eternal life. We will examine the significance of these parallels in the next section.

Comparing Ancient Near Eastern and Biblical Materials

Even the brief descriptions of the ancient Near Eastern legal and narrative texts provided here reveal many obvious similarities between the ancient Near Eastern and biblical texts. Such similarities have led some scholars to conclude that the biblical materials are largely borrowed from the ancient Near Eastern materials. Some argue that the biblical account of creation, for example, represents little more than an ancient Israelite "spin" on a familiar, mythological account of creation found in the *Enuma Elish* or Atrahasis. Similarly, the legal material in the Pentateuch is sometimes seen as reflecting the same patterns and values of the ancient Near Eastern legal codes, with a similar degree of bloodthirstiness.

How should we understand the similarities between the ancient Near Eastern material and the biblical texts? Should we conclude that the biblical texts simply have adopted the ancient Near Eastern texts and modified them slightly to fit ancient Israelite sensibilities? Or is there another possibility?

We should note, first, that the similarities between the materials really are not all that surprising. As we saw earlier, the ancient Israelites were part of the ancient Near Eastern world, and their texts consequently reflect the worldview of that cultural milieu. Just as other ancient peoples reflected on the question of creation and the activities of the gods they believed exercised dominion over their lives, so too the ancient Israelites wrestled with such questions. In the same way, ancient Israelite laws address situations that are similar to those experienced and expected in the ancient world. Thus, it should not be surprising that the materials are similar.

We also must note, however, that the similarities can be *vastly* overstated. Indeed, a careful reading of the ancient Near Eastern and biblical materials reveals many significant differences between them as well. In fact, at several points it may be argued that the biblical texts are directly engaging with the ancient Near Eastern texts in an effort to refute the claims found in them. Similarity, then, is not the end of the matter.

Rather than concentrating on superficial similarities between ancient Near Eastern and biblical texts, we will analyze the theological claims being made in them. In doing so, we can begin to see important differences between the materials.

A close examination of the creation accounts in Genesis, *Enuma Elish*, and Atrahasis reveals striking contrasts. The creation account in Genesis appears to know the ancient Near Eastern accounts and seeks to refute the claims being made there. In Genesis, everything worshipped as gods by ancient Near Eastern people is created by Yahweh, the God of Israel. Moreover, Yahweh creates through the power of his word (Gen. 1:3).[47] Conflict among the gods does not lead to creation, as in the *Enuma Elish*; in Genesis Yahweh creates on his own. Whereas in the *Enuma Elish* Ea uses words to powerfully cast a spell on Apsu (thus allowing him to be killed), in Genesis Yahweh uses words to make worlds appear.

Moreover, in the *Enuma Elish* the earth is literally a part of the divine, having been fashioned by Marduk from the corpse of Tiamat. In Genesis, the earth is a reflection of Yahweh's intentionality but is in no way a part of the divine realm. In addition, Yahweh is utterly in control of events in creation. He is not surprised that Noah survives the flood, since he ordered the flood and commanded the construction of the ark for the preservation of Noah's family and the animals (and, according to Genesis 7:16, even shut the door to the ark!). This contrasts starkly with the gods in Gilgamesh; they are terrified by the flood they send, and Enlil is completely unaware of the machinations of Ea to save anyone.

Finally, we see differences in terms of the creation of human beings and their relationship with God/the gods. In each of the Babylonian texts described above, human beings are created to relieve the gods of the drudgery of work, which is seen as beneath their dignity. In addition, when people become numerous, their noise causes the gods to plan their destruction via flood (and other methods). In contrast, in Genesis Yahweh actively creates. Work is not drudgery to be avoided but the act of a sovereign God. He creates human beings in his image, which is best understood

---

47. Creation by word is part of Egyptian creation mythology as well. See Gordon H. Johnston, "Genesis 1 and Ancient Egyptian Creation Myths," *Bibliotheca Sacra* 165 (2008): 178–94.

as suggesting that they will serve as his representatives on the earth.[48] They are not insignificant beings created to relieve Yahweh of the drudgery of work but creatures elevated to the pinnacle of creation as the only ones privileged to be his image-bearers and entrusted with being stewards of all he made.

The flood narrative further illustrates the significance of human beings in Genesis and therefore the contrast with the ancient Near Eastern accounts. In Genesis, Yahweh himself commanded human beings to be fruitful and multiply, and to fill the earth (Gen. 1:28); a populous earth was a sign of obedience to the divine command, not an unforeseen nuisance to be dealt with. In the ancient Near Eastern parallels, the gods destroy humans because they are too noisy. By contrast, in Genesis the moral failures of human beings lead to their destruction. Humans matter in Genesis.

Even many superficial similarities appear to have been deliberately reworked in order to make a theological point.[49] Both Genesis and Gilgamesh narrate accounts of humanity, using certain common thematic elements (snake, humans, and a life-giving plant). We noted above that a snake steals immortality from Gilgamesh by stealing the life-giving plant. In Genesis, however, the same elements appear but with vastly different significance. The loss of access to the Tree of Life is not an unfortunate accident but rather divine judgment on the sinful actions of human beings. It is possible, if not likely, that Moses seeks to persuade listeners familiar with the story of Gilgamesh that Genesis, not Gilgamesh, presents the truth of what caused humans to lose access to immortality and to foster reflection on the solution to that problem.

These differences all point to the fact that the Pentateuch conceives of Yahweh as an utterly different kind of God. The gods of the ancient Near East in the Babylonian accounts we have considered are not particularly moral creatures, or even all that powerful. They are, to be sure, more

---

48. The meaning and significance of the image of God in humans is a complex, though important, topic. For more on its meaning in Genesis, see Gordon J. Wenham, *Genesis 1–15*, WBC (Waco: Word, 1987), 29–32; and Bruce K. Waltke and Cathi J. Fredricks, *Genesis: A Commentary* (Grand Rapids: Zondervan, 2001), 65–66. For a more general discussion, see David J. A. Clines, "The Image of God in Man," *Tyndale Bulletin* 19 (1968). See also the discussion in chapter 2 on the seriousness of sin as developed in Genesis.

49. That is not to suggest that the events described did not happen. I believe that the biblical narratives describe events that actually did occur, and they occurred as described. The shaping of the narrative, however, reflects a desire to communicate particular truths to a particular audience. Moreover, this is part of the author's intentionality that is the key to interpretation. See Grant R. Osborne, "Historical Narrative and Truth in the Bible," *JETS* 48, no. 4 (2005): 673–88.

powerful than human beings, but they are limited, and, like humans, tied to the created realm. There is no sense of transcendence on the part of the gods of the ancient Near East. Yahweh, in contrast, is transcendent, moral, and all-powerful.

The radical nature of the biblical worldview may be seen when comparing the creational "systems" envisioned in the ancient Near Eastern and biblical creation accounts. The ancient Near Eastern cosmologies all presuppose a closed system, in which the gods, humans, and nature all exist together. There is nothing "outside" of the created order in which gods, humans, and nature all coexist. The system envisioned by the ancient Near Eastern texts is depicted in figure 4.

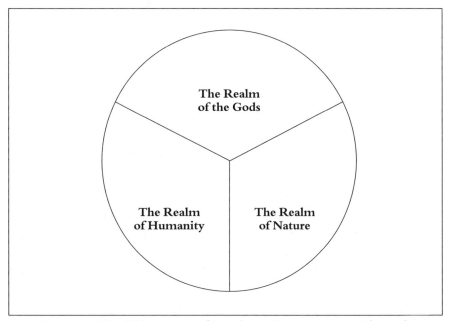

Figure 4: World System of Ancient Near Eastern Thought

Taken from Bill T. Arnold, *Encountering the Book of Genesis* (Grand Rapids: Baker, 1998), 49. Used by permission.

The biblical depiction of creation is very different. There, Yahweh is transcendent. He intervenes in events within the created order, but he himself is "outside" of it. The forces of nature are all under his control, not only because he created them, but also because he is not "in" nature in the way the gods of the ancient Near East are in it. So, he is never overwhelmed by the power of nature, and he is not subject to spells, as were the ancient Near Eastern gods. The system envisioned by the biblical text is portrayed in figure 5.

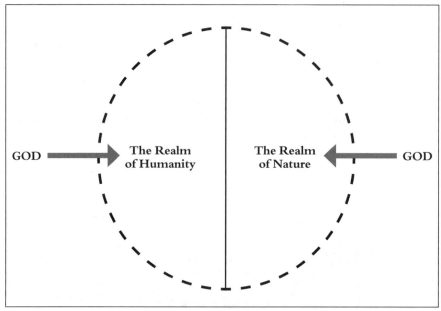

Figure 5: World System of Israelite Thought

Taken from Bill T. Arnold, *Encountering the Book of Genesis* (Grand Rapids: Baker, 1998), 50. Used by permission.

These two figures show how radical the Israelite conception of Yahweh and his relationship to creation were. Contemporary readers often miss this because we have been steeped in the biblical worldview. For Moses and his audience, however, the claims of the Pentateuch were radical and countercultural. The Pentateuch serves, in part, to shape the worldview of the Israelites by arguing against the ancient Near Eastern conceptions on the grounds that Yahweh is a radically different kind of God compared to the ancient Near Eastern gods.

Similarly, the differences between ancient Near Eastern and biblical laws point to the supremacy and "otherness" of Yahweh. We have already noted that the ancient Near Eastern laws provide for commutation of punishments based on human decisions; in the biblical law codes, no such commutation is possible because God is the offended party. More generally we can note that the biblical laws are said to have come from Yahweh and therefore reflect his understanding of what is right and wrong. In fact, as noted in chapter

1, the Torah is best understood not as a "job description" but as a doctor's prescription for how human beings can and should live in relationship to a holy God. Torah is given to Israel so the people can be a **paradigm** of how to live. Part of the function of the law is to set Israel apart from the nations in many areas of life. Torah observance, then, serves to foster a unique community of God's people; the people live out a different kind of society because they know and worship a different kind of God.

In this way, even practices known and carried out by others in the ancient Near Eastern world take on new significance. For example, we know that circumcision was practiced in other ancient cultures, often in connection with puberty or marriage.[50] The practice, then, is not new and certainly not "magical" in any way. Nevertheless, circumcision functions in a unique way for the Israelites. It serves as the sign of Yahweh's covenant with Abraham and marks the Israelite men as belonging to the people of Yahweh. Moreover, this identification includes (in theory, at least) an embrace of the claim that Yahweh is the one, true God. So, circumcision for the Israelites was an important statement of identity: the circumcised man was a member of God's special people, chosen by the one, true God for relationship in order to be a blessing to the nations.

BIBLIOGRAPHICAL HELPS AND TOOLS FOR INTERPRETATION

There are a number of resources that will assist in the interpretation of the Pentateuch. The following are of particular value.

Introductions and General Works

Alexander, T. Desmond. *From Paradise to Promised Land: An Introduction to the Pentateuch*. 2nd ed. Carlisle: Paternoster, 2002. An introduction to the themes of the Pentateuch, emphasizing its coherence. Critical issues are dealt with, but the focus is a synchronic examination of pentateuchal themes and theology. Alexander's work is particularly helpful for its discussion of how these themes lay the foundation for New Testament ideas.

---

50. John H. Walton, Victor H. Matthews, and Mark W. Chavalas, *The IVP Bible Background Commentary: Old Testament* (Downers Grove, IL: InterVarsity Press, 2000), 49–50.

Clines, David J. A. *The Theme of the Pentateuch*. 2nd ed. Sheffield: Sheffield Academic Press, 1997. An updated edition of a classic study of the Pentateuch as a whole. Clines maintains that the theme of the Pentateuch is the partial fulfillment (and partial nonfulfillment) of the promises to the patriarchs.

Hamilton, Victor P. *Handbook on the Pentateuch: Genesis, Exodus, Leviticus, Numbers, Deuteronomy*. 2nd ed. Grand Rapids: Baker, 2005. Provides a helpful overview of the Pentateuch, focusing on content rather than methodology. Important theological themes are developed in some detail, and the work as a whole provides the reader with a solid understanding of the Pentateuch as a coherent whole.

Wenham, Gordon J. *Exploring the Old Testament: A Guide to the Pentateuch*. Downers Grove, IL: InterVarsity Press, 2003. An extremely user-friendly introduction to the Pentateuch, including engagement with critical issues. Important topics such as the Levitical sacrificial system are dealt with in dialogue with the latest scholarship but presented in a clear and understandable way.

Whybray, R. Norman. *Introduction to the Pentateuch*. Grand Rapids: Eerdmans, 1995. A concise introduction, focusing on examination of a variety of approaches to the Pentateuch. Students seeking to understand critical approaches to the Pentateuch will find this work particularly useful.

————. *The Making of the Pentateuch: A Methodological Study*. JSOTSup 53. Sheffield: JSOT Press, 1987. A rigorous challenge to the classical **documentary hypothesis** from a critical perspective. Whybray tentatively proposes a relatively late provenance for the Pentateuch by a single skilled author.

Text Criticism

Brotzman, Ellis R. *Old Testament Textual Criticism: A Practical Introduction*. Grand Rapids: Baker, 1994. A brief yet useful introduction to Old Testament textual criticism. Includes an indispensable twenty-one-page English key to the Latin terminology used in the textual apparatus of *BHS*.

Jobes, Karen H., and Moisés Silva. *Invitation to the Septuagint*. Grand Rapids: Baker, 2000. An orientation to the LXX and its use in interpretation of the Old Testament. Provides a guide to using the LXX in Old Testament textual criticism.

Tov, Emanuel. *Textual Criticism of the Hebrew Bible*. 2nd ed. Minneapolis: Fortress, 2001. A well-regarded, technical treatment of textual criticism. Includes extremely detailed discussion of all aspects of textual criticism.

Wegner, Paul D. *A Student's Guide to Textual Criticism of the Bible*. Downers Grove, IL: InterVarsity Press, 2006. An accessible yet thorough introduction to textual criticism. Provides many helpful examples to assist in learning the mechanics of textual criticism.

Interpretation of Biblical Law

Crüsemann, Frank. *The Torah: Theology and Social History of Old Testament Law*. Translated by A. W. Mahnke. Minneapolis: Fortress, 1996. An examination of the purpose and theology of the Torah, with an emphasis on understanding the relationship among the legal codes of the Pentateuch. Interpretations of specific texts in their social settings are particularly useful.

Kaiser, Walter C., Jr. *Toward Old Testament Ethics*. Grand Rapids: Zondervan, 1983. Advocates for deriving moral principles from Old Testament laws that, with appropriate awareness of the vastly changed circumstances between the original setting and the modern world, can be applied to today.

Lalleman, Hetty. *Celebrating the Law? Rethinking Old Testament Ethics*. Milton Keynes, UK: Paternoster, 2004. A brief yet thorough and accessible argument for a paradigmatic approach to the interpretation of Old Testament law. Provides a good overview of the various approaches to law with a balanced critique of their strengths and weaknesses.

Patrick, Dale. *Old Testament Law*. Atlanta: John Knox, 1985. A helpful, though increasingly dated, perspective on the interpretation of law using form-critical and tradition-critical methodologies.

Watts, James W. *Reading Law: The Rhetorical Shaping of the Pentateuch*. Biblical Seminar 59. Sheffield: Sheffield Academic Press, 1999. Examines the rhetorical aspects of the Torah in an effort to discover how the rhetorical interests of the author shaped the form of the Pentateuch. Argues that the Pentateuch was intentionally designed to persuade post-exilic Jews of the need for allowing Torah to define their identity as the people of God.

Wright, Christopher J. H. *Old Testament Ethics for the People of God*. Downers Grove, IL: InterVarsity Press, 2004. Presents a thorough case for a paradigmatic approach to the interpretation of law that emphasizes Israel's role as being a light to the nations. Wright's work is marked by careful interaction with other scholarly approaches and fair evaluation of them.

Interpretation of Biblical Narratives

Alter, Robert. *The Art of Biblical Narrative*. New York: Basic Books, 1981. A useful introduction to the interpretation of Hebrew narrative. Alter notes the high degree of literary skill with which the biblical authors shaped their narratives. He examines the literary techniques used, including type scenes, repetition, **characterization**, and dialogue. While widely acknowledged as a masterful and foundational work on the literary characteristics of the Hebrew Bible, some evangelical readers may be uncomfortable with his characterization of much of the biblical narratives as fictional.

Chisholm, Robert B., Jr. *Interpreting the Historical Books: An Exegetical Handbook*. Handbooks for Old Testament Exegesis. Grand Rapids: Kregel, 2006. A concise, accessible guide to understanding the features of historical biblical narratives and how they convey the author's intentionality. Many examples from the biblical text make this an especially useful work, particularly for the beginning student.

Sternberg, Meir. *The Poetics of Biblical Narrative: Ideological Literature and the Drama of Reading*. Bloomington: Indiana University Press, 1985. Considered by many to be the standard work on the interpretation of biblical narratives. Sternberg notes that narratives shape and are shaped by worldviews, and examines the ways in which they do so.

Wenham, Gordon J. *Story as Torah: Reading the Old Testament Ethically*. Old Testament Studies. Edinburgh: T & T Clark, 2000. Argues that the narrative texts of the Old Testament provide instruction in righteous living, through both positive and negative examples. Wenham emphasizes the attitudes of the authors of the texts considered rather than the specific actions of the characters in them. He also examines how the attitudes demonstrated through the texts compare to attitudes expressed by New Testament authors, concluding that they are not as different as sometimes maintained.

Sociohistorical Background to the Pentateuch

Gaining familiarity with the broader culture in which the Pentateuch was written must be part of an ongoing learning process; it is not something best done quickly as a "crash course." There is a place for an intensive examination of culture prior to interpreting a particular text, but this is ideally a supplement to an ongoing process of education about the worldview of the authors and audiences of the biblical texts. The following resources are a useful place to start in the study of ancient Near Eastern culture and the intellectual environment that forms the backdrop for the Pentateuch.

Block, Daniel I. *The Gods of the Nations: Studies in Ancient Near Eastern National Theology.* 2nd ed. Grand Rapids: Baker, 2000. An examination of ancient Near Eastern concepts of how the gods related to the land and the people living in it, with an emphasis on how this relationship was lived out.

Hallo, William W., and William K. Simpson. *The Ancient Near East: A History.* 2nd ed. Fort Worth: Harcourt, 1997. The standard reference on the history of the ancient Near East. Analyzes Mesopotamian and Egyptian history separately and includes a survey of the culture of the Mesopotamian world.

Matthews, Victor H., and Don C. Benjamin. *Social World of Ancient Israel 1250–587 BCE.* Peabody, MA: Hendrickson, 1993. A careful analysis of five areas of daily life in ancient Israel, with an emphasis on the ways in which proper understanding of these aspects of life contributes to comprehension of the biblical texts.

von Soden, Wolfram. *The Ancient Orient: An Introduction to the Study of the Ancient Near East.* Grand Rapids: Eerdmans, 1994. An Assyriologist's analysis of ancient Near Eastern culture. Includes examination of artistic, agricultural, intellectual, economic, political, and social life in the ancient Near East.

Walton, John H. *Ancient Near Eastern Thought and the Old Testament: Introducing the Conceptual World of the Hebrew Bible.* Grand Rapids: Baker, 2006. A comprehensive examination of the worldview of the ancient Near East and the Old Testament. Walton demonstrates how Israel is similar to, yet distinct from, the broader culture of the ancient Near East. This book is accessible to the beginning student yet engages with the latest scholarship in a sophisticated and in-depth way.

————. *Ancient Israelite Literature in Its Cultural Context: A Survey of Parallels Between Biblical and Ancient Near Eastern Texts*. Grand Rapids: Zondervan, 1989. Analysis of ancient Near Eastern texts that parallel Old Testament texts. Especially helpful are Walton's discussion of similarities and differences between the source texts and his citation of a variety of ancient Near Eastern texts and genres.

Walton, John H., Victor H. Matthews, and Mark W. Chavalas. *The IVP Bible Background Commentary: Old Testament*. Downers Grove, IL: InterVarsity Press, 2000. A useful introduction to the cultural background of biblical texts. Presented as a commentary, this study provides relevant cultural insights on particular passages in canonical order.

Primary Sources of Ancient Near Eastern Literature

The following resources provide translations of ancient Near Eastern literature. These allow the student of the Old Testament to directly gain an appreciation for the similarities and differences between the Old Testament and ancient Near Eastern literature.

Dalley, Stephanie. *Myths From Mesopotamia: Creation, the Flood, Gilgamesh and Others*. Oxford: Oxford University Press, 1989. A noted Assyriologist provides translation as well as extensive introduction and notes to ten ancient Near Eastern texts.

Hallo, William W., ed. *The Context of Scripture*. 3 vols. Leiden: Brill, 1997–2002. A comprehensive collection of texts from the ancient Near East, including canonical compositions, historical and archival texts, and monumental inscriptions. Each selection is introduced by the translator, and all include extensive bibliographical references. These volumes are emerging as the standard reference for ancient Near Eastern texts.

Matthews, Victor H., and Don C. Benjamin. *Old Testament Parallels: Laws and Stories from the Ancient Near East*. 3rd ed. New York: Paulist Press, 2007. Helpful excerpts of key ancient Near Eastern texts presented in a readable translation. Each selection includes introduction to the text, including identification of provenance and its relevance to Old Testament interpretation.

Pritchard, James B., ed. *Ancient Near Eastern Texts Relating to the Old Testament*. 3rd ed. Princeton: Princeton University Press, 1969. A classic reference with excellent translations of many key ancient Near Eastern texts.

Individual Books

In addition to the resources listed above, commentaries on particular biblical books are important tools in interpretation. In this section I recommend some of the most important commentaries on each book in the Pentateuch. Rather than provide an annotation for each book listed here, I will simply describe the series in which the books appear and allow that to orient you to the individual works.

The Word Biblical Commentary (WBC) series features in-depth analysis of the book with extensive bibliographies. The series is broadly evangelical and focuses on exegesis. Similar to this series is the Apollos Old Testament Commentary (AOTC) series, the New International Commentary (NICOT) series, the New International Biblical Commentary (NIBC) series, and the New American Commentary (NAC) series. The Jewish Publication Society Torah (JPS Torah) commentary series presents interpretations of texts from a Jewish perspective. Two commentary series that approach the text from a nonevangelical perspective are the Anchor Bible (AB) series and the Old Testament Library (OTL) series. In general, commentaries in these series will focus to a great extent on source-critical issues rather than a synchronic reading of the text.

Genesis

Commentaries

Hartley, John E. *Genesis*. NIBC. Peabody, MA: Hendrickson, 2000.
Mathews, Kenneth A. *Genesis 1–11:26*. NAC. Nashville: Broadman & Holman, 1996.
————. *Genesis 11:27–50:26*. NAC. Nashville: Broadman & Holman, 2005.
Sarna, Nahum. *Genesis* בראשית: *The Traditional Hebrew Text with the New JPS Translation*. JPS Torah. Philadelphia: JPS, 1989.
Waltke, Bruce K., and Cathi J. Fredricks. *Genesis: A Commentary*. Grand Rapids: Zondervan, 2001.
Wenham, Gordon J. *Genesis 1–15*. WBC. Waco: Word, 1987.

————. *Genesis 16–50*. WBC. Dallas: Word, 1994.

Additional Studies

Longman, Tremper, III. *How to Read Genesis*. Downers Grove, IL: Inter-
Varsity Press, 2005. A highly accessible guide to the interpretation of
Genesis. Orients the reader to reading the book in light of its genre and
cultural context, rather than in light of modern assumptions seeking
answers to modern questions.

Wittmer, Michael E. *Heaven Is a Place on Earth: Why Everything You Do Matters
to God*. Grand Rapids: Zondervan, 2004. A popular-level application of
the book of Genesis to the Christian life. Very useful in understanding
how the ancient message of Genesis is relevant to a modern audience.

Exodus

Commentaries

Cassuto, Umberto. *A Commentary on the Book of Exodus*. Translated by
I. Abrahams. Jerusalem: Magnes, 1967.

Childs, Brevard S. *Exodus: A Commentary*. OTL. Philadelphia: Westminster,
1974.

Durham, John I. *Exodus*. WBC. Waco: Word, 1987.

Propp, William H. C. *Exodus 1–18: A New Translation with Introduction and
Commentary*. AB. New York: Doubleday, 1999.

————. *Exodus 19–40: A New Translation with Introduction and Commentary*.
AB. New York: Doubleday, 2006.

Sarna, Nahum M. *Exodus* שמות: *The Traditional Hebrew Text with the New
JPS Translation*. JPS Torah. Philadelphia: JPS, 1991.

Stuart, Douglas K. *Exodus*. NAC. Nashville: Broadman & Holman, 2006.

Additional Studies

Hoffmeier, James K. *Israel in Egypt: The Evidence for the Authenticity of the
Exodus Tradition*. Oxford: Oxford University Press, 1996. An examination of the evidence for the historical accuracy of the Exodus account
of the Israelites in Egypt, and their departure, from the perspective of
an Egyptologist.

Sprinkle, Joe M. *The "Book of the Covenant": A Literary Approach*. JSOTSup 174. Sheffield: Sheffield Academic Press, 1994. A detailed examination of Exodus 20:22–23:19 and its place in the book of Exodus as a whole. Sprinkle identifies where and how a literary approach to the book is preferable to a source-critical one and demonstrates the intentionality of the inclusion of the Book of the Covenant in Exodus.

Leviticus

Commentaries

Hartley, John E. *Leviticus*. WBC. Dallas: Word, 1992.

Kiuchi, Nobuyoshi. *Leviticus*. AOTC. Downers Grove, IL: InterVarsity Press, 2007.

Levine, Baruch A. *Leviticus* ויקרא: *The Traditional Hebrew Text with the New JPS Translation*. JPS Torah. Philadelphia: JPS, 1989.

Milgrom, Jacob. *Leviticus 1–16: A New Translation with Introduction and Commentary*. AB. New York: Doubleday, 1991.

———. *Leviticus 17–22: A New Translation with Introduction and Commentary*. AB. New York: Doubleday, 2000.

———. *Leviticus 23–27: A New Translation with Introduction and Commentary*. AB. New York: Doubleday, 2001.

Rooker, Mark F. *Leviticus*. NAC. Nashville: Broadman & Holman, 2000.

Wenham, Gordon J. *The Book of Leviticus*. NICOT. Grand Rapids: Eerdmans, 1979.

Additional Studies

Jenson, Philip P. *Graded Holiness: A Key to the Priestly Conception of the World*. JSOTSup 106. Sheffield: Sheffield Academic Press, 1992. A landmark work examining the system of graded holiness and its rationale.

Numbers

Commentaries

Budd, Philip J. *Numbers*. WBC. Waco: Word, 1984.

Cole, R. Dennis. *Numbers*. NAC. Nashville: Broadman & Holman, 2000.

Levine, Baruch A. *Numbers 1–20: A New Translation with Introduction and Commentary*. AB. New York: Doubleday, 1993.

———. *Numbers 21–36: A New Translation with Introduction and Commentary*. AB. New York: Doubleday, 2000.

Milgrom, Jacob. *Numbers* במדבר: *The Traditional Hebrew Text with the New JPS Translation*. JPS Torah. Philadelphia: JPS, 1990.

Wenham, Gordon J. *Numbers: An Introduction and Commentary*. TOTC. Downers Grove, IL: InterVarsity Press, 1981.

Additional Studies

Douglas, Mary. *In the Wilderness: The Doctrine of Defilement in the Book of Numbers*. Sheffield: Sheffield Academic Press, 1993; reprint, Oxford: Oxford University Press, 2001. Analyzes the structure of Numbers from the perspective of an anthropologist. Douglas argues that Numbers reflects a well-ordered structure in which law and narrative sections are arranged in a ring, with each pair having a corresponding pair on the other side.

Deuteronomy

Commentaries

Christensen, Duane. L. *Deuteronomy 1:1–21:9*. 2nd ed. WBC. Nashville: Thomas Nelson, 2001.

———. *Deuteronomy 21:10–34:12*. WBC. Nashville: Thomas Nelson, 2002.

Craigie, Peter C. *The Book of Deuteronomy*. NICOT. Grand Rapids: Eerdmans, 1976.

McConville, J. Gordon. *Deuteronomy*. AOTC. Leicester: Apollos, 2002.

Merrill, Eugene H. *Deuteronomy*. NAC. Nashville: Broadman & Holman, 1994.

Nelson, Richard D. *Deuteronomy*. OTL. Louisville: Westminster John Knox, 2002.

Tigay, Jeffrey H. *Deuteronomy* דברים: *The Traditional Hebrew Text with the New JPS Translation*. JPS Torah. Philadelphia: JPS, 1996.

Weinfeld, Moshe. *Deuteronomy 1–11: A New Translation with Introduction and Commentary*. AB. New York: Doubleday, 1991.

Wright, Christopher J. H. *Deuteronomy*. NIBC. Peabody, MA: Hendrickson, 1996.

Additional Studies

Millar, J. Gary. *Now Choose Life: Theology and Ethics in Deuteronomy*. Grand Rapids: Eerdmans, 1999. An engaging and helpful analysis of Deuteronomy, noting its "journey" motif. Millar argues for the relevance of Deuteronomy for the modern Christian.

Olson, Dennis T. *Deuteronomy and the Death of Moses: A Theological Reading*. Eugene, OR: Wipf & Stock, 2005. An examination of the message of Deuteronomy and the centrality of the death of Moses. Sees Deuteronomy as catechesis, or instruction in proper living.

4

INTERPRETING
THE PENTATEUCH

WE ARE NOW READY to examine the specifics of interpreting the Pentateuch. Ideally, at this point, we have translated the text[1] (or, if facility in Hebrew is not part of your interpretive "toolbox," selected a couple of good modern-language translations, preferably representing two different translation philosophies[2]) and considered the best reading of the text based on comparison with other textual traditions where relevant. In addition, we should have a fairly good sense of the ancient Near Eastern cultural environment against which the Pentateuch was written.

UNITY AND DIVERSITY IN THE PENTATEUCH

People approach the interpretation of the Pentateuch in a variety of ways. Some see multiple sources used in the composition of the Pentateuch and focus their interpretation largely on identifying and classifying those

---

1. See Robert B. Chisholm Jr., *Interpreting the Historical Books: An Exegetical Handbook*, HOTE (Grand Rapids: Kregel, 2006), 150–58, for a concise guide to translation.
2. For a discussion of translation philosophy and a guide to selecting versions for exegesis, see Gordon D. Fee and Mark L. Strauss, *How to Choose a Translation for All Its Worth: A Guide to Understanding and Using Bible Versions* (Grand Rapids: Zondervan, 2007).

sources. Others seek to engage with the text as a unified whole. We need to examine these differing approaches, as they affect how the interpreter will engage the text of the Pentateuch.

The Documentary Hypothesis

Prior to the mid-eighteenth century, it was widely agreed by both Jewish and Christian scholars that the Pentateuch was largely, if not entirely, written by Moses. Beginning in the late eighteenth century, scholars began to consider alternatives to the traditional association of the Pentateuch with Moses.[3]

Because multiple names for God are used at various places in the Pentateuch, some scholars questioned whether the Pentateuch was the result of a single author or whether multiple authors may have been at work at differing time periods. The best-known early presentation of this view is that of W. M. L. de Wette, who argued in a lengthy footnote in an 1805 dissertation that Deuteronomy is best associated with the Josianic reforms of the seventh century B.C. He further argued that the oldest parts of the Pentateuch should be dated to the time of David, obviously well after the time of Moses.

Modern study of the Pentateuch saw significant development later in the nineteenth century through the work of Julius Wellhausen, who argued for the existence of four hypothetical sources in the Pentateuch: J, E, D, and P.[4] The J source is so named because of its preference for the name Jehovah (**Yahweh**). The E source is named for its preference for the divine name Elohim. D refers to the Deuteronomistic source, and P refers to the Priestly source.

The earliest source, JE or J,[5] was understood to date to around 840 B.C. (when E was seen as a separate source, it was dated to around 700 B.C.). D was understood as originating near the time of Josiah in about 623 B.C., and P was seen as the product of the early exilic period, about

---

3. It is also the case, however, that questions arose at an earlier period. The medieval Jewish scholar Abraham Ibn Ezra noted some aspects of the Pentateuch that he viewed as inconsistent with Mosaic authorship. See David W. Baker, "Source Criticism," in *DOTP*, 800.

4. Julius Wellhausen, *Prolegomena to the History of Israel* (Edinburgh: Black, 1885; reprint, Atlanta: Scholars Press, 1994).

5. Though Wellhausen saw a single source JE, later scholars saw two separate sources, J and E. More recently, adherents to this view have begun to again question the independence of E.

500–450 B.C.[6] Wellhausen himself acknowledged that this idea was not unique to him.[7] Some of his conclusions were anticipated by others (notably Eduard Reuss and Karl Graf), but these scholars did not publish widely, and so Wellhausen is rightly credited with popularizing the now-famous "**documentary hypothesis**" and articulating the significance of this view for understanding Israel's history and the development of the literature of the Pentateuch.

More important than the dates of the sources, however, was how these various hypothetical sources were seen as reflecting the evolution of the thinking and theology of ancient Israel. The J source, for example, was understood as being very primitive in its conception of Yahweh. It presented Yahweh in a very anthropomorphic way, ostensibly reflecting the less sophisticated thinking of its time. In contrast, the later sources were more sophisticated and, to some extent, repudiated the theology and worldview of the earlier sources. For Wellhausen and those who followed, identification and examination of these sources was useful particularly because they contributed to understanding the development of ancient Israelite thinking.

In addition to the differing names for God used in the Pentateuch, the presence of doublets provided evidence for the documentary hypothesis. Doublets are stories that are very similar to each other. Examples include the dual accounts of Abraham presenting his wife as his sister, the repeated accounts of a patriarch or his representative meeting a bride at a well, and the apparent duplications in the flood **narrative**.[8]

The documentary hypothesis was widely embraced and indeed became the dominant approach to the interpretation of the Pentateuch, despite opposition from conservative Christian and Jewish interpreters. Wellhausen's original model was refined somewhat, but the consensus of most Old Testament scholars was that the Pentateuch was an amalgamation of hypothetical sources put together in its present form much later than the time of Moses.

---

6. Some scholars have questioned whether or not P should be seen as later than or contemporaneous with the D source. Weinfeld, for example, maintains that D and P are contemporaneous. See Moshe Weinfeld, *Deuteronomy and the Deuteronomic School* (Oxford: OUP, 1972; reprint, Winona Lake, IN: Eisenbrauns, 1992), 180–83.

7. Wellhausen, *Prolegomena to the History of Israel*, 4.

8. For a thorough analysis of all the criteria used to identify sources in the documentary hypothesis, see Norman Whybray, *The Making of the Pentateuch: A Methodological Study*, JSOTSup 53 (Sheffield: JSOT Press, 1987), 43–131.

This dominant view of the origins of the Pentateuch began to face serious challenge in the latter part of the twentieth century. Though conservative Christian and Jewish scholars had long questioned the validity of the documentary hypothesis, it lost its hegemony in Old Testament studies only when contested by those who were considered part of the scholarly mainstream. One of the most notable challenges to the documentary hypothesis came from Norman Whybray, whose 1987 book, *The Making of the Pentateuch: A Methodological Study*, presents a comprehensive analysis of the bases and criteria used to support the classical understanding of the Pentateuch's origins. Whybray concludes that the documentary hypothesis as usually understood fails to adequately account for the features of the text in light of its ancient Near Eastern context and suffers from an inconsistent use of data at many points. Moreover, he notes, the idea that the Pentateuch was created by amalgamating a variety of sources is utterly unknown in the ancient Near Eastern world.[9] Other scholars also challenged the validity of the documentary hypothesis on different grounds.[10]

As a result of these challenges, there is no longer a consensus as to how the Pentateuch came to be. Wenham notes that "the academic community is looking for a fresh and convincing **paradigm** for the study of the Pentateuch, but so far none of the new proposals seems to have captured the scholarly imagination."[11]

An Alternative Approach

For many evangelicals, the traditional association of the Pentateuch with Moses remains a viable understanding of the way in which the Pentateuch came to be. While there are many good reasons for holding this view, we must examine some considerations as to what this does—and does not—mean.[12]

---

9. Ibid., 129–31.
10. For a helpful survey of recent challenges to the documentary hypothesis, see T. Desmond Alexander, *From Paradise to the Promised Land: An Introduction to the Pentateuch*, 2nd ed. (Grand Rapids: Baker, 2002), 42–61.
11. Gordon J. Wenham, "Pondering the Pentateuch: The Search for a New Paradigm," in *The Face of Old Testament Studies: A Survey of Contemporary Approaches*, ed. David W. Baker and Bill T. Arnold (Grand Rapids: Baker, 1999), 119.
12. This is not intended as a comprehensive defense of Mosaic authorship. For more thorough discussion of the bases for that view, see Roland K. Harrison, *Introduction to the Old Testament* (Grand Rapids: Eerdmans, 1969), 495–541; and, more recently, John H. Sailhamer, *The Pentateuch as Narrative: A Biblical-Theological Commentary* (Grand Rapids: Zondervan, 1992), 1–25; and Duane A.

Intellectual honesty demands that we acknowledge the diversity evident in the Pentateuch. Different styles are clearly found in certain portions, particularly in Genesis, along with the use of multiple names for God, people, and places. None of these excludes the idea that Moses is responsible for the writing of the Pentateuch, but we must acknowledge that Mosaic authorship is more easily asserted than conclusively demonstrated.

Some of these features of the text can be explained by the fact that Moses may have used certain sources in the composition of the Pentateuch, particularly Genesis. Even as we take seriously the idea that Moses is the author of the Pentateuch, we need to bear in mind that Moses was not present for any of the events in Genesis and therefore had to rely on some external source for his information about these events. Whether these were oral or written sources is unknown (and unknowable), but it is clear that some source material (including direct divine revelation) was used in the composition of the Pentateuch.

Moreover, we know with certainty that sources *were* used at points because the Pentateuch refers to them. Numbers 1 describes census lists, and it seems apparent that these were recorded at the time the census was taken. Similarly, there are lists of plunder (Num. 31:26) and an itinerary of the journey taken by the Israelites (Num. 33:1–2). Exodus recounts the inventory of materials used in the construction of the tabernacle (Exod. 38:21–31). In addition, the various law codes in the Pentateuch[13] were available in a later composition. The **Decalogue** was written on tablets at the time of its revelation (Deut. 5:22), and Exodus 24:4 notes that Moses "wrote down all the words of Yahweh" at the time they were given to him. We even find a written source specifically identified in Numbers 21:14: "The Book of the Wars of Yahweh." Though we know nothing about this source beyond this reference, it clearly was used in the composition of Numbers as Moses sought to tie in the experiences of the wilderness generation with texts known in other sources.[14] Finally, we note the presence of songs in Exodus 15, Numbers 21:17–18, and Deuteronomy

Garrett, *Rethinking Genesis: The Sources and Authorship of the First Book of the Pentateuch* (Grand Rapids: Baker, 1991; reprint, Fearn by Tain, Scotland: Mentor, 2003).

13. These include the Book of the Covenant (Exod. 20:22–23:33), the two presentations of the Ten Commandments (Exod. 20; Deut. 5), the Holiness Code (Lev. 17–26), and the legal material in Deuteronomy 12–26.

14. See R. Dennis Cole, *Numbers*, NAC (Nashville: Broadman & Holman, 2000), 353.

31:30–32:44 that were sources used in the composition of their respective books.

Clearly, then, sources *were* used in the composition of the Pentateuch, though not the hypothetical sources envisioned by the documentary hypothesis. Noting the use of these sources and positing other sources used for information about events that occurred prior to Moses' birth helps to partially explain the differences in style that are undeniably present. Moreover, none of these sources is inconsistent with the idea that Moses is the author of the Pentateuch.

Later editors also likely inserted additional material. It is very improbable that Moses wrote the account of his own death in Deuteronomy 34, for example. But other examples of editorial insertions exist as well. Numbers 12:3 says that Moses was "more humble than any person on the face of the earth." The sense of this statement is greatly undermined if it is understood that Moses wrote this concerning himself!

Moreover, Genesis 14:14 states that Abram went to rescue Lot, pursuing Lot's captives "as far as Dan." But Judges 18:29 notes that the city of Dan was originally Laish and was changed to Dan *after* the Israelites entered the land, in honor of their ancestor. Since this was hundreds of years after Abram's time, the reference to "Dan" in Genesis 14:14 must be understood as a later editorial insertion, perhaps to clarify the location for a later audience who would not have been familiar with a reference to the original name of the city (presumably Laish).

Finally, we should note that there was a fairly comprehensive updating of the language of the Pentateuch at some time in the first millennium B.C. This may be seen by the fact that it is similar to the language used in the rest of the Old Testament, with a few exceptions.[15] This fairly widespread grammatical and orthographical update makes certain archaic elements, such as poetic forms, names used, and so on, all the more significant.

What does all this mean with regard to the authorship and unity of the Pentateuch? In light of subsequent editorial activity and the demonstrable use of sources, can we still speak of Mosaic authorship in any meaningful way?

---

15. The Pentateuch tends to spell words with fewer **vowel letters** than elsewhere in the Old Testament. In addition, the third-person masculine singular pronoun הוא is used as a third-person feminine singular pronoun (see, e.g., Gen. 3:15, where הוא is used to refer to Eve). Many scholars see this as an ancient form, and it is found primarily in the Pentateuch. Finally, a variant of the third-person feminine singular pronoun, הִוא, is found only in the Pentateuch.

I believe we can. The fact that sources were used in the composition of the Pentateuch does not mean that the author is relegated to an insignificant role. Rather, authors can take existing materials and shape them according to their communicative purposes. The fact that Moses presumably had access to oral or written sources describing events in the lives of the patriarchs, for example, does not mean that he simply "stitched together" the accounts, resulting in the book of Genesis. Given the thematic and theological unity of the book, it seems more likely that Moses took the sources available to him and shaped the narratives and the book as a whole to accomplish his communicative purposes for his audience (the post-Exodus generation of Israelites). In doing this, he included some things from his original sources and presumably left out other things that didn't advance his purpose in writing. Thus, even with the fairly extensive use of sources in Genesis (which was necessary since Moses was not an eyewitness to any events in Genesis), we can rightly think of Moses as an "author," not simply an editor or compiler of existing sources. His firsthand experience of the events described in Exodus to Deuteronomy allowed greater freedom for him to convey his communicative intentions there.

Neither do subsequent editorial additions deny the authenticity of Moses as an author. Most of the editorial insertions are relatively small and fairly insignificant, such as the example of Dan/Laish already mentioned.

In a contemporary setting, we accept these sorts of changes without challenging the authorship of a text. Christensen and Narucki helpfully note that the hymn "Come, Thou Fount of Every Blessing" originally included the line, "Here I raise mine Ebenezer." Yet most current hymnbooks change the line to say, "Here I raise to Thee an altar." The reason, they explain, is that contemporary audiences are less familiar with the story of the "Ebenezer"—which means "stone of help"—in 1 Samuel 7. But we still correctly consider Robert Robinson the author of the hymn, as he was responsible for its composition and most of the words are his.[16] The subsequent editorial changes seek only to help clarify the original intentionality.

I conclude, then, that the Pentateuch is rightly seen as a product of a single author, who creatively used some sources available to him to

---

16. Duane L. Christensen and Marcel Narucki, "The Mosaic Authorship of the Pentateuch," *JETS* 32, no. 4 (1989): 468–69.

accomplish his purposes in writing to his intended audience. His choice of what to include and leave out of the original material was made based on what would best allow him to communicate his intentions to the original audience. Subsequent editorial additions and linguistic updating do not detract from the idea of Moses as author but in some respects enhance his role, as the changes ensured that his intentions would be understandable to later audiences.

INTERPRETING LAW

Preliminary Considerations

We may now examine some guidelines for interpreting law. Before turning our attention to the guidelines, we should note that interpretation of *any* **genre** is not a mechanical process. That is, it is not the case that an interpreter can simply apply a particular set of "rules" and the correct interpretation of the text will automatically come forth. Rather, interpretation is a dynamic process that is both science and art and requires sound methodology as well as instincts honed through practice (and many mistakes!). It also requires sensitivity and vigilant awareness of the **implied reader** and the social-historical context in which the text was written.

In approaching law, we must always be aware of the nature of law, discussed in chapter 1. We noted there that law for the Israelites was *not* about earning salvation through the keeping of a set of rules but was a means by which God's people were to live out relationship with God as a witness to a watching world. The specific stipulations were intended to help the people live lives pleasing to and centered on God and were further intended in many instances to foster a unique identity of his people.

Another consideration we must keep in mind is that we contemporary readers are not Israel. This is an obvious point, to be sure, but one that is nevertheless important. I have argued against the view that says that the law is not applicable to the Christian, or is perhaps only partially applicable (e.g., the civil and ceremonial laws are not applicable, but the moral law is), and in favor of the view that the entire law *is* relevant and applicable for the Christian. But while I believe that to be true, I also believe that the life, ministry, death, resurrection, and exaltation of Christ have profound implications for the identity of the people of God and, consequently, our relationship to the law. We will be discussing this in some detail below.

Guidelines for Interpretation

In light of the above considerations, I suggest the following guidelines for interpreting law.

Determine the Contexts of the Passage

Identification of the context of the passage is a vital consideration in interpreting law. Both the social-historical context and the literary context (often referred to as **co-text** to distinguish it from the social-historical setting) must be identified.

In identifying the social-historical context, we must determine who is being addressed and what major issues they are dealing with. While the whole of the Pentateuch was written to the post-Exodus Israelites, we can be a bit more specific in some instances.

For example, Deuteronomy obviously presents many of the same laws that appear in Exodus and Leviticus. But it would be a mistake to consider Deuteronomy simply a repetition of the earlier material, though it has sometimes been popularly understood that way. Rather, Deuteronomy represents a **recontextualization**[17] of the earlier material, as Moses addresses a different audience from those who heard the law given at Sinai/ **Horeb**. Though we can't know for certain when the materials in Exodus and Leviticus were finalized, we know that Deuteronomy is presented as a compilation of Moses' speeches given to the people on the plains of Moab, as they were about to enter the Promised Land. This was a significant moment of transition for them, and Deuteronomy presents Moses' teaching in order to help them deal with the challenges facing them in the land. Knowing this contextual information helps ensure that we ask the right questions of the text.

More generally, we know that the whole of the Pentateuch is addressed to Israel. Part of the purpose of the Torah was to inculcate in the Israelites a particular worldview that had at its center an awareness of who Yahweh

---

17. For a discussion of recontextualization, see Jeannine K. Brown, *Scripture as Communication: Introducing Biblical Hermeneutics* (Grand Rapids: Baker, 2007), chaps. 11–12.

is and who they were in relationship to him and the rest of humanity. We must consider how the text we are interpreting develops that worldview and in what ways it reflects that worldview.

Identifying the co-text of the passage is important in ensuring that we are aware of breaks in the author's thought, which further helps identify the communicative intention. For example, Numbers 5 contains a number of regulations concerning clean and unclean people, most of which have been presented elsewhere. Rather than see this as a random insertion of legal material, we need to note that Numbers 5 is part of the broader narrative of Numbers 1–10, which details the scrupulous obedience of the people to Yahweh's commands and their transformation from a ragtag group of frightened, escaped slaves into a nation with an identity and a mission.

Identify the Kind of Law(s) Involved

After having determined the context and co-text of the text in question, it can be helpful to identify the types of law that are present. This may be done in a number of ways.

Laws often are categorized according to their form. **Casuistic law** is case law. It presents a particular case and describes punishments associated with it. An example is found in Exodus 22:14–15, which states, "If anyone borrows an animal from a neighbor and it is injured or dies while the owner is not present, restitution must be made. But if the owner is with the animal, the borrower will not have to pay. If the animal was hired, the money paid for the hire covers the loss" (TNIV). **Apodictic law**, on the other hand, is categorical assertions of right and wrong. Apodictic laws are not presented in the form of cases ("If . . . then . . .") but as declarations. The Ten Commandments are all apodictic laws (though there are other examples found in the Torah). No case is provided; the listener is simply commanded, "You shall not commit adultery" (Exod. 20:14 ESV).[18]

A second way of categorizing or classifying laws is to assign them to the traditional categories of civil, ceremonial, or moral laws. As I argued in chapter 1, however, these categories are not particularly useful for interpretation.

---

18. For a fuller discussion of these two types of law and some proposed nuancing of how they might best be understood, see Dale Patrick, *Old Testament Law* (Atlanta: John Knox, 1985), 21–24.

A third way of classifying laws is according to their type. In the Torah, there are laws of many different sorts. The following outlines some of the major kinds of laws:[19]

- *Criminal laws* specify offenses that are regarded as contrary to the best interests of the community (e.g., Exod. 21:16; 23:1; Deut. 19:14).
- *Case laws* describe particular cases and how they should be resolved (e.g., Exod. 22:5–15).
- *Family laws* regulate relationships within families and responsibilities of members of a family, including the role of the patriarch (e.g., Exod. 20:12; 21:17; Deut. 21:15–17).
- *Sacrificial laws* detail the regulations concerning sacrifices, including when they must be done and how they are to be carried out (e.g., Lev. 1–7; Deut. 17:1).
- *Symbolic laws* describe and establish the system of clean and unclean, which may be understood as culturally appropriate "object lessons" designed to remind the people of their relationship with Yahweh and their mission to be a paradigmatic witness to the Gentiles (e.g., Lev. 11–15; Deut. 14:1–21).
- *Sacred calendar laws* regulate the Sabbath and other feasts and festivals that provide a rhythm to Israel's life in relationship to Yahweh (e.g., Exod. 20:8–11; 23:10–17; Lev. 25:1–22; Deut. 5:12–15; 16:1–17).
- *Compassionate laws* regulate how the people in community are to treat one another (e.g., Exod. 22:21–27; Lev. 19:9–10, 13–18; 25:35–38; Deut. 15; 24:10–22).

In my estimation, it is most helpful to think primarily in terms of the third approach when it comes to categorizing laws.[20] Identifying the kind of law helps orient the interpreter to the communicative intention of the author.

---

19. The categories used here are taken from Christopher J. H. Wright, *Old Testament Ethics for the People of God* (Downers Grove, IL: InterVarsity Press, 2004), 288–301, though I have modified their descriptions somewhat.
20. The types listed here are more useful than the categories of civil/ceremonial/moral laws because they provide greater specificity and they don't limit the moral aspect of law only to laws in that category. As we have seen (see "The Seriousness of Sin" in Leviticus in chapter 2), there is a moral aspect to adhering to laws of clean/unclean, though they are usually seen as ceremonial laws.

We also should note at this point that not all laws are "equal" in terms of their priority for Israel. Some laws deal with weightier matters, and violation of them was understood as a particularly serious offense. Laws related to the Ten Commandments, for example, assign the death penalty for their violation when presented casuistically outside the Decalogue. Other laws, such as compassionate laws, are important priorities but are not the sort of things that could be easily adjudicated. For example, Deuteronomy 24:14–15 states, "You shall not oppress a hired servant who is poor and needy, whether he is one of your brothers or one of the sojourners who are in your land within your towns. You shall give him his wages on the same day, before the sun sets (for he is poor and counts on it), lest he cry against you to the LORD, and you be guilty of sin" (ESV). The implication is that Yahweh would hear the oppressed servant's cry and bring about judgment on the oppressor. It would be a mistake to conclude, however, that the absence of a penalty indicates that the law is unimportant. Though it is difficult (if not impossible) to adjudicate failure to care for the poor, such care was a vital measure of whether the Israelites were succeeding at being the people of God, even if no state-sanctioned penalty is mandated for violation of these laws.[21]

Determine the Nature of the Legal Requirement

The next consideration is what, exactly, the people were being asked to do or not to do. This can be fairly simple, as in the case of the command, "Do not murder" (Exod. 20:13; Deut. 5:17). At first glance, there is not much ambiguity about what is being required in this instance. We should note, however, that the translation "Do not murder" reflects an interpretation of the requirement (which can be seen when noting the difference between the ESV and the KJV, which reads, "Thou shalt not kill"). Determining the nature of what exactly was prohibited means evaluating whether or not such a command forbids capital punishment, which is obviously killing. So even a fairly straightforward prohibition such as this requires some evaluation.[22]

---

21. See Peter T. Vogt, "Social Justice and the Vision of Deuteronomy," *JETS* 51, no. 1 (2008): 35–44.

22. Genesis 9:6 mandates capital punishment prior to the giving of the law at Sinai, which must be considered when determining what, exactly, is prohibited in Exodus 20:13 and Deuteronomy 5:17.

Other cases are even more challenging. Deuteronomy 13:9 (v. 10 in the Hebrew text) says of the person who has sought to entice someone to worship other gods in secret, "You must certainly put them to death. Your hand must be the first in putting them to death, and then the hands of all the people" (TNIV). Some argue this mandates immediate summary execution of the offender by the person who was being asked to worship other gods.[23] Others maintain that this text presumes the completion of legal proceedings, the culmination of which was the imposition of the death penalty.[24] These vexing questions can be resolved only by careful study and analysis. But in seeking to properly understand the relevance of the text for a contemporary audience, it is clearly necessary to begin with a proper understanding of exactly what the law is requiring or forbidding.

Describe the Purpose of the Law in Israel

Once the nature of the legal requirement has been established, we can examine the purpose of the law in Israel. Laws are established in any society to preserve the good of the community, for protection, to establish and maintain a sense of equity among competing interests, and to promote social objectives. Examining the purpose of the law helps determine how it may be relevant in a different setting.

There are a number of probative questions that can help determine the purpose of a law or set of laws. At bottom, the question we are seeking to address is, "Why was this law or set of laws given? What objective is it seeking to accomplish?"[25] To get at these issues, the following questions might be helpful:

- What kind of situation was this law designed to prevent or promote?
- Who would have benefited from this law, and why?
- Is this law designed to restrict someone's power? How? Why?
- What values or moral principles may be seen as underlying this law?

23. See Bernard M. Levinson, *Deuteronomy and the Hermeneutics of Legal Innovation* (Oxford: Oxford University Press, 1997), 134.
24. Peter T. Vogt, *Deuteronomic Theology and the Significance of Torah: A Reappraisal* (Winona Lake, IN: Eisenbrauns, 2006), 63–64. See also Jeffrey H. Tigay, *Deuteronomy* דברים: *The Traditional Hebrew Text with the New JPS Translation* (Philadelphia: JPS, 1996), 132.
25. Wright, *Old Testament Ethics*, 322.

The motivation is God's Love for us, & to help us Love Him appropriately & each other.

- What vision of society is being promoted or pursued in the inclusion of this law?
- What penalty (if any) is prescribed for violating this law?
- What does the penalty show about the seriousness of the law and its objective?[26]

7. Seeking to answer these questions can give us a better idea about the motivation for the laws we are considering. Here, again, determining context and co-text is absolutely essential to proper analysis of the text.

Let's consider again the example of the regulations dealing with an incitement to apostasy (Deut. 13:6–11). We want to consider why this law was included and what its purpose was.

In addressing these matters, we can apply some of the above questions. The law was seeking to prevent the people of Israel from being divided in their loyalties and worshipping other gods. The beneficiary of this law was the community as a whole (see v. 11), which would remain pure through the people's devotion to Yahweh by the identification and elimination of idolaters. The law seems to be promoting a vision of Israelite society in which the people were united in their total devotion to Yahweh and would not tolerate even a hint of disloyalty to him. (Note that the idolatry hasn't actually taken place. This is describing an *enticement* to apostasy, not the actual act.) The seriousness of the situation is readily seen in that state-sanctioned death was commanded for the offender and the person approached was to be the first to cast a stone. The seriousness is further highlighted by the fact that the offender is described as a brother, child, wife, or best friend. Even those close relationships in which heartfelt loyalty was expected were secondary to the need for showing total loyalty to Yahweh.

So what conclusions can we draw about these requirements? Why are they included? The purpose seems to be to inculcate a sense of the tremendous importance of showing absolute loyalty to Yahweh. Even the closest human relationships must be abandoned if the person entices one to follow after other gods. Loyalty to Yahweh was paramount for Israel (Jesus cites Deut. 6:5 as the first and greatest commandment in Matt. 22:37–38), and the relationship between Israel (and individual Israelites) and Yahweh was

---

26. Ibid., 323. Wright presents more questions than I include here, partly because I have incorporated some of his questions into my analysis of what the law requires, discussed in the previous guideline.

He makes it sound like these are the laws of Men. They're not. They're God's Laws.

This is a good parallel for our Christian lives

more important than any human relationships. This sense of total devotion to Yahweh was necessary for Israel's survival and success as the people of God. Israel could not be a paradigm for the nations in terms of what it means to be human in relationship with God if the people were just like the nations in terms of idolatry.

Identify Applicability of the Purpose in a Contemporary Context

The final step is to determine how the law is applicable in our context. Here, we must consider how the purpose of the law can be preserved in a vastly different context. In addition, we will be looking to determine what changes are necessary in light of Jesus' redefinition of the people of God.

In seeking to identify the applicability of an Old Testament law in a contemporary setting, we must begin by asking questions about our own context that are similar to those we asked about the law itself. That is, we should seek to identify situations that are similar and discern ways in which the people of God today are facing issues like those faced by the original audience. This is not always easy or straightforward, but it is necessary to ensure a proper application of the biblical law to a contemporary setting. As Wright notes, the advantage of engaging in this sort of analysis is that we are able to engage "with our context equipped not merely with highly generalized and abstract principles but with much more sharply articulated objectives derived from the paradigm of the society God called Israel to be."[27]

We must be cautious, however, to bear in mind the distinction between Israel on the one hand and the people of God in the New Testament and beyond on the other hand. Whereas the Old Testament included a national political identity for the people of God in the **theocratic** state[28] of Israel, the theocratic aspect was eliminated in the **Christocentric** redefinition of God's people that Jesus effectuated.[29] As a result, certain elements of the

---

27. Ibid., 323.

28. As mentioned before, the word *state* in reference to ancient Israel is somewhat anachronistic but is still a useful way of referring to national political entities.

29. Evangelicals differ in terms of their understanding of the future of ethnic Israel. Dispensationalists—both classical and progressive—view Israel in the New Testament age as distinct from the church and see a temporal, political future for Israel, though the two groups differ on the exact meaning and implications of the relationship between Israel and the church. Others, notably many amillennialists and Reformed theologians, see the church, to a large degree, as redefining Israel such that the temporal promises to Israel have been/will be fulfilled in the church. There are also nuanced and mediating positions. One is that, while Jesus (and therefore his followers) is the

legal system are not applicable in our context, as they assume or require a state in order for them to be carried out. Imposition of the death penalty for religious offenses, for example, is something that was required of the theocratic state of Israel. But as a result of the redefinition of the people of God, no state can claim that identity today. Neither can the church carry out such executions, as that is a state function. These considerations must be a part of our analysis.

Let's turn again to Deuteronomy 13:6–11 to see how this law might be applicable in a different context. We noted above in our discussion of the purpose of the law that for Israel the law was designed to foster an awareness of the need for total loyalty to Yahweh and that relationship with Yahweh was more important than any human relationship. Moreover, we noted that this law was intended to develop and preserve the unique identity of the people of God against an environment in which many other gods were worshipped. The seriousness of the requirement was seen in the fact that even a close friend, child, wife, or brother was to be executed merely for incitement to apostasy.

How, then, does this relate to a contemporary audience? First, we should note that the law in question was addressed to the people of God. Though the nations at times were indicted for failure to adhere to Yahweh's standards (e.g., Amos 1:2–2:3), this law was meant for the Israelites. It was addressed to the elect nation to help them know how they were to live out their relationship with Yahweh. We can conclude, then, that just as this law was not immediately applicable to every society at the time it was originally written and promulgated, it is not one that is universally applicable today but is addressed to the community of believers.

Second, it is apparent that much of the law in Deuteronomy 13 is relevant for the people of God today. The need for total loyalty to God is as necessary for the Christian as it was for the ancient Israelite. Moreover, the rationale for this total loyalty is the same. The people of God, *by definition*, must be totally loyal to him. It makes no sense to speak of believers

---

fulfillment of Israel, ethnic Jews are preserved and will experience salvation (through identification with the Messiah, Jesus) in large numbers in the last days. This is my view. For overviews of these views and the exegetical and theological bases for them, see Darrell L. Bock, ed., *Three Views on the Millennium and Beyond* (Grand Rapids: Zondervan, 1999); and Stanley J. Grenz, *The Millennial Maze: Sorting Out Evangelical Options* (Downers Grove, IL: InterVarsity Press, 1992). See also Thomas R. Schreiner, *New Testament Theology: Magnifying God in Christ* (Grand Rapids: Baker, 2008), 675–754; and N. T. Wright, *Paul in Fresh Perspective* (Minneapolis: Fortress, 2005), 108–53.

who worship God *and* other gods. The call to be God's people means abandoning all other gods in favor of loyalty to God himself. In addition, Deuteronomy's emphasis that loyalty to Yahweh must supersede even the closest human relationships is echoed in the New Testament, when Jesus says, "If anyone comes to me and does not hate father and mother, wife and children, brothers and sisters—yes, even life itself—such a person cannot be my disciple" (Luke 14:26 TNIV).

Clearly, then, the law in Deuteronomy has relevance for the contemporary believer. But what about the penalty? Should we, as some **theonomists** argue,[30] seek to ensure that the death penalty is carried out in present-day societies even for religious offenses such as these?

Here, again, we need to note the importance of Jesus' ministry in relation to this question. As a result of Jesus' ministry,[31] the new community of the people of God is not centered primarily in any one nation or state but rather is found in *all* nations and is inclusive of all people groups.

The purpose of the law in Deuteronomy 13 was to ensure the purity of the people in terms of their loyalty to Yahweh. That, of course, is relevant to the contemporary believer. But some elements were unique to Israel's situation as the political identification of the people of God. The purity of the Israelites' devotion to Yahweh was singularly important for the nation. Israel was called to act on the world stage as a nation representing Yahweh. Thus, there were political implications involved. No state today can claim the divine mandate that Israel had, since no state is "Israel" as understood in the Old Testament. Accordingly, certain aspects of state functions (such as the imposition of the death penalty) cannot be carried out by the church.

Interestingly, there is at least one example of this approach to law in the New Testament. In 1 Corinthians 5:1–3, Paul refers to a man who had engaged in sexual relations with his father's wife. This is specifically forbidden in Leviticus 18:8, and Leviticus 20:11 mandates that the death penalty be imposed on the offenders. In writing to the Corinthians, however, Paul demands that the offender be handed over "to Satan for the destruction of the flesh, so that his spirit may be saved in the day of the Lord" (1 Cor. 5:5 ESV).

---

30. See, e.g., Greg L. Bahnsen, *Theonomy in Christian Ethics*, 2nd ed. (Phillipsburg, NJ: Presbyterian and Reformed, 1984), 435–68.

31. Jesus appears to have self-consciously sought to identify himself as the fulfillment of Israel, as seen through his "I am" sayings in the Gospel of John, the selection of twelve apostles, and the use of the Isaiah servant image and texts for his mission.

[Handwritten annotations in margins:]

While the sin is still sin, the punishment isn't the same as in the Law.

He could have used the story of the woman caught in adultery.

Could it be that stories were to (simply?) so people who follow the Holy Spirit without the need of a Law? But maybe that Paul should he writes we need all should the posted all Sabbaths as the Holy Spirit leads?

Could it be that stories were to simply... Could it be forgot? Paul maybe... Should we follow that... words that can I forget?

Though interpreters do not all agree, most New Testament scholars maintain that Paul's intention here is that the person will be excommunicated
from the fellowship of believers.[32] Further, what likely was *not* intended was
that the offender be executed either by the state or the church of which he
was a part. It appears, then, that Paul did not see the sanctions of the Old
Testament law as something that was to be carried out in the context of the
church, presumably because it is not a state.[33]

In this way, the sanctions of Leviticus have been recontextualized for
the altered circumstances of a Christian community following Jesus' ministry. In seeking to interpret the laws of the Old Testament, we must be
sensitive to the ways in which this redefinition will affect our application
of the laws.

INTERPRETING NARRATIVE

Preliminary Considerations

The Pentateuch is primarily narrative. Even those other genres that
appear in the Pentateuch, such as poetry and law, are embedded within a
narrative framework. It is important, then, that we think carefully about
how to interpret narratives.

Because narratives are so prevalent, and we are familiar with stories told
in our own culture, we are often very comfortable working with them.
Unfortunately, this familiarity sometimes has led to misinterpretations of
biblical texts. Too often, contemporary interpreters have sought to ex-
trapolate an easily applicable moral from the biblical accounts and paid too
little attention to the ways in which the author intended the text to be understood by the original audience. But proper interpretation demands that
authorial intention govern interpretation. At times this may necessitate

---

32. For a discussion of the issues involved in the interpretation of this passage, see Gordon D.
Fee, *The First Epistle to the Corinthians*, NICOT (Grand Rapids: Eerdmans, 1987), 208–13;
Anthony C. Thiselton, *The First Epistle to the Corinthians*, NIGTC (Grand Rapids: Eerdmans,
2000), 392–400.

33. Some have maintained that Paul's intention was that the offender would die as a result of being
handed over to Satan for the destruction of the flesh. This is unlikely, however, as the purpose of
the action is restoration. (See Fee, *First Epistle*, 209.) Moreover, even if this is true, the offender
was not to be killed by agents of the church or the state but rather by Satan. The elimination of
the role of the state in favor of action by Satan is understandable in light of the elimination of a
national political identity for the people of God.

our letting go of cherished understandings in favor of an interpretation centered on the author's communicative intention.

Here we will consider some useful guidelines for interpreting narratives. As we noted above, however, this is not a mechanical process but rather a dynamic one. We might find that we draw certain conclusions that must be revised later in light of subsequent analysis of the text. It is important that interpreters not become committed to a particular understanding too quickly but instead be willing to see where the data of the text take them.

Guidelines for Interpretation

Establish the Co-text of the Passage

We must begin by establishing the boundaries of the text in question. Since the chapter, verse, and paragraph divisions all were added well after the text attained its final form, they are not accurate or helpful guides as to where a text begins or ends. We are looking for breaks in the author's thought that give some indication that a new section of the narrative has begun.

Sometimes, the author has used structural markers that can assist in identifying sections of a text. In Genesis, for example, the repeated use of the word תּוֹלְדוֹת ("generations") marks various sections of the book. The word appears in variations of the phrase אֵלֶּה תּוֹלְדוֹת ("these are the generations") in Genesis 2:4; 5:1; 6:9; 10:1; 11:10; 11:27; 25:12; 25:19; 36:9; and 37:2 as structural markers in the book.

Not every book or section has such obvious markers, however, and even with sections noted in this way there are various subsections. The material on Abraham, for example, is contained in one major section (Gen. 11:27–25:11) introduced by וְאֵלֶּה תּוֹלְדוֹת and subdivided into a number of **pericopes**.

Identifying sections, or pericopes, is usually fairly easy to do. We need to look for major changes in where the action takes place, who is involved, and the nature of the action itself. These will indicate that the author has shifted attention from one narrative cycle to another.

Consider Numbers 13. The previous chapter describes the rebellion of Miriam and Aaron against Yahweh's choice of Moses for a special relationship with himself. The narrative ends with Miriam being restored from her leprosy and the people leaving Hazeroth and going to Paran. Numbers 13 begins with Yahweh commanding Moses to send spies into the land of Canaan. No longer is the rebellion of Aaron and Miriam in view; a new pericope has begun. The narrative of the spies continues until Numbers 14:38, after which the attention shifts to an untimely attempt at obedience. This, too, indicates that a new section has begun.[34]

This narrative contains other sections as well. Numbers 13:25 introduces the report of the spies and the response of the people. This clearly represents a shift from the focus of verses 1–24, which concentrates on the commissioning of the spies and their work in the land of Canaan. The people involved and the nature of their activity has changed, at least somewhat. Similarly, the rebellion of the people and its aftermath is best seen as a new section. Though the same people are involved (Moses, the twelve spies, and the Israelites), the attention is on their responses (their actions).

The value of this analysis is that it helps us to better see the priorities of the author. Moses was not concerned with a detailed description of the spies' activities, as he narrates forty days in just fifty-eight words in the Hebrew text. Given this lack of attention to the activities of the spies in those days, we can safely presume that that was not the focus of Moses' attention.

duh!

Identify and Label the Scenes in the Narrative

Once the text's boundaries have been identified and a sense of the narrative's place within the book has been established, we can turn our attention to the passage itself. Just as identification of the co-text of the passage helped determine the priorities of the author, noting the scenes within a narrative can be a useful means of identifying those things that the author felt were important to convey to the audience. *again — duh!*

In many respects, identifying scenes is similar to establishing the boundaries of the narrative itself. That is, we need to be looking for changes in where the action takes place, who is involved, etc.[35] This was introduced in chapter 1.

Analyze the Plot

The next consideration of a narrative text is the plot. Tracing the tension in a narrative helps us to see the issues the author wanted to raise.

---

34. For a somewhat different assessment of the structure of Numbers, see Cole, *Numbers*, 36–42.

35. For a more detailed discussion of how to identify scenes and their importance to interpretation, see Shimon Bar-Efrat, *Narrative Art in the Bible*, JSOTSup 70 (Sheffield: Sheffield Academic Press, 2000), 184–96.

This always must be done, to the best of our abilities, from the perspective of the implied reader, remembering that our concerns may well be different from those of the implied reader.

Focusing on the tension as part of plot helps us to see what was important to the author. By identifying the **climax** of the narrative—which was defined in chapter 1 as the point at which the implied reader has questions about what will happen but no answers (the questions are usually resolved after the climax)—we can identify the author's priorities. This helps us avoid a tendency to read our questions and concerns into the text or to derive "morals" from the text that are not a primary part of the author's communicative intention.

Does he really think biblical authors thought about all of this? This I never ask question.

Examine the Details of the Scenes

Following analysis of the co-text, scenes, and the plot, attention can be turned to the question of how the author developed his ideas. This involves a careful examination of the details of the scenes, noting the ways in which characters are developed, the point of view, the use of dialogue, and the stylistic devices employed.

Characterization. **Characterization** refers to the kind of information that is provided about an actor in the narrative. Characterization takes one of two forms. **Explicit characterization** about the character is information provided directly by the **narrator**. An example of this is found in Genesis 39:6, which notes that Joseph was "well-built and handsome" (NIV). **Implicit characterization** is what is conveyed about the character of the actors through what they do, what they say, and how others respond to them.[36] We learn of a certain impetuousness in Esau when, in Genesis 25:29–34, he sells his birthright for some lentil stew. Another example may be seen in Genesis 34:4, when Shechem says to his father, "Get me this girl for my wife" (ESV). The lack of respect he shows to his father cements the negative reputation he earned with his rape of Dinah, and it prepares the reader for his (and his father's) deceitfulness in speaking to his fellow citizens in verses 20–23.

Point of view. Point of view is the perspective of the **implied author**. As with characterization, this may be presented explicitly, in the form of explicit statements about a person, action, or situation. For example,

---

36. For more on characterization, see Robert Alter, *The Art of Biblical Narrative* (New York: Basic Books, 1981), 114–30, and Bar-Efrat, *Narrative Art in the Bible*, 47–92.

Me thinks he analyzes way too much.

Numbers 11:1 says, "When the people complained, it displeased the LORD. When the LORD heard it, his anger burned, and so the fire of the LORD burned among them and consumed some of the outer parts of the camp" (NET). No question remains as to how God (and the implied author) feels about the people's actions.

Point of view also may be expressed implicitly and must be discerned through analysis of what is said and how it is portrayed. The silence of Jacob in the face of Dinah's rape in Genesis 34, coupled with the repeated emphasis on the fact that she is his daughter, communicates that the author is not endorsing his actions or attitudes.[37]

Use of dialogue. Dialogue is often a key to the proper understanding of a biblical text. Through dialogue, we learn about the characters (implicit characterization) and, sometimes, the point of view of the implied author. Numbers 11:4–5 recounts the complaint of the Israelites in direct speech: "And the people of Israel also wept again and said, 'Oh that we had meat to eat! We remember the fish we ate in Egypt that cost nothing, the cucumbers, the melons, the leeks, the onions, and the garlic" (ESV). This use of dialogue highlights their lack of character and devotion to Yahweh, as they reminisce about the good food they had to eat and how inexpensive it was—while living as slaves in Egypt!

Stylistic devices. Finally, we should note the use of stylistic devices. The biblical authors employed various techniques in order to heighten the interest of the hearer/reader and to ensure that their intentionality was communicated successfully.

These stylistic devices include such things as repetition, irony, foreshadowing, and type scenes. Repetition is used in Numbers 9 to show the people's obedience to Yahweh's commands. The phrase עַל־פִּי יהוה ("at the command of Yahweh") occurs seven times in verses 18–23. Such frequent use of the term highlights their unfailing obedience to Yahweh and sets up a contrast with the actions of the people in Numbers 11.

An example of irony occurs in the early chapters of Genesis, where Adam and Eve are seduced by the serpent, who entices them with the promise that they will become "like God" (Gen. 3:5) when they have eaten the forbidden fruit. This is ironic in that Genesis 1 indicates that they were already "like God," having been created in his image (1:27).

---

37. Bear in mind the discussion in chapter 1 on the need for caution in determining the author's point of view.

Foreshadowing is a technique in which something is referred to briefly in an early part of the narrative and then taken up in greater detail later. We see this in Genesis 25:27–28, which describes Esau and Jacob: "The boys grew up, and Esau became a skillful hunter, a man of the open country, while Jacob was content to stay at home among the tents. Isaac, who had a taste for wild game, loved Esau, but Rebekah loved Jacob" (TNIV). This sets the stage for the conflicts that will later ensue between the two brothers, and it also helps explain the actions of Isaac and Rebekah in their dealings with their sons.

Finally, type scenes are formulaic presentations of certain key events. Comparison and contrast between the type scenes helps identify the author's intention. An example of a type scene is the "meeting a woman at a well." This occurs in Genesis 24, where Abraham's servant meets Rebekah at a well, and again in chapter 29, where Jacob meets Rachel. Certain elements are the same: A traveler comes upon a well and sees a beautiful local girl there. She is revealed to be from the tribe the traveler is seeking. Marriage is then arranged. But there are important differences that help communicate the author's intentions. In Genesis 24:12–14, the servant asks Yahweh to grant him success in his quest, whereas in Genesis 29 Jacob offers up no such prayer. The deviation from the pattern conveys important information about the characters and the author's point of view.[38]

Identify the Communicative Intention of the Author

Having engaged with the details of the text, always bearing in mind the crucial hermeneutical question of, "How would this have been understood by the original author and audience?" we are now in a position to draw some conclusions about the meaning of the text. Here, we are seeking to address the questions, "What did the original author intend to communicate by presenting this text in this way?" and "Why is this text here?"

Ideally, a careful analysis of the details of the text and examination of its co-text will lead to greater awareness of why it is included. Remember that at this point we are always thinking of the past. That is, we are concerned with what the text *meant* to the original audience.

---

38. For more on type scenes and their function in communicating the intention of the author, see Alter, *Biblical Narrative*, 47–62.

One important consideration in addressing the questions about the author's communicative intention is the purpose and message of the whole book in which the text appears. It is important to remember that the biblical authors did not usually write isolated narratives that were envisioned as "stand-alone" texts.[39] Rather, they were responsible for books, which have coherent themes and messages in them. So, we can interpret the whole in light of the parts as we draw conclusions about what overall message and themes the author wanted to communicate. But the parts also must be interpreted in light of the whole, as the overarching message derived from the parts then helps govern how the individual texts are shaped. Consequently, it is important to consider how the narrative in question relates to and supports the development of the message and themes of the book as a whole.

Consider, for example, the creation account in Genesis 1–2. Too often interpreters have read the creation account as a "stand-alone" text, without consideration for how it (and the **primeval history** as a whole) relates to the rest of the book of Genesis. But Genesis focuses more on the history of the patriarchs than on the primeval history, and the book as a whole develops important themes of the sovereignty of Yahweh, his character as a God of grace, and the seriousness of sin. And it does so in contrast to and in figurative dialogue with the ancient Near Eastern worldview. Thus the creation account in Genesis 1–2 shows *who* created all that is and *what* he created. Moreover, the Genesis creation account portrays Yahweh as utterly unlike the gods of the ancient Near Eastern world.[40] He is a God whose speech is powerful and literally reality-shaping. He is a moral God, whose intentions result in a creation that is, according to Genesis 1:31, טוֹב מְאֹד ("very good" or "perfect").[41]

All this helps set the stage for the patriarchal history in chapters 12–50. We know from the primeval history in general and the creation account in particular that Yahweh is a God who can and will accomplish his pur-

---

39. It may be the case that certain narratives were written as isolated accounts, but even those have been incorporated into a collection that reflects an author's intentions. So, regardless of the provenance of a particular account, we are concerned with its use in the larger book of which it is a part.

40. This was introduced in chapter 2.

41. The sense of "perfection" comes from the use of the absolute superlative of degree as well as the emphatic use of הַנֵּה. See B. K. Waltke and M. O'Connor, *An Introduction to Biblical Hebrew Syntax* (Winona Lake, IN: Eisenbrauns, 1990), 268; and Gordon J. Wenham, *Genesis 1–15*, WBC (Waco: Word, 1987), 34.

poses in the world. Thus, when he speaks to Abram in Genesis 12:1–3 and promises that he will make him a great nation through whom all other nations will be blessed, we know from the creation account that Yahweh's word is powerful and that he is able to accomplish that which he says he will do.

When we ask of the creation account, "Why is this narrative here, and why is it presented in this way?" we need to consider the broader book in which it appears. If we do not, we might conclude that the text is present simply to explain the *how* of creation. Recognizing that it is part of a much more expansive narrative (along with awareness of the cultural backdrop of the ancient Near Eastern world) points us in a somewhat different direction, one that is more in keeping with Moses' communicative intention.

Recontextualize the Text for a Contemporary Setting

Once the text has been analyzed carefully and the author's intended meaning has been identified (at least tentatively!), we are in a position to analyze its relevance for a contemporary audience. Note that this can come only *after* careful engagement with the meaning of the text and proper consideration of the hermeneutical questions described above.

As we consider the text's contemporary relevance, we must remember that the text can't mean something for today that it didn't mean to the original author and audience. There must be coherence between the meaning intended by the author and the **contextualization** of the text by the contemporary reader.

As we have noted frequently, the biblical texts are addressed to a particular audience. To put it a bit more technically, the author's communicative intention is contextualized for the implied reader. We noted that the author uses conventions that would have been familiar to the audience, writes in a language they would understand, and makes reference to things they would know about (events, places, people, etc.). This is contextualization.

The interpreter has the task of *re*contextualizing the text in a contemporary setting. That means we must ask how the communicative intention of the author is relevant in a setting vastly different from the original one. Addressing this question means being aware of the nature of the contemporary setting and, as we have seen, assumes proper knowledge of the original context of the text. We must also consider the altered situation that obtains as a result of Jesus' redefinition of the people of God around himself, as was the case with law. Clearly, a measure of "cultural exegesis" of contemporary civilization is necessary to properly recontextualize the Old Testament text. It is challenging, but it is also a vital aspect of proper interpretation, as it helps prevent us from inappropriately applying the text in our setting.[42]

Let's consider as an example Numbers 11:31–35, which deals with God's response to the people's desire for meat. Applying all the previous guidelines for interpretation ideally would lead us to conclude that Moses sought to remind his audience of the need for showing total loyalty to Yahweh. In this pericope, the people are faced with a stark choice. They could remain within the camp, in the shelter of Yahweh's presence, which also meant they would eat only manna. Or they could travel a day's journey outside the camp, where they would find an abundance of quail to eat. The problem was that leaving the camp meant leaving—decisively—Yahweh's presence and protection and entering the realm of death. Shockingly, many people preferred to have meat instead of Yahweh! Moses includes this account in order to highlight the need for trusting in and showing loyalty to Yahweh. No matter how uncomfortable or incomprehensible Yahweh's plans might have been, the Israelites were expected to follow after him.

As we seek to recontextualize this text for today, we must ask how the meaning of the text is relevant in our very different circumstances. We must recognize that we are not ancient Israel with its unique calling to be the people of God. Though we are not in the position of eating only manna each day, we are nevertheless dependent on God for his provision and on his wisdom for knowing what we need. We may find ourselves tempted to want things—even good things!—that God has not provided for us. We may find ourselves wanting better vacations, larger homes, or other manifestations of success in North American society. Sometimes God blesses us by giving us those things; other times he chooses not to. Like the Israelites, we must choose between showing loyalty to God and having what we want. In some situations, pursuing what we want may take us from God's presence. The message of Numbers 11:31–35 is relevant even in our changed circumstances.

---

42. See the discussion on (re)contextualization in Brown, *Scripture as Communication*, chaps. 11–12.

Once we have identified the author's communicative intention and investigated its relevance for the contemporary reader, we can examine how it can best be communicated. We will turn our attention to that in the next chapter.

5

COMMUNICATING THE
GENRES OF THE PENTATEUCH

WE HAVE NOW EXAMINED the way in which we go about discerning the author's communicative intention for a biblical text. To this point, the focus has been on the past: what the author intended to communicate to the original audience.

But the relevance of Scripture is not confined to its meaning in the original setting. Indeed, if that were the only purpose for engaging with Scripture, the Bible would function more as an artifact in a museum. Rather, the message of Scripture is important and powerful for readers today, despite the fact that it is the product of a very different context. Part of the interpretive process includes developing awareness of the text's significance for today, particularly in light of the changed circumstances of the people of God since Jesus' life and ministry.

All that careful exegesis and study is useless, however, if the truth of Scripture cannot be effectively communicated to contemporary audiences. In this chapter, we turn our attention to how law and **narrative** texts can be communicated today. Though the language I use often will be that of "preaching" the texts, we should note that the principles discussed here are applicable in other contexts as well. The teacher of Scripture, no less than the preacher, must think carefully about how the truth of the text can be communicated effectively. And even those who are not engaged in "public" proclamation should reflect on the principles discussed here, as the focus is on communication, not simply public proclamation, important though that is.

PRELIMINARY CONSIDERATIONS

Before examining some specific principles that may be helpful in communicating narrative and law, we will first look at some potential obstacles to effective communication of these **genres**.

Attitudes Toward the Old Testament

One consideration to keep in mind is that most contemporary readers are often suspicious about the relevance of the Old Testament, and they even question its necessity at times. Though the following attitudes may not often be expressed, it is my experience that they are held by many Christians today.

- "The Old Testament describes a world that doesn't exist anymore. The people living in Old Testament times fought with swords and chariots, knew little or nothing about other peoples and cultures, and could not conceive of the world as we know it today. Consequently, anything the Old Testament has to say is probably irrelevant to us, who live with the threat of terrorists using weapons of mass destruction and are in communication with people around the world instantly. Whatever the Old Testament says about the human condition is hopelessly out of date, as it reflects a world that is gone."
- "The Old Testament is rigid and narrow in its conceptions of right and wrong. Its zealotry and patriarchal attitudes (and institutions) are simply incompatible with the more enlightened worldview that we know. It is consistently guilty of one of the most egregious contemporary sins: intolerance."
- "The 'God of the Old Testament' is of a different character than the 'God of the New Testament.' The Old Testament God is capricious, vengeful, and bloodthirsty, whereas the God of the New Testament is loving and merciful."

These attitudes amount to what I call a "functional Marcionism" in many of our churches. As you may recall from chapter 1, Marcion was a heretic who believed that the father of Jesus Christ (i.e., the God of the New Testament), was *not* **Yahweh**, the God of Israel (and, consequently, the God of the Old Testament). Accordingly, he rejected the Old Testament, believing that it had *no* relevance for the Christian. Though Marcion's views were repudiated (he was excommunicated in A.D. 144), remnants of his thinking continue to afflict the contemporary church.[1]

It may be helpful to briefly address these attitudes, as they can be a significant barrier to understanding the message of the biblical text. First, we should note that while it is true that the Old Testament reflects a very different time and worldview from our own, this does not mean that the Old Testament is irrelevant to our situation. People today certainly know more about the world around them and are able to communicate more quickly with people around the world, but it would be difficult to maintain that this has resulted in appreciably greater understanding or reduced the tendency toward hatred, fear, or intolerance. A simple examination of any daily newspaper shows that human sin remains a significant problem, our technological prowess notwithstanding. Our enhanced technological abilities have resulted in more efficient ways of harming or killing one another; our technology has *not* changed human propensity to sin. And we should note that the Old Testament addresses the problems of the human condition. The manifestations of human sin are clearly presented against the backdrop of the ancient Near Eastern world, but the proclivity toward sin is presented as universal. Thus, the changed circumstances of the contemporary reader don't negate the importance of the message of the Old Testament in any way.

Second, we can and should acknowledge that the Old Testament (and the New Testament, for that matter) is in fact fairly rigid and narrow in its conception of right and wrong and is intolerant of many things. But that raises a question: is this necessarily a bad thing? Contemporary American culture maintains that tolerance and acceptance are two highly prized virtues. But that is a culturally influenced view. In other societies, emphasizing "truth," "morality," and "goodness" might be more culturally

---

1. For more on Marcion and his views, see Kenneth Scott Latourette, *A History of Christianity*, vol. 1, *Beginnings to 1500*, rev. ed. (New York: Harper Collins, 1975), 125–28; and Justo L. González, *The Story of Christianity*, vol. 1, *The Early Church to the Beginning of the Reformation* (New York: Harper Collins, 1984), 61–66.

valuable. The point is that the value of the Old Testament should not be determined by how well it conforms to our cultural norms and values but by how well it reflects the morality and perspective of God.[2]

The question of worldview is relevant here. As we noted in chapter 2, the Pentateuch presents a particular worldview. In that view Yahweh, the God of Israel, is portrayed as sovereign, holy, and just. Moreover, he is the creator of all that is, and creation originally reflected his intentionality perfectly. Human sin marred that. In giving instructions (or Torah) to his people, God was simply advising them of how they were to live in order to be happy, healthy, and successful (from his perspective, not necessarily from a human one). So, from the perspective of the Pentateuch itself, its "rigid" constructions of right and wrong are part of God's gracious gift to human beings. He instructs them in how they must live in relationship to a holy God who is present with his people. In the worldview of the Old Testament the "rigid" and "narrow" conceptions of right and wrong derive from the character and holiness of a gracious God, who desires that people live as they were created to live.

An illustration might help here. If you buy a piece of electronic equipment, the instruction manual will include all sorts of "dos" and "don'ts," all of which are designed to help you maximize the benefits of the product and to ensure its long life. When the manual says, "Do not immerse in water," the product designers are not intending to deprive you of the fun of immersing the product in water or being overly rigid and narrow. Rather, they want you to avoid doing something that will damage the product (and yourself!). The "rigid" and "narrow" tenets of the Pentateuch function in much the same way. Certain prohibitions exist because humans weren't made for those behaviors. Exalting oneself rather than God, for example, is behavior forbidden in the Old Testament. It is not because God is arrogant or wants to deny us the thrill of self-exaltation. Rather, we aren't "wired" for that behavior, and it will ultimately harm us, since it can never be true that we are equal to or above God.

The Pentateuch maintains that Yahweh is at the center of everything. He is the creator, sustainer, and ruler of all that is. Human sin is fundamentally a rejection of that truth and represents a desire to supplant God's rightful place in favor of independence and self-sufficiency. The Torah,

---

2. This, of course, is a controversial statement, and one should be very cautious in claiming to speak authoritatively for God. Nevertheless, the primary criteria by which the relevance of the Old Testament is judged should not be those of our contemporary culture.

and the perspective of the entire Old Testament, teaches that such self-sufficiency is impossible, no matter how desperately we pursue it. From that perspective, then, the most loving thing God could do is to ensure that humans know their rightful place in the universe and understand how to relate to Yahweh properly. Intolerance of other perspectives is not arbitrary; other perspectives are rejected because they simply aren't true. Being "tolerant" of such views is *not* loving, since the actual reality is that Yahweh alone is God.[3]

It is true that the worldview of the Pentateuch is presented against the backdrop of a society in which women were afforded few rights and slave ownership was permitted and regulated. But this fact highlights the importance of paying careful attention to the author's intentions. Part of the interpretive process, as we saw in the last chapter, involves determining how the contextualized message of the original author is applicable in vastly different circumstances. In many instances, objectionable aspects of the ancient Near Eastern society and culture are accepted but not endorsed by the biblical authors. Intellectual honesty demands that those "countercultural" features of the text are acknowledged.

One example is the remarkable inclusion of women in the community of God's people in Deuteronomy 15:12, which reads: "If your brother, a Hebrew man or a Hebrew woman, is sold to you, he shall serve you six years, and in the seventh year you shall let him go free from you" (ESV). Against an ancient Near Eastern backdrop that is pervasively patriarchal (elements of which are present in Israelite society as well), Moses explicitly notes that women are to be considered "brothers" in this new community. This radically countercultural stand must be acknowledged in evaluating the nature of the Pentateuch and the point of view of its author.[4]

Finally, we should note that the idea that the "God of the Old Testament" is different from the "God of the New Testament" simply cannot be sustained from the data of the Bible itself. The New Testament and Jesus himself assume that the God of Abraham, Isaac, and Jacob is the father of Jesus Christ. The extensive use of the Old Testament by

---

3. Many people choose to reject the worldview of the Old Testament, but it is much harder to argue that this is not what the Old Testament claims.

4. For a discussion of the hermeneutical implications of engaging with the countercultural trends in Scripture, and the means by which the point of view of the author may be discerned in the text, see Robin Parry, "Feminist Hermeneutics and Evangelical Concerns: The Rape of Dinah as a Case Study," *Tyndale Bulletin* 53, no. 1 (2002): 1–28.

the New Testament writers (and in Jesus' teachings) demonstrates that such a view was foreign to the thinking of the early church. Moreover, the Old Testament itself won't support such a view, as Yahweh is consistently portrayed as loving and gracious.[5]

Ignorance of the Old Testament

A second consideration to remember when thinking about how the message of the Pentateuch can be effectively communicated is the lack of knowledge about the Old Testament that exists even among Christians. Studies have confirmed what has long been known anecdotally: there is widespread ignorance of the contents of the Bible as a whole in contemporary American society, including (sadly) many Christians.

For example, surveys show that only half of all adults know that the book of Jonah is part of the Bible.[6] Moreover, fully 80 percent of adults believe that the Bible teaches that "God helps those who help themselves."[7] When Jay Leno surveyed his audience one evening (admittedly not a scientific study!), nobody in attendance could name a single apostle. When asked to name the Beatles, the four members were quickly identified.[8] Clearly, there is a great degree of biblical illiteracy among adults in our society.

Why does this matter? In seeking to communicate the message of the Pentateuch, the speaker must know that the audience understands something of the framework from which he or she is speaking. Barna notes that even among born-again Christians, just 60 percent could offer a correct definition of the word *gospel*.[9] If that is the case, it seems likely that many people in our churches will have an inadequate conception of important

5. It is also true that the differences between the Testaments can be vastly overstated. For example, in Acts 5:1–11, Ananias and Sapphira are struck dead immediately for their untruthfulness to Peter. This hardly seems consistent with the understanding that the "New Testament God" does not judge, as did the "Old Testament God." Moreover, when we note that God gave the Canaanites more than four hundred years to turn from their idolatry before they were judged (the most common evidence cited in favor of the capriciousness of the "God of the Old Testament"), yet apparently gave Ananias and Sapphira no opportunity to repent, one could perhaps argue that the "God of the New Testament" is even quicker to judge!

6. George Barna, *The Index of Leading Spiritual Indicators* (Dallas: Word, 1996), 79.

7. Ibid., 80. The quote is from Benjamin Franklin, not the Bible!

8. Clayton Hardiman, "Bible Literacy Slipping, Experts Say," Newhouse News Service, March 28, 2001, http://www.lexisnexis.com/.

9. Barna, *Spiritual Indicators,* 78.

Old Testament concepts and words, such as covenant or Torah. If we are to communicate effectively with the people attending our churches, then we must ensure that we don't "talk past" people by assuming knowledge of terms and concepts that they probably aren't familiar with.

Suppose, for example, someone was teaching or preaching on Deuteronomy 29, which deals with the covenant renewal on the Plains of Moab. Describing the responses to Yahweh's judgment of the people for their failure to remain loyal to him, Deuteronomy 29:25 says, "Then people will say, 'It is because they abandoned the covenant of the LORD, the God of their fathers, which he made with them when he brought them out of the land of Egypt" (ESV). Given what Barna and other researchers have found, the speaker could not count on everyone in the audience having a proper understanding of what the covenant is and its significance for Israel and for proper understanding of the Old Testament. Similarly, they may not have a good grasp of whom "the fathers" refers to, and the significance of that reference for understanding the passage. Accordingly, the speaker will have to ensure that the message or lesson is presented in such a way as to explain those things to the audience, in order to ensure that Moses' communicative intention is properly conveyed to the listeners.

Similarly, the speaker cannot assume that the listener understands the historical events that precede or follow a particular event. Some of the subtleties in the theology and argument in Deuteronomy, for example, are based on the "blending" of the generations of Israelites after the exodus. The book is addressed to the Israelites gathered on the Plains of Moab. This is the second generation of Israelites following the departure from Egypt, the first having been forbidden to enter the Promised Land because of the their rejection of Yahweh at Kadesh Barnea (Num. 14). Thus, Moses is addressing the *next* generation of Israelites in his sermons recorded in Deuteronomy. But he at points seems to maintain that his audience was at Sinai, when in fact they were not. Deuteronomy 5:3 makes this explicit, saying, "Not with our ancestors did Yahweh make this covenant, but with us, with all of us who are alive here today." This blending of generations is deliberate on Moses' part, and understanding it is a necessary part of understanding his communicative intention. He does it again in Deuteronomy 29:14–15: "It is not with you alone that I am making this sworn covenant, but with whoever is standing here with us today before the LORD our God, and with whoever is not here with us today" (ESV). Moses wants his audience to understand the continuity between the generations of Israelites and the responsibilities that each generation has in ensuring that Israel succeeds at being God's people.[10] The speaker will likely have to explain this to a contemporary audience.

All this suggests that the task of communicating the meaning of pentateuchal texts is more complicated than simply presenting the meaning in an engaging way (challenging though that alone is!). Instead, effective communication means being aware of what the listeners do and do not know about the contents, history, and theology of the Old Testament in general and the Pentateuch in particular. This will vary from setting to setting and won't even be uniform within one particular setting, but effective communication means being aware of this issue.

Lack of Awareness of the Old Testament's Coherence

The final preliminary consideration we will examine is very much related to the previous one. Part of the challenge of communicating the Old Testament message is that many people are unaware of its coherence (and the entire Bible's, for that matter). That is, many people are unaware of how the sections and books of the Old Testament, though written by different authors in very different contexts, nevertheless show remarkable consistency in themes, theology, and worldview. As we noted in chapter 2, the Old Testament presents a coherent **metanarrative**. Part of communicating the message of the pentateuchal texts includes demonstrating how the text in question contributes to and advances that metanarrative.

One way in which this can be seen is in the relationship of the Pentateuch to the prophetic material. The prophets rightly have been understood as "preachers of Torah," since the prophetic books are firmly grounded in an understanding of the Pentateuch. As Stuart notes in the introduction to his commentary on Hosea–Jonah, the evidence "supports the conclusion that the OT prophets carried on their inspired ministries within a tradition that consciously and directly went back to the ancient Mosaic covenant expressed in the Pentateuch, i.e., its first statement in Exodus–Leviticus–Numbers and its renewal in Deuteronomy."[11] Effective

---

10. On the significance of this in Deuteronomy, see J. Gary Millar, "Living at the Place of Decision: Time and Place in the Framework of Deuteronomy," in *Time and Place in Deuteronomy*, ed. J. Gordon McConville and J. Gary Millar, JSOTSup 179 (Sheffield: Sheffield Academic Press, 1994), 15–88.

11. Douglas Stuart, *Hosea–Jonah*, WBC (Waco: Word, 1987), xxxii.

communication of the biblical texts demands an awareness of the overall consistency of the Old Testament.

In the Pentateuch itself, we see something similar. As noted in the previous section, Deuteronomy 29:25 makes reference to the covenant with Yahweh and to the "fathers" of the people. Both references demand awareness of preceding material if they are to be properly understood. In Deuteronomy, Moses simply assumes that the **implied reader** was familiar with the stories about the making of the covenant, if not the texts themselves, and that the reference to the "fathers" did not need explanation. Indeed, one can't really conceive of "Israel" as a nation without understanding the importance of the election and call of Abram in Genesis 12:1–3 and the amplification of these promises into the Abrahamic covenant (Gen. 17) and Yahweh's solemn oath in Genesis 22.

Here, once again, effective communication of the message of the Pentateuch demands that the speaker highlight these things for the listener. During my years as a teacher of graduate students, I have been shocked at how many students have never read the whole of the Pentateuch. Given that they perhaps have never read the whole book of Numbers, for example, it is not surprising that they sometimes miss the development of the metanarrative in the Pentateuch.[12] If many highly motivated graduate students who sense a call to Christian ministry have never read the books of the Pentateuch in their entirety, and therefore miss its coherence, how much more likely is it that a nominal Christian or unbeliever in our churches will be more familiar with these things? Clearly, successful articulation of the message of the biblical text entails addressing this lack of awareness of the Pentateuch's coherence and its relationship to the Bible as a whole. While this undoubtedly makes the communicator's job more difficult, it contributes to more effective understanding.

COMMUNICATING LAW

Law is always a challenging genre to communicate to a contemporary

---

12. It is for this reason that I require my students to read each biblical book covered in the course in one sitting. Through this (admittedly challenging) exercise, they are able to see how the individual books develop important themes and ideas, as well as note how the ideas of one book are amplified and developed in other ones (especially in the case of the Pentateuch, which is best seen as a coherent whole). Often, students who dreaded the thought of having to read each book in one sitting found that that exercise alone opened their eyes to intricacies and consistency in the text that they had never seen before.

audience. In this section, we will examine some strategies that will help overcome this challenge.

Strategies for Communication

Address the Cultural Connotations of Law

Part of the challenge of communicating law stems from the fact that the cultural connotations of law are different when comparing the context of ancient Israel and contemporary American society. For Americans, law is primarily about rules. Anyone violating the law is a criminal, someone guilty of an offense. As in the ancient Near Eastern context, law in contemporary society serves to preserve and foster a society in which people can expect fair and equitable treatment. Consider the preamble to the U.S. Constitution, which establishes the framework within which our laws are made and enforced. It says, "We the People of the United States, in Order to form a more perfect Union, establish Justice, insure domestic Tranquility, provide for the common defence, promote the general Welfare, and secure the Blessings of Liberty to ourselves and our Posterity, do ordain and establish this Constitution for the United States of America."

Typically we don't associate the law with righteousness, and few laws mandate specific action that must be taken as a matter of righteousness. For example, no laws (that I am aware of) exist in the United States that mandate care for the poor on the part of citizens of the nation. Laws can provide incentives for such behavior, as in the case of tax deductions for charitable contributions, but they don't demand the behavior. "Good Samaritan" laws in many jurisdictions protect people from being sued if they attempt to help someone in need, but they don't mandate that everybody give help.[13] Indeed, in our legal system, "there is no duty to aid a person who is in distress or danger . . . even if the rescue can be accomplished at no cost to the rescuer. . . . In other words, the law imposes no liability upon those who stand idly by and fail to rescue a stranger who is in danger."[14]

Similarly, law in American society expressly protects the right to hold—

---

13. This can vary from jurisdiction to jurisdiction. See *American Jurisprudence*, 2nd ed., "Negligence § 106," (updated May 2007) http://www.westlaw.com. I am grateful to two attorneys, my brother Rick Vogt and Professor Craig Stern, for their work in helping me understand some of the intricacies of American jurisprudence.

14. Ibid.

and express—offensive opinions, and no laws prohibit covetousness, lust, and hatred. The law prevents *acting* on those impulses (in the form of theft, rape, and murder), but the impulses or desires themselves are not prohibited or punishable.

This contemporary connotation of law stands in marked contrast to the ancient Near Eastern conceptions of law, and the biblical sense in particular. Old Testament law not only restrained negative behavior but also mandated righteous behavior. Perhaps the contrast between American law and the requirements of the Torah may be seen most starkly in Deuteronomy 22:4, which says, "If you see someone's donkey or ox fallen on the road, do not ignore it. Help the owner get it to its feet" (TNIV). Here, unlike in American law, assistance to another was *required*, and someone failing to render assistance violated the commands of Yahweh to his people. Or, to put it another way, the Israelites *were* their brothers' keepers!

Similarly, laws such as the laws of release in Deuteronomy 15 promoted a society in which righteousness could be and was lived out. With the emphasis on community in those laws, Deuteronomy sought to foster a society in which there was an awareness of each person's obligations to the other. This was vital to the identity of the people of God.[15]

These differing connotations must be noted for the audience. Since the likely assumption on the part of the listeners will be that Torah in Israel functioned in much the same way as law functions in our society, it is helpful to address this issue directly. This can be done through illustrations, comparisons between laws, and/or preliminary sermons or lessons on the nature of Torah in ancient Israel.

Note the Purpose of the Law in Its Original Setting

An important second strategy for communicating law is to set forth the purpose of the law in its original setting. As we noted in chapter 4, identifying the purpose of the law is necessary for proper understanding of it. That purpose also must be communicated to the audience in order to help the listeners understand the relevance of the ancient text.

In seeking to help the audience understand the purpose of the law, it is not necessary to address every one of the seven questions suggested

---

15. For further discussion of the role of social justice in the identity of the people of Yahweh, see Peter T. Vogt, "Social Justice and the Vision of Deuteronomy," *JETS* 51, no. 1 (2008): 35–44.

in chapter 4. Rather, the speaker can simply summarize the conclusions drawn from the analysis.

For example, Deuteronomy 14:21 says, "Do not eat anything you find already dead. You may give it to an alien living in any of your towns, and he may eat it, or you may sell it to a foreigner. But you are a people holy to the LORD your God" (NIV). Careful analysis of the law should lead us to conclude that its purpose was to inculcate a sense of the uniqueness of Yahweh's people. The people were to abstain from the nations' eating practices. The prohibition against eating anything found dead is probably because the Israelite could not know if the blood was drained properly. According to Leviticus 17:14 (and amplified in Deut. 12:16, 23), the blood of an animal was not to be eaten by the Israelites, because "the life of every creature is in its blood." This does not mean that there is something "magical" about the blood. Rather, the blood prohibition is a culturally appropriate "object lesson" to remind the Israelites that Yahweh is the God of life and he rules all of creation. He determines what is acceptable for food and what isn't, and he is the giver of life. Since animals killed by other animals would not have had the blood drained properly, such meat was forbidden to the Israelites. Forgoing such meat reminded the Israelites that they were different from the nations around them, since they, and they alone, were the people of Yahweh, chosen to be a paradigmatic witness to the nations.[16]

Moreover, this is tied to the tripartite division of humanity into the categories of priests, Israelites, and Gentiles. The food laws, including this one, derive from a correspondence in the animal world to this division of humanity, such that animals are classified as sacrificial, clean, or unclean.[17] These categories of animals were related to the division of humanity, such that sacrificial animals went to the priest (and Yahweh), the clean animals were for the Israelites, and the unclean animals were for the Gentiles.[18] So, food prohibitions were designed to remind the Israelites that as the people of Yahweh they were different (set apart—קָדוֹשׁ) from the nations.

In seeking to communicate the sense of Deuteronomy 14:21, one must convey the original purpose to the audience. Depending on the

---

16. See Douglas K. Stuart, *Exodus*, NAC (Nashville: Broadman & Holman, 2006), 522–23.

17. See Joe M. Sprinkle, *Biblical Law and Its Relevance: A Christian Understanding and Ethical Application for Today of the Mosaic Regulations* (Lanham, MD: University Press of America, 2006), 101–23.

18. For more on this, see Gordon J. Wenham, *The Book of Leviticus*, NICOT (Grand Rapids: Eerdmans, 1979), 18–25, 165–71; and idem, *Exploring the Old Testament*, vol. 1, *A Guide to the Pentateuch* (Downers Grove, IL: InterVarsity Press, 2003), 91–93.

communicative situation, the speaker might choose to be fairly elaborate in the explanation. Alternatively, one might need to simply summarize the purpose of the law. For example, a Sunday school teacher might have more time to communicate the purpose of the law and go into some detail on the food laws, their relationship to the division of humanity, the blood prohibition, and so on. On the other hand, someone preaching a thirty-minute sermon on Deuteronomy 14:3–21 may not have much time to go into detail on each of the laws and their purposes, though he or she would need to devote at least some time to communicating these purposes.[19] In any event, the purpose of the law should be communicated to the audience in order to help the listener understand the particular law.

Discuss the Implications of Jesus' Ministry for the Law's Relevance

In communicating the meaning and message of legal texts, it is also important to discuss the ways in which Jesus' life, death, resurrection, and exaltation affect the relevance of the law in question. As we have seen, Jesus redefined the people of God around himself and thus eliminated certain aspects of the identification of the people of God. These differences must be communicated to a contemporary audience, lest the listener erroneously conclude that the law as given to the Israelites is *directly* applicable to the contemporary Christian in the same way it was applicable to the original recipients. In other words, the speaker must address the fact that the contemporary people of God are not Israel.

It may be helpful to continue thinking about Deuteronomy 14:21. We noted that the purpose of that law was to foster an awareness of the people's identity and to highlight Yahweh's sovereignty and role as the God of life. In their everyday choices of what to eat and what to avoid, the Israelites were confronted with their calling to be the people of Yahweh.

As a result of Jesus' ministry, the "object lessons" used to inculcate an awareness of that identity for the Israelites were no longer necessary. Consequently, Mark maintains that Jesus "declared all foods clean" (Mark

---

19. It should be readily apparent that much time could be spent on just a single law in Deuteronomy 14! While the decision as to how much time should be spent on any text, chapter, or book depends very much on the context of the church in which the text is presented, I am very much in favor of spending more, rather than less, time in exposition of the biblical texts. This will foster a greater sense of the relevance of the Old Testament and help combat the "functional Marcionism" described above.

7:19 ESV). That the food laws had their basis in the tripartite division of humanity and were unnecessary following Jesus' ministry may be seen further in Acts 10, in which Peter's vision confirms the dissociation of food laws and separation from the Gentiles.

As a result of Jesus' transformation of the identity of God's people, this identity was no longer primarily associated with ethnicity.[20] Accordingly, the associated reminders for the people (such as the food laws) were no longer necessary. This has implications for the contemporary relevance of Deuteronomy 14:21, as there is no longer a pressing need for God's people to keep certain food laws as a means of separating themselves from the Gentiles. It is important to clarify this for a listening audience to prevent misunderstanding of the author's intention and an inappropriate application of the text.

Here, again, how this is done will depend greatly on the ministry context. Some churches heavily emphasize theology and will have no real problem integrating these ideas into the theological environment. Other settings are marked by a lack of awareness of theological ideas, and the challenge there will be to communicate these theological ideas in a way that is appropriate for that context.

Regardless of how it is done, the theological significance of Jesus' ministry and its implications for application of Old Testament legal texts must be communicated to the contemporary audience. Not to do so is to invite misunderstanding and erroneous application of the text.

Address the Applicability of the Law in a Contemporary Setting

The final strategy for communicating the message of pentateuchal legal texts is to address how the text *does* relate to a contemporary audience. In a sense, this is really drawing conclusions from the analysis already done and conveying them to the audience.

It is important here to ensure that the speaker is prepared to illustrate the point with concrete, relevant examples. It is not enough simply to allow listeners to draw their own conclusions about the applicability of a particular law; it is too easy for erroneous conclusions or applications to be drawn. So, the speaker should provide illustrations of ways in which the legal text is relevant to a contemporary audience.

---

20. This point is made firmly by Paul in Romans 11:17–24, as well as Ephesians 2:11–3:13. See Thomas R. Schreiner, *Paul, Apostle of God's Glory in Christ: A Pauline Theology* (Downers Grove, IL: InterVarsity Press, 2001), 79–85.

Let's continue with Deuteronomy 14:21. As we have seen, the purpose of this text was to foster an awareness of the identity of God's people against the backdrop of the ancient Near Eastern world and to highlight Yahweh's supremacy (through the avoidance of eating blood). We also have noted that the redefinition of the people of God around Jesus has important implications for the relevance of this text. Specifically, since the basis for the food laws was the tripartite division of humanity and they served as reminders to the Israelites of their unique status as the people of Yahweh, does the **Christocentric** redefinition of the people render this law obsolete or entirely irrelevant for the Christian?

The answer is no, not at all. This law continues to have relevance, though not in the direct way that it did for Israel (since the modern-day people of God—the church—are not Israel). The law is applicable in any situation in a contemporary context that would parallel the situation of the original setting (with appropriate consideration for the changes wrought by Jesus' ministry). If, for example, in a contemporary context, eating a certain type of food might associate a Christian with idolatrous practices, then this is to be avoided. Like the Israelites, Christians are called to be different from those around them, and this law points to one way that this can be manifested. Under this law, Christians should avoid eating foods that would prevent someone from recognizing that they are Christians. What those foods are—and even the existence of any such foods in a given culture—will vary from context to context, even within a single culture.

For example, in some Asian cultures, food is sometimes offered to idols, which represent either spirits or the ancestors. Christians in those cultures need to carefully consider whether eating such food could cause someone to think that they believe in appeasing the spirits (which is incompatible with a Christian worldview, which holds that Christ has triumphed over *all* the spirits) or venerating ancestors as an important spiritual act of devotion. In those contexts, eating the food might lead someone to conclude that the person eating is *not* a Christian or to misconstrue the claims Christianity makes about Christ's sufficiency and power. This is akin to the Israelite eating food allowed only for the Gentiles, the context of Deuteronomy 14:21.[21] It is not that there is anything inherently "wrong" with the food

---

21. In citing this example, I am not suggesting some sort of legalism. Each individual in each context will need to evaluate the situation and come to a conclusion as to what is best, right, and proper in that given situation. It is possible that eating the food would actually enhance one's witness and therefore be a positive thing. The key is to be sensitive to the context, as well as to other people

itself in either instance. Rather, the issue is what impact eating the food may have on the believer's awareness of who he or she is as a person of God, and how others may perceive the believer.[22]

Communicating law requires a clear treatment of its relevance for a contemporary setting. This helps the listeners to have a better sense of how the law is applicable in their circumstances.

COMMUNICATING NARRATIVE

As we have seen, narrative is the most common literary genre in the Old Testament, and one that most people feel fairly comfortable with. We also have noted that Old Testament narratives are often more complex and subtle than usually recognized, which can make their interpretation somewhat challenging. It also makes communicating the meaning of the text more difficult, as the communicator is often in the position of having to challenge (either implicitly or explicitly) comfortable, familiar understandings of well-known texts.

As a genre, narrative is particularly powerful as a means of shaping, challenging, or reinforcing worldviews. Stories are disarming yet effectively convey important ideas. Communicating narrative can have the same powerful effect. In this section, we will be examining some strategies for effectively communicating the meaning of biblical narrative texts.

Strategies for Communication

Let the Story Speak for Itself

Biblical narratives are complex literary compositions. But this does not detract from their status as inspired texts. Simply put, the biblical narratives are more than great literature, to be sure, but they are not less than

---

(cf. 1 Cor. 8). This is particularly true in situations in which form and meaning are not easily separated. For more on this, see Charles H. Kraft, *Anthropology for Christian Witness* (Maryknoll, NY: Orbis, 1996), 132–47. I am grateful to my colleague Wilbur Stone for discussing this issue with me and helping me understand more about the important relationship between form and meaning.

22. In addressing this issue in 1 Corinthians 8, Paul makes it clear that the overriding concern is the well-being of someone else. That is, the concern is not what the believer is allowed to do but what will be best for another person. Similarly, the apostles' letter to the Gentiles in Acts 15 includes prohibitions of eating blood. This may be because doing so would offend the Jewish believers in the church. The point is that the concern is for someone else in each instance. That should be part of our analysis as well.

that either. Moreover, they were intended to engage the readers/listeners and draw them into the story. Awareness of these two characteristics of the genre can enable more effective communication.

The power of narrative comes in *showing* rather than *telling*. As we noted earlier, the authors of biblical narratives don't always tell the listeners what they should think about a particular person, action, or episode. Rather, they expect the listeners to be able to engage with those ideas on their own. Communication of the biblical narratives should follow the same practice to some degree. That is, the speaker should not always draw conclusions for the listeners but rather should point toward the conclusion without explicitly identifying it. "Narratives are most effective," Haddon Robinson notes, "when the audience hears the story and arrives at the speaker's ideas without the ideas being stated directly."[23] Allowing the biblical story to "speak for itself" is a powerful means of communication.

As an example, let's consider Genesis 12:10–20. Following a remarkable step of faith in leaving everything to follow the call of Yahweh and be the progenitor of the people of God, Abram demonstrates tremendous fear as he and Sarai journey to Egypt. Afraid that he will be killed because of the Egyptians' desire for his wife, Abram instructs her to say that she is his sister, not his wife. She does so, and Sarai is then taken by Pharaoh. Eventually, as a result of plagues Yahweh sends on Pharaoh's household, Sarai is returned to Abram, and they leave Egypt with greater riches.

One of the most important aspects of Moses' communicative intention here is to show the importance of trusting in Yahweh and his faithfulness. Despite the explicit promise of Yahweh's protection in verses 1–3, Abram feels the need to rely on his own "wisdom" in dealing with a dangerous situation. Ultimately, Yahweh resolves the situation, not because of Abram's righteousness, but in order to ensure that his plan is carried out as he intended.[24] Thus, this text points to Yahweh's sovereignty and the need for trusting in his sovereign rule.

In seeking to communicate this aspect of Moses' intended meaning, one could explicitly state the conclusions, much as I have done here. But a more effective strategy would be to allow the text to speak for itself. That

---

23. Haddon W. Robinson, *Biblical Preaching: The Development and Delivery of Expository Messages*, 2nd ed. (Grand Rapids: Baker, 2001), 130.

24. Much more could be said about this brief but complex passage. In particular, the differences between this Pharaoh and the one in Exodus are especially noteworthy. For more on this pericope, see Gordon J. Wenham, *Genesis 1–15*, WBC (Waco: Word, 1987), 290–92.

[handwritten margin note: Showing w/o telling is dangerous. They may not get it. This is more 'an example' that can make what "is told" easier to understand & remember.]

is, the speaker could relate the facts of the narrative, as well as highlight the promise of protection in verses 1–3. The audience would then see the disconnect between what Abram was promised and how he lived out his trust in that promise.[25] Their discovery of this disconnect (i.e., *showing*) is far more memorable and effective than if it were stated to them (*telling*). This communicative strategy seeks to capitalize on the nature of and the strengths of the genre of narrative.

Tie in Contemporary Parallels to the Biblical Story

The next strategy for communicating narratives effectively is to find contemporary parallels to the story. This allows the listener to see the relevance of the experience of ancient people for their lives in a vastly different world.

In many instances, an exact parallel of the situation described in the biblical text will not be readily available. For example, in communicating the meaning of Genesis 22, which discusses the sacrifice of Isaac, we are unlikely to find an example of God asking someone to sacrifice his or her son! To some, this means that the text is largely irrelevant for a contemporary audience. But if we can identify parallels (not replicas) of the situation described there, we will be able to help the listener have a better sense of the significance of the text.

One might, for example, be able to identify situations in which God asks a person to give up some important aspect of that person's calling. In Genesis 22, the challenge of Yahweh's demand is not limited to its moral repugnance (significant though that is); rather, the challenge comes because Abraham is asked to sacrifice *Isaac*, the child of promise. In asking Abraham to kill Isaac, Yahweh is asking Abraham to give up any sense of understanding how Yahweh's plan for restoration could possibly be fulfilled. Analogously, a situation in which a person unmistakably called to a particular ministry is then asked to give it up would be a contemporary parallel that can help illustrate Moses' intention in Genesis 22.

At first blush, it may seem difficult to come up with appropriate parallels

---

25. One obstacle is a tendency on the part of many readers to assume that the actions of the biblical "heroes" are always and unequivocally good. I have had students try to defend Abram's behavior and frame it as good, simply because they did not want to conceive of a patriarch of his stature as having flaws. That, however, is part of what is remarkable about Yahweh's plan of redemption: he uses fallen, frail human beings to help restore the creation that we ourselves corrupted!

to illustrate the point of the narrative. As you train yourself to think this way, however, you will likely find that it becomes easier. Robinson notes that "all theological questions show up in life somehow, somewhere."[26] We simply need to look for them and think carefully about the events of our own lives. Being intentional about identifying parallels will help foster more effective communication of the narrative texts.

Communicate Literary Artistry

Another communication strategy for narrative texts is to show the literary artistry of the text under consideration. This helps the listener learn how and why you came to the conclusions you arrived at and ultimately enables them to be more independent interpreters of the biblical text themselves.

We noted earlier that the biblical authors were clearly very highly skilled. They used a number of important literary techniques to communicate their intentions. Recognizing and understanding these techniques helps us understand the message of the texts more clearly. In the same way, communicating to contemporary listeners how these techniques work contributes to their understanding of the text.

One of the most important literary characteristics of the biblical narratives is the authority and omniscience (from a literary perspective) of the **narrator**. The narrator in biblical texts knows the private thoughts, motivations, and actions of everyone. Thus, the narrator is authoritative in his assertions, and the reader should not question what the narrator says. For example, if the narrator says someone is speaking deceitfully (as he indicates the sons of Jacob did in Gen. 34:13), the reader should not question that assertion. From a literary perspective, the narrator is omniscient and knows what the reader does not or cannot know.

Suppose, for example, you are leading a Bible study focusing on Genesis 21:8–14. It is possible that someone might try to mitigate Abraham's displeasure (v. 11), since it might reflect poorly on Abraham, particularly since Yahweh commands Abraham to comply with Sarah's demand. However, such an attempt to avoid acknowledging Abraham's anger cannot be justified, since the literarily omniscient narrator states that "Abraham was very

---

26. Robinson, *Biblical Preaching*, 128. See also David L. Larsen, *Telling the Old, Old Story: The Art of Narrative Preaching* (Grand Rapids: Kregel, 1995), 241–54, for more on stimulating creativity and imagination.

displeased" (וַיֵּרַע הַדָּבָר מְאֹד בְּעֵינֵי אַבְרָהָם).[27] The conventions understood by the author and audience do not allow for "second-guessing" the narrator. Helping the contemporary listener understand this aspect of the narrative will allow for proper understanding of the text.

I am not suggesting that sermons or Bible studies become lectures on literary techniques. However, it can be very effective to point out certain features of the text as they arise and note the significance of them. This, then, helps listeners learn to interpret the text for themselves, not merely listen to someone else's interpretation.[28]

Allow for Ambiguity

The final strategy we will consider for communicating the meaning of narratives is to allow for ambiguity. In many ways, this is related to the first suggestion about letting the text speak for itself. This goes beyond that, however.

We have noted that the biblical narratives are subtle in terms of conveying point of view. I suggested that it can be useful to allow the listener to draw conclusions, rather than stating them explicitly. But there are times when it really isn't clear what the author intended in some aspect of a text. Rather than seek to answer or address every possibility, it often can be more effective to allow the ambiguity to remain. In some instances, the author intended to be ambiguous. If so, then allowing the ambiguity to remain is the most responsible course of action. This is not always the author's intention, however; we don't need to seek out ambiguity in every instance.

We see an example of ambiguity in Genesis 34. At the end of the account of the rape of Dinah, Jacob confronts his sons. They reply (v. 31), הַכְזוֹנָה יַעֲשֶׂה אֶת־אֲחוֹתֵנוּ ("Should he have treated our sister like a prostitute?"). The grammar here is straightforward: the verb is a third masculine singular ("he"). But what is less clear is who, exactly, the brothers are

---

27. Gordon J. Wenham, *Genesis 16–50*, WBC (Dallas: Word, 1994), 83, notes that this is the only place in which "very displeased" is used. When God is merely "displeased," death often follows. This highlights Abraham's anger.

28. It is my conviction that men and women called to leadership in the church have an obligation to see themselves also as teachers of interpretation. That is, we are not simply to do interpretation but are also called to teach interpretation. Moreover, we should note that "teaching moments" occur every time we use Scripture in our ministries. The question that we need to consider is: What kind of interpretation are we teaching?

referring to. One obvious possibility is that they are referring to Shechem, who sought to marry Dinah after raping her. In this view, the brothers are justifying their actions to their father, on the grounds that the people of Shechem deserved their fate due to the abhorrent actions of their prince. After defiling her, he offers a bride price as high as they demand, which is tantamount to prostitution in their eyes.[29]

Another possibility is that Simeon and Levi are referring to their father. This, too, is grammatically possible and is most consistent with the flow of the narrative to this point. Shechem has not been mentioned at all in the dialogue, and the brothers' question is the only one in chapter 34 that does not specify who is being addressed. In this view, the brothers suffered Jacob's accusations silently, then justified their actions to each other on the grounds that *Jacob* had treated Dinah like a prostitute, presumably by his lack of concern for his own daughter after she had been violated.

In this situation, both interpretations are grammatically possible. The second is more consistent with other biblical narratives in that Shechem has not been mentioned in the dialogue. Typically, Hebrew narratives use the pronoun only after making the referent explicit. On the other hand, the first option is possible, given the fact that Shechem's actions are fairly easily described as treating Dinah like a prostitute.

In my estimation, Moses has deliberately ended the narrative on a note of ambiguity. Given the lack of grammatical or contextual clues and the overall negative portrayal of Jacob in the passage, it is possible that Moses sought to leave the door open. In the end, *both* Jacob and Shechem treated Dinah like a prostitute. To be sure that does not justify the actions of Jacob's sons, but it is possible that Moses wanted the listener to wrestle with this very question by leaving some ambiguity as to who is addressed in verse 31. His purpose may well have been to get the reader to conclude that both have done so.[30]

In seeking to communicate the message of Genesis 34 to a contemporary audience, it is important not to "iron out" all ambiguity. If Moses intended the reader/listener to wrestle with the question of who is addressed

---

29. See Meir Sternberg, *The Poetics of Biblical Narrative: Ideological Literature and the Drama of Reading* (Bloomington: Indiana University Press, 1985), 474–75.

30. If this is the case, then it is another example of how the author isn't explicit in stating how he feels about a person or situation. Rather, by encouraging the listener to wrestle with this question and conclude that both Jacob and Shechem have treated Dinah like a prostitute, he is showing rather than telling.

in verse 31, then any attempt to communicate his intention in this chapter must preserve that ambiguity. After all, if Moses wanted to specify who was in view, he easily could have done so. The contemporary communicator of the meaning of the text must respect the author's intention, even when it may be more satisfying to resolve all ambiguity.

We must be cautious, however, not to allow our own uncertainty about which of two viable options is correct to be conveyed as ambiguity on the part of the author. In the example above, the case for ambiguity is strengthened when we note factors such as Jacob's apparent ambivalence toward the situation, his relationship with Leah and her sons, and the fact that there are no unmitigated heroes in this account.

This aspect of communication is often particularly challenging in a contemporary Western setting. American audiences, in particular, want everything neatly resolved (preferably, as in our television shows, in thirty minutes or an hour!). We don't always appreciate ambiguity. Nevertheless, if ambiguity is present in the text, that too must be communicated to the audience.

ADDITIONAL RESOURCES

In this chapter we have examined just a few strategies for communicating the meaning and message of the Pentateuch. I am not a preacher however. Though I do preach a number of times each year, my vocation is teaching the Old Testament in an academic setting. Accordingly, I include here some resources from experts in homiletics that may be useful as you consider more deeply the questions and issues raised in this chapter. There are many other outstanding resources to assist in this endeavor; these are ones that I have found helpful, and they represent a place to start.

Gibson, Scott M., ed. *Preaching the Old Testament*. Grand Rapids: Baker, 2006.

Kaiser, Walter C., Jr. *Preaching and Teaching from the Old Testament: A Guide for the Church*. Grand Rapids: Baker, 2003.

Larsen, David L. *Telling the Old, Old Story: The Art of Narrative Preaching*. Grand Rapids: Kregel, 1995.

Robinson, Haddon W. *Biblical Preaching: The Development and Delivery of Expository Messages*. 2nd ed. Grand Rapids: Baker, 2001.

6

PUTTING IT
ALL TOGETHER

In the previous chapters, we examined some important considerations in interpreting and communicating the **genres** of law and **narrative**. We will now look at two examples, to see how the process might work from beginning to end.

In looking at these examples, it is important to bear in mind the caveat noted earlier: Interpretation is not a mechanical process; rather, it is a science *and* an art. In these examples, I will attempt to demonstrate why I make the interpretive decisions I do, in the hope that you will have a better sense of how this process works.

INTERPRETING AND COMMUNICATING
A LEGAL TEXT: LEVITICUS 19:28

Leviticus 19 contains many legal stipulations covering a variety of topics. In many ways, this chapter, more than other texts found in the Torah, seems to be a collection of miscellaneous laws, many of which are usually seen as irrelevant to contemporary believers. Verse 28 presents a particularly challenging law. It says,

Do not cut your bodies for the dead or put tattoo marks on your-selves. I am the LORD. (TNIV)

We will apply the methodology described previously and determine how this text may be relevant to the contemporary reader of Leviticus.

Interpreting the Text

We will start with the guidelines from chapter 4 for interpreting law.

Determine the Contexts of the Passage

The first consideration is the context of the passage. As you may recall, this includes the sociohistorical setting as well as the literary placing of the text (also called **co-text**).

The text we are examining is obviously part of the book of Leviticus. While some erroneously conclude that Leviticus is addressed primarily to the priestly tribe, that is not the case. White, for example, argues that the **Holiness Code** in Leviticus, "was written for priests only, and its pri-mary intent was to set the priests of Israel over and against priests of other cultures."[1] This cannot be the case, as the second verse of the book states, "Speak to the people of Israel and say to them" (Lev. 1:2 ESV). Moreover, Leviticus 19:1–2 further identifies who is being addressed, as **Yahweh** speaks to Moses and says, "Speak to the entire assembly of Israel and say to them: 'Be holy because I, the LORD your God, am holy" (TNIV). Clearly, the text is addressed to the people, as part of the instructions of Leviticus.

If we take seriously the idea that Moses is the author of the Pentateuch, and therefore of Leviticus, we can conclude that the text was written at some point following the exodus and prior to Israel's entry and settlement in the land. Leviticus was given at Sinai, as part of Yahweh's instructions as to how the people were to live as a paradigmatic witness to the nations. Part of the overall purpose, then, was to help shape the Israelites' self-understanding as the people of Yahweh and thus their worldview.

We also need to bear in mind that the Israelites were formerly slaves in Egypt. They were oppressed by the Egyptians (Exod. 1:11–14; 2:11) as

(not in glossary)

---

1. Mel White, *What the Bible Says—and Doesn't Say—About Homosexuality* (Lynchburg, VA: Soulforce, n.d.), 13; electronic version available at http://www.soulforce.org/article/homosexuality-bible (ac-cessed July 16, 2007).

well as dependent on them (Exod. 5:10–21). Part of the purpose of the Pentateuch, including Leviticus, was to help transform the Hebrews from an oppressed, frightened collection of former slaves into Israel—the nation of God's chosen people.

Further, we must remember that the Israelites were part of the broader ancient Near Eastern culture. We have seen what that means for their conception of God versus the gods and their understanding of what it means to be human. Moreover, we must consider the likelihood that the **implied reader** of Leviticus was familiar with the tenets of the ancient Near Eastern worldview.[2] If we remember that the Israelite audience of Leviticus had only recently escaped slavery in Egypt, where they were surrounded by people who shared the ancient Near Eastern view of the world and the gods, we will have a better sense of Moses' intentions in Leviticus. It is against this backdrop that Yahweh gave his instructions.

We also must consider the co-text of our verse. Leviticus 19 is part of what has been called the "Holiness Code" (H) by some critical scholars, who maintain that it is related in some way to the hypothetical source P. Some see P as incorporating H, while others think H edited and incorporated P.[3] While I don't believe that the evidence supports the view that Leviticus was composed from disparate sources after the time of Moses, it may be helpful to think of Leviticus as a whole as a "Holiness Code." After all, the purpose of the book is to foster an awareness of the need for holiness on the part of the people.

This also may be seen in Leviticus 19:2, which says, "Speak to the entire assembly of Israel and say to them: 'Be holy because I, the LORD your God, am holy" (TNIV). Thus, the co-text of Leviticus 19:28 consists of laws that detail how the people were to be holy (קְדוֹשׁ), "set apart," to Yahweh.

We should note, too, that the co-text also includes the famous command in Leviticus 19:18 that says, "You shall not take vengeance or bear a grudge against the sons of your own people, but you shall love your neighbor as yourself: I am the LORD" (ESV). The emphasis throughout the chapter on proper concern for others (vv. 9–18) suggests that another part of the communicative intention is to build awareness of what it means to love one's neighbor.

---

2. See the discussion in chaps. 2 and 3.
3. See Nobuyoshi Kiuchi, "Leviticus, Book of," *DOTP*, 523.

Awareness of the context and co-text helps us to understand this. If, for example, we maintain that the text in question was addressed to priests alone, that expectation would shape our perception of the text's meaning. For this reason, we must carefully consider the context and co-text and allow the evidence, not our presuppositions, to determine what conclusions we draw.[4] The evidence suggests that in this chapter (including the law in question in v. 28), the author explicated what it means to be set apart (holy) to Yahweh and how God's people were to live out love for their neighbors. Given the primacy of the blessing to the nations in the call of Abram in Genesis 12:1–3, it seems likely that these two intentions are interrelated.

Identify the Kind(s) of Law Involved

We must next determine the kind of laws involved here. The major consideration should be the type of law, rather than the form.

This law belongs to the category of *symbolic law*.[5] Like the other laws of this type (such as laws establishing the system of clean and unclean), this law seeks to regulate behavior to preserve the Israelites' identity as the unique people of Yahweh. It is designed to make the people stand out and be different from the people around them.

We also should note that there is no penalty explicitly associated with this law. That is, it doesn't say, "You shall not make any cuts on your body for the dead or tattoo yourselves. I am Yahweh. If you do, you must offer a sacrifice of a male goat without blemish," as other laws might. That does not mean that this law is optional, insignificant, or incidental. Rather, as we will see, it is an important part of being identifiable as the people of Yahweh, which, in turn, is vital to the success of Israel's mission to the nations.

In terms of other ways of classifying the laws, this is an **apodictic law**. It does not present a particular case; it simply says what the people are not to do. Apodictic law often is said to derive from the character or will of the lawgiver, in this case, Yahweh.

---

4. For more detailed treatments of the role of presuppositions in interpretation, see J. Scott Duvall and J. Daniel Hays, *Grasping God's Word: A Hands-on Approach to Reading, Interpreting, and Applying the Bible*, 2nd ed. (Grand Rapids: Zondervan, 2005), 87–96; Jeannine K. Brown, *Scripture as Communication: Introducing Biblical Hermeneutics* (Grand Rapids: Baker, 2007), 121–28; Craig L. Blomberg, "The Globalization of Hermeneutics," *JETS* 38, no. 4 (1995): 581–93.

5. See chapter 4. See also Christopher J. H. Wright, *Old Testament Ethics for the People of God* (Downers Grove, IL: InterVarsity Press, 2004), 297–99.

Determine the Nature of the Legal Requirement

Next, we must determine what, exactly, is being prohibited in this legislation. This allows us to better understand the author's communicative intention.

In this text, there are two prohibitions. The first says:

וְשֶׂרֶט לָנֶפֶשׁ לֹא תִתְּנוּ בִּבְשַׂרְכֶם

("You must not cut your bodies for the dead")

The second says:

וּכְתֹבֶת קַעֲקַע לֹא תִתְּנוּ בָּכֶם

("You must not incise a tattoo on yourselves")

Ritualistic cutting in mourning was known throughout the ancient Near Eastern world. The *Curse of Agade,* an epic poem written between 2200 and 2000 B.C. about the vicissitudes of a Mesopotamian empire, describes the mourning of the people following the destruction of their city by the god Enlil. It says:

The chief lamentation singer who survived those years,
For seven days and seven nights,
Put in place seven . . . drums, as if they stood at heaven's base, and
Played . . . drums for him (Enlil) among them . . .
The old women did not restrain (the cry) "Alas my city!"
The old men did not restrain (the cry) "Alas its people!"
The lamentation singer did not restrain (the cry) "Alas the Ekur!"[6]
Its young women did not restrain from tearing their hair,
Its young men did not restrain their sharp knives.
Their laments were (like) laments which Enlil's ancestors
Perform in . . . the holy lap of Enlil.
Because of this, Enlil entered his holy bedchamber, and lay down
    fasting.[7]

---

6. Ekur was the city of Enlil, which had been destroyed earlier by Naramsin, the king of Agade. It was in retaliation for this attack that Enlil destroyed Agade.
7. *The Curse of Agade,* 4:196–209. Translation from Jerrold S. Cooper, *The Curse of Agade* (Baltimore: Johns Hopkins University Press, 1983), 59, 61.

The reference to the young men not restraining their sharp knives probably refers to the practice of cutting.[8] This was done to placate the offended god, Enlil, or perhaps to attract the attention of another god who could intercede on behalf of the mourners.[9] The origin of this practice may lie in the belief that the gods cut themselves in mourning (for reasons that are not clear). A text from **Ugarit**, for example, describes the ritual mourning by the god El following the death of Baal. It says:

> "The prince, lord of the earth, has perished."
> Thereupon Latipan kindly god
> came down from his throne . . . sat on the footstool;
> and from the footstool, he sat on the ground . . .
> He poured straw of mourning on his head
> dust of wallowing on his crown. . . .
> For clothing he covered himself with a loincloth . . . ,
> he cut his skin with a stone . . .
> incisions with a razor,
> he gashed (his) cheeks and chin
> he raked the bone of his arm
> he plowed his chest like a garden
> Like a valley he raked his back.
> He raised his voice and shouted:
> Baal is dead.[10]

The idea that mourners would cut themselves to attract a god's attention or to placate an angry god makes sense in light of the fact that, as we noted previously, the gods of the ancient Near East were not understood to be omniscient or even, at times, particularly interested in the affairs of human beings. This is supported by the description of the practice in a cultic context among the priests of Baal in 1 Kings 18:28, which obviously is about getting the attention of Baal.

The Old Testament further shows that the practice of cutting in mourning was carried out among the nations in the ancient Near Eastern

---

8. Xuan Huong Thi Pham, *Mourning in the Ancient Near East and the Hebrew Bible*, JSOTSup 302 (Sheffield: Sheffield Academic Press, 1999), 17.

9. Cooper, *The Curse of Agade*, 251.

10. *KTU* 1.5, translation by Jacob Milgrom, *Leviticus 17–22*, AB (New York: Doubleday, 2000), 1693.

world. Reference to the practice among the Gentiles is found in Jeremiah 47:5, and cutting in a cultic (not mourning) context is described in 1 Kings 18:28, as just noted.

Despite the prohibition of the practice in Leviticus 19:28, cutting was known in Israel as well. Jeremiah 41:5 describes eighty men as coming to the ruins of the temple[11] after the fall of Jerusalem with shaved beards, torn clothes, and cuts on their bodies. Similarly, Jeremiah 16:6 notes that following Yahweh's judgment of the nation, "Both high and low will die in this land. They will not be buried or mourned, nor will people cut themselves or shave their heads for them" (TNIV). These references suggest that cutting was practiced in Israel as well as the nations, though it was specifically forbidden in Leviticus 19:28.[12]

In light of the cultural context and parallels elsewhere in the Old Testament, we can conclude that Leviticus sought to prohibit the Israelites from engaging in cutting as a mourning practice in an effort to attract the attention of Yahweh. Such cutting would have suggested that Yahweh was like the gods of the nations, needing dramatic actions to gain his attention or turn away his wrath.

The second part of Leviticus 19:28 prohibits tattooing oneself. The term קַעֲקַע appears only here in the Hebrew Old Testament, so it is not exactly clear what is intended. Most likely, it refers to cutting the skin and inserting pigment.[13]

The purpose of this practice was probably to identify the marked person as belonging to a particular group.[14] In some ancient Near Eastern contexts, the name of a god would be tattooed on a devotee in order to signify that the person belonged to (or was a "slave" to) that particular god.[15]

The second prohibition in Leviticus 19:28, then, forbids the Israelites to permanently mark themselves to identify themselves as followers of Yahweh. We will examine the rationale behind this law in the next section.

---

11. See Charles L. Feinberg, "Jeremiah," in *Expositor's Bible Commentary*, ed. Frank E. Gaebelein (Grand Rapids: Zondervan, 1986), 6:630–31.

12. Though the terminology is different in the other verses, using גָּדַד ("penetrate, cut") rather than שָׂרַט, ("cut"), there is no significant difference in terminology. Both words refer to incising or cutting oneself.

13. *EncJud*, s.v. "tattoo."

14. John H. Walton, Victor H. Matthews, and Mark W. Chavalas, *The IVP Bible Background Commentary: Old Testament* (Downers Grove, IL: InterVarsity Press, 2000), 134.

15. Milgrom, *Leviticus 17–22*, 1694.

Describe the Purpose of the Law in Israel

The next consideration is the purpose of the law in Israel. We have noted that Leviticus 19:28 is a *symbolic law*. As such, it differentiated the Israelites from the people around them. Being different from the nations allowed the Israelites to better demonstrate the uniqueness of the God they served. If Israel did not maintain its unique identity but instead simply began to be like the nations around it, accomplishing its mission to the nations would become impossible.

In particular, this law distinguished Israel from the nations around it in its mourning practices and identification with God.[16] In this area of life, as in all others, Israel's relationship with Yahweh demanded they be different from other people.

More specifically, the problem with the mourning practices of the peoples of other ancient Near Eastern nations was that they presupposed a worldview rejected as inadequate or false by the Old Testament. The practice of cutting most likely was practiced in other ancient Near Eastern cultures in order to attract the attention of the gods. The gods of the ancient Near Eastern world were not understood as being consistently loving, merciful, or even mindful of the peoples of their lands. Accordingly, one might need to "act out" in order to get the attention of the gods to comfort the mourner and/or to protect and preserve the spirit of the deceased in the afterlife.

In contrast to the ancient Near Eastern gods, Yahweh is loving and compassionate toward his people (Exod. 34:6–7) and is mindful of them and their needs. In addition, Yahweh knows the goings on in his creation, and thus does not need dramatic acts such as cutting to get his attention.

Consider, for example, the fact that the Torah itself provides for a thirty-day period for a captive woman to mourn the loss of her parents before she can be married to an Israelite soldier (Deut 21:13).[17] This

---

16. Milgrom argues that the purpose of this law is to eliminate slavery in Israel. Since tattoos often were used to mark or brand slaves, the prohibition of tattooing is best seen as an attempt to eliminate the practice of slavery entirely. See ibid., 1694–95. This is unlikely, however, as the context is clearly that of mourning. Moreover, the text prohibits the people from tattooing themselves (וּכְתֹבֶת קַעֲקַע לֹא תִתְּנוּ בָּכֶם "You must not incise a tattoo on yourselves"), which makes it less likely that this intends to prohibit the practice (permitted in Exod. 21:6 and Deut. 15:17) of marking a permanent slave. Indeed, those verses describe piercing the ear, not tattooing. Thus, it seems rather unlikely that this statute bans slavery altogether.

17. This is the same length of time the people mourned Moses, a significant Israelite leader (Deut. 34:8). This further demonstrates the compassion Yahweh has for the captive woman—her parents are to be mourned as fully as an Israelite leader!

reflects an awareness of the sorrows experienced by the captive woman; she does not need to engage in ritualistic cutting in order to cause God to take notice of her suffering. After all, Yahweh (through Moses) is the one who instituted this period of mourning! Similarly, we should note that the word זָכַר ("remember") in some form appears frequently in the Pentateuch. When God is the subject, it often has the sense of considering carefully, rather than simply recalling something or someone; and the word frequently associates the remembrance with action.[18] So, in contrast to the ancient Near Eastern flood accounts, God "remembered" Noah and the animals in the ark (Gen. 8:1). Likewise, he "remembered" Abraham and consequently spared Lot, Abraham's nephew, from destruction in Sodom (Gen. 19:29), and he "remembered" Rachel and granted her a child (Gen. 30:22). Each of these examples demonstrates that Yahweh is mindful of the needs of his people and carefully considers them.

Israelites in mourning who engaged in cutting would be tacitly denying that Yahweh is the kind of God that the Old Testament claims he is. They would be implying that he is similar to the gods of the nations, needing dramatic actions to capture his attention. In short, to engage in cutting would be to treat Yahweh like the gods of the nations. The prohibition on cutting seeks to prevent that from happening.

Similarly, the law in Leviticus 19:28 prohibits tattooing oneself. We noted above that this was most likely to identify the mourner as the devotee ("slave") of a particular god. It may be that the tattoo was necessary primarily to remind the gods of who belonged to them.

But the people of Yahweh were to be identified by means of the unique community they established and maintained. This radically different kind of community, marked by brotherhood, was to be the primary "mark" of the people of God, as seen in the compassionate laws (e.g., Exod. 22:21–27; Lev. 19:9–10; 13–17; 25:35–38; Deut. 15; 24:10–22). While external markers were part of that unique identity (e.g., ways of dressing, haircuts, phylacteries, and circumcision), these were to be external marks of an internal reality. The people were to have "circumcised hearts" (Deut. 10:16; 30:6) that marked their devotion to Yahweh and was the primary means of identifying them as his people. Israelites engaging in cutting or tattooing in mourning were seeking to be identified primarily by externals.

Moreover, the Pentateuch is explicit in noting that in contrast to the

---

18. Leslie C. Allen, "זכר," *NIDOTTE*, 1:1103.

ancient Near Eastern conceptions, humans are the pinnacle of Yahweh's creation and are privileged to be created in his image (Gen. 1:26–28). In his sovereignty, Yahweh determined how humans would reflect his image. Intentional, permanent disfigurement would mar God's intention and suggest that Yahweh's purposes and plans were somehow deficient and in need of "improvements." Prohibitions on permanent disfigurement in mourning were designed to maintain the Israelites' awareness of who Yahweh is and their unique place in his plans.[19] This anticipates Paul's argument in 1 Corinthians 6:12–20, where he notes that the body is the temple of the Holy Spirit and must be cared for accordingly.

In short, the first part of Leviticus 19:28 ensured that Israel did not mourn like those who had no hope. Rather, they were to live as people who knew Yahweh and the unique claims the Pentateuch made about him in comparison to the gods of the ancient Near Eastern world. Mourning itself was not discouraged.[20] Instead, the people were to mourn while recognizing that Yahweh was their God and he cared deeply about them. In this way, the Israelites would be set apart from the nations and would serve as an example of what it means to be human in relationship to Yahweh.

The second part of our verse, the prohibition on tattooing, reminded the Israelites of Yahweh's constant presence and concern for them and of the uniqueness of Yahweh and their relationship with him. Their religious identity was not to be manifested by tattoos but in the ways that Yahweh established. These included circumcision, manner of dress, acceptable foods, and the broader social structure of Israel. Moreover, they were to live out their awareness of the uniqueness of human beings created in God's image by respecting the body he created.

Identify the Applicability of the Original Purpose in a Contemporary Context

Once we have analyzed the purpose of the law in Israel, we can determine how that original purpose is relevant in a contemporary context. The key here is to look for true parallels to the original situation. This

---

19. Cf. Gordon J. Wenham, *The Book of Leviticus*, NICOT (Grand Rapids: Eerdmans, 1979), 272.

20. Examples of deep mourning are found in Genesis 23, Genesis 50:1–13, and Deuteronomy 34:8. In addition, the law requiring a period of mourning for a foreign woman captured in war (Deut. 21:13) points to a regular period of mourning in Israel, as does the prohibition from eating the tithe while in mourning (Deut. 26:14).

helps avoid the well-intentioned but nevertheless erroneous tendency to be overly broad in applying legal stipulations from the Torah.

In this instance, the original purpose may be fairly easily applied in a contemporary context. As was the case in ancient Israel, there are today competing understandings of the destiny of the dead, and even of God's attentiveness to the suffering of those in mourning. The purpose of Leviticus 19:28 in fostering a unique identity is still relevant today. Just as the Israelites were to mourn as those who had hope because of the character and power of Yahweh, the contemporary believer is to mourn in the same countercultural way. Likewise, the call to honor God as Creator through not disfiguring the body is relevant today.

We should note, moreover, that nothing in the New Testament calls this into question. The **Christocentric** redefinition of the people of God does not in any way eliminate an awareness of the uniqueness and power of God. Indeed, the New Testament makes even more explicit the hope that the dead in Christ will be raised to a glorious existence of relationship with him in meaningful service in the new heavens and the new earth (e.g., Matt. 22:23–33; 1 Cor. 15).[21]

So the legislation from Leviticus 19:28 *is* readily applicable in a contemporary setting. Like the ancient Israelites, contemporary believers must avoid any practices in mourning that would suggest that Yahweh is *not* a loving, sovereign God. He cares about his people, and there is no need for them to try to catch his attention by dramatic demonstrations.

What about the controversial issue of tattooing? Can the believer today get a tattoo? In my estimation, believers today also must seek to live out their identity primarily through internal transformation, not through external markings. Moreover, humans still are created in the image of God despite the Fall and must not substitute human wisdom for God's as to what is proper appearance. Thus, tattooing would be forbidden for the believer today, for the same reasons it was forbidden for the ancient Israelites.

---

21. Though this is not always popularly understood, the Christian hope is not for an eternal existence in heaven. Rather, Scripture (both Old Testament and New) makes clear that the hope is for a glorified existence in a restored creation. This has important implications for understanding the purpose and importance of this life, as it is best understood as preparing us for a future existence. It is not a "waiting room" that we inhabit as we wait for the time when we will be taken to our "real" lives. For a helpful introduction to this concept, see Michael E. Wittmer, *Heaven Is a Place on Earth: Why Everything You Do Matters to God* (Grand Rapids: Zondervan, 2004). See also Philip S. Johnston, *Shades of Sheol: Death and Afterlife in the Old Testament* (Downers Grove, IL: InterVarsity Press, 2002), for a discussion of Old Testament understandings and hopes for existence following death.

We should note that this law is normally assigned to the category of ceremonial law under traditional approaches to law and consequently is not seen as binding upon the Christian (though it may be relevant in learning about God's character and values). In the approach to law taken here, however, the **paradigm** is recontextualized in light of the altered circumstances of a contemporary audience. Thus, the law *is* applicable, even if recontextualized.

We now have a sense of the author's intentions for this law and the relevance of the text for a contemporary audience. We will now turn our attention to how the message of the text and its relevance can be communicated effectively to a contemporary audience.

Communicating the Text

Address the Cultural Connotations of Law

As we have noted, the first consideration in communicating the message of Leviticus 19:28 is to address the ancient cultural connotations of law. We saw in chapter 5 that contemporary listeners will have a sense of law as related to criminality and will not associate the regulations of Torah with righteousness. Moreover, the audience may well (wrongly) believe that Torah adherence is about earning salvation. The connotations of the author and audience must be addressed.

To communicate the message of Leviticus 19:28, you must address the way in which law functioned in ancient Israel by drawing distinctions between the ancient law and modern conceptions of law. Specifically, you will need to note that there is no exact parallel to this sort of law in a contemporary context, since no modern state is an exact parallel to ancient Israel. You must address the overall purpose of Torah to show that adherence to it was not part of a program of earning salvation. Finally, you will have to address the importance for the Israelites of maintaining a unique identity, as that impinges on proper understanding of Israelite law.

Note the Purpose of the Law in Its Original Setting

The second strategy for communicating a legal text is to address the purpose of the law in its original setting. This can be integrated well with addressing the cultural connotations of law, depending on your ministry setting and the communicative situation.

As we noted in the previous section, the first part of Leviticus 19:28 was given to ensure that the Israelites did not mourn in the same way as the nations around them. They had to be different, since they worshipped a radically different God than the nations did. The prohibition on tattooing also ensured that external signs of identification with Yahweh were limited to those he established.

To show the purpose of the law in its original setting, the communicator may be more or less elaborate, depending on the communicative context. Stories can be used to enhance effective communication. For example, to highlight the prohibition on cutting, I might choose at this point to briefly relate "A Tale of Two Mourners," in which I describe the mourning rituals of a fictional person from an ancient Near Eastern setting. The goal would be to convey the sense of helplessness and the concern that the gods might not care about—or be able to help—the situation. I might then introduce an Israelite mourner, who, though deeply saddened by the loss of a loved one, nevertheless is able to trust in Yahweh's goodness and power. To properly note the "missional" aspect of the law, the story could end with the two meeting and the Israelite being able to explain *why* he or she mourns so differently. Such a story can be a powerful tool in conveying the purpose of the law for the Israelites.

Discuss the Implications of Jesus' Ministry for the Law's Relevance

Next, we must note the impact of Jesus' life and ministry on how the law applies to the contemporary believer and then address the question of the impact of the Christocentric redefinition of the people of God.

This is important because there can be a tendency among many in our churches to see either a radical break from the Old Testament to the New Testament or, on the other hand, to see a direct line from the Old Testament to the New Testament. The reality is that the issues are more complex than these two simple positions allow.

Addressing the unique place of **theocratic** Israel in God's plan requires a great deal of wisdom and skill, however, as in certain contexts raising the issue may be seen as being "anti-American."[22] But it is necessary to ensure proper understanding of the biblical text.

---

22. In every course I teach, I am very careful to avoid addressing partisan political issues. In one class, a student lamented the fact that the professor's "partisan political views" were so transparent. In talking later to students from the class, it became apparent that the student felt that because I was

The Christocentric redefinition of the people of God has less impact on Leviticus 19:28 than on many other texts. This is because there is little here unique to Israelites as an ethnic identity or for the nation of Israel as a political entity.

As we noted above, the issue in Leviticus 19:28 is differentiation of the people of Yahweh from the nations in order to highlight Yahweh's supremacy. For the ancient Israelites, this differentiation was lived out in the context of a theocratic state, Israel. And this assumes that the people of God are primarily ethnically related (i.e., they have a common ancestor in Abraham), though this is not a necessary aspect of the legislation.[23] Unlike the food laws, for example, the differentiation of Israel from the nations in Leviticus 19:28 is not predicated on ethnicity. In the same way, this law does not demand a theocratic state for it to function, as did certain other laws (imposition of the death penalty for serious offenses, for example). In this case, then, the Christocentric redefinition of the people of God does not have a significant impact on how the legislation might be relevant today.

Address the Applicability of the Law in a Contemporary Setting

The final issue concerns *how* the law is relevant today. This may be more or less challenging, depending on the extent to which the law requires the political and spiritual context of ancient Israel to be effective.

As we have noted, in a paradigmatic approach to law such as that advanced here, the question is not, "Is the law binding?" but rather, "How is the law to be lived out?" The point is that the purpose of the law is still to be lived out in most instances, even if the specific application of it may not reflect the ancient context in which the law was originally promulgated and applied. Communicating how the law is applicable to listeners helps them to better understand the author's intention as well as understand and experience the power of God's Word.

In this case, although the context of the law in Leviticus 19:28 was ancient Israel, compliance with the law does not require a theocratic nation or a largely ethnically interrelated people of God. Rather, the law

---

unable to assert that the United States was a Christian nation, I was taking a partisan "political" stand against the United States!

23. It is also the case that, though assuming ethnic relationships, the Old Testament in general assumes that foreigners could and would enter into the people of God through conversion to Yahwism. This is the point of Ruth, for example, as well as many other texts.

demands that the Israelites live differently from their neighbors because of their relationship with Yahweh.

The goal is not to communicate some set of rules that would be applicable everywhere in the exact same manner in a legalistic sense but rather to foster a sensitivity to the demand for living a life of total devotion to God and to how that can be done most effectively in any given setting. We must find contemporary situations that similarly reflect the situation addressed by the law in its original setting.

One example that comes to mind stems from burial laws in my home state, Minnesota. Due in part to the severe changes in weather throughout the year, Minnesota requires that burial vaults be purchased for all gravesites, whether a casket or simply an urn is to be interred there. Though not required by law, many cemeteries and funeral homes sell vaults that are guaranteed to be leakproof for up to a hundred years. This raises a number of issues.[24] Why would it be important for the vault to be dry for a hundred years? What does that say about the hope of the deceased (or their families)?

A Christian contemplating the purchase of such a vault might well want to consider the relevance of Leviticus 19:28. As the people of God, our hope is not in the preservation of the body but rather in Christ, who will ensure its resurrection when he returns. God is able to resurrect the body and perfect it no matter what its state of decay. And since the hope for the believer is to experience the joy of fellowship with God immediately upon death and until the resurrection (cf. 1 Cor. 15; 2 Cor. 5:8), the earthly condition of the old body is unimportant. The danger is that nonbelievers might conclude that the Christian who purchases a "a hundred-year vault" believes that the ongoing condition of the body somehow matters or that God is incapable of accomplishing the resurrection if the body is too decomposed.

The law in Leviticus 19:28 represented an opportunity for the ancient Israelite to proclaim, "I don't need to cut my body for the dead, because Yahweh is a different kind of God from the gods of the nations." Similarly, it serves to offer an opportunity for the contemporary believer to proclaim, "I don't need to worry about hundred-year vaults for my loved one who died in Christ. Her hope was in God, who is surely able to do what

---

24. I realize that the issues surrounding death and mourning are legion, and this is not an attempt to be exhaustive in addressing the issue. Rather, I am seeking to address one aspect of the issue that may be affected by the paradigmatic purpose of the regulations in Leviticus 19:28.

he promised and resurrect this body to a glorified existence." In both instances, the law demands that the person of God mourn as one who has hope and as a witness to a watching world.

The second prohibition in our text is also applicable today. A believer contemplating getting a tattoo should consider the rationale for the prohibition in Leviticus 19:28. The context of our text concerns tattoos that serve to identify the religious loyalty of the bearer. Tattooing was prohibited because Yahweh established other external (circumcision, dress, phylacteries, etc.) marks for his people, as well as the more important countercultural aspects to Israelite society that were to be the marks of his people. In addition, the prohibition on tattoos served to remind the people that human beings are created in the image of God. If a believer today wanted to get a tattoo of a cross as a means of identifying herself as a follower of Christ, that would be inconsistent with the paradigm established by Leviticus 19:28. Similarly, if someone wanted to tattoo himself with an image of a heart and the name of his wife, that also would be inconsistent with the paradigm, since it entails permanent disfigurement to the human body that is created in the image of God and, for the believer, is the temple of the Holy Spirit.

Even beyond the question of the purpose of the law, however, the overriding principle should be concern for others in the context in which you live and minister. Would wearing even a nonreligious tattoo become a stumbling block for others? If so, then Paul's reminder to the Corinthians becomes relevant: "'I have the right to do anything,' you say—but not everything is beneficial. 'I have the right to do anything'—but not everything is constructive" (1 Cor. 10:23 TNIV).

INTERPRETING AND COMMUNICATING A NARRATIVE TEXT: GENESIS 39

Genesis 39 is one of the stories from Genesis that is familiar to many readers. After being sold into slavery, Joseph ends up in the household of Potiphar, one of Pharaoh's officials. There, because of Yahweh's presence, he prospers. When ordered to sleep with his master's wife, Joseph refuses and is falsely accused of attempted rape. He is thrown into prison, where he again prospers because of Yahweh's presence with him.

Because of the familiarity of the story, communicating this text is both easier and more difficult than it is with many other texts. It is easier because listeners are familiar with the characters and contents of the story. That fact, however, makes it more difficult as well. Listeners have ideas about what the text means that may or may not be in keeping with the author's intention. Encountering a different perspective may be challenging for listeners, as they may feel that their understanding is being challenged or critiqued. Effective communication of the text demands sensitivity when popular understandings or perceptions are being challenged.

No, this should make it more interesting.

Interpreting the Text

In chapter 4, we examined guidelines for the interpretation of narrative. Here, we apply those guidelines to an examination of Genesis 39.

Establish the Co-text of the Passage

We begin with analysis of the co-text of the passage. The concern here is to identify where the author's thought begins and ends. Since chapter, verse, and paragraph divisions were added much later, we need to identify natural breaks in the narrative through our own analysis of the text.

In Genesis 39, a shift in the author's thought is apparent at the outset. The previous chapter is primarily concerned with Judah, while chapter 39 opens with a resumption of the Joseph account from chapter 37. While all of Genesis 37–50 is a coherent section dealing with the "generations" (תּוֹלְדוֹת) of Jacob,[25] chapter 39 represents a new **pericope** in the life of Joseph.

The section that opens in verse 1 continues to the end of the chapter in verse 23. Though some see the end of this pericope at verse 20,[26] it is more likely that the section reflects a **chiastic** structure as follows:[27]

A Joseph Prospers in Potiphar's House (vv. 1–6a)
  B Potiphar's Wife Seduces Joseph (vv. 6b–19)
A' Joseph Prospers in Pharaoh's Prison (vv. 20–23)

---

25. See Tremper Longman III, *How to Read Genesis* (Downers Grove, IL: InterVarsity Press, 2005), 63–64.
26. Gordon J. Wenham, *Genesis 16–50*, WBC (Dallas: Word, 1994), 372–73.
27. Kenneth A. Mathews, *Genesis 11:27–50:26*, NAC (Nashville: Broadman & Holman, 2006), 729–30. The presence of the chiasm and the repeated language in the A and A' sections suggest that the pericope continues to verse 23.

That Genesis 39 is a discrete unit is further seen when noting that Genesis 40:1 begins וַיְהִי אַחַר הַדְּבָרִים הָאֵלֶּה ("some time after these things"). This indicates that a new pericope is beginning. Indeed, though the setting in chapter 40 is clearly the same as that in chapter 39, the focus in subsequent chapters is on Joseph's rise to power in Egypt.

In this instance, then, the section we are interpreting begins in verse 1 and ends in verse 23. Though the analysis demonstrates that the section corresponds to the chapter division, that is not always the case; you must not assume that because there is a chapter or verse division, there is therefore a break in the author's thought.[28]

More broadly, we should note that this text falls into the larger section dealing with the "generations" (תּוֹלְדוֹת) of Jacob (Gen. 37:2–50:26). That entire section is part of the patriarchal narratives in Genesis (Gen. 12–50), which describe God's activities on behalf of the descendants of Abraham, who was chosen to be the "tool" through which Yahweh would bless all nations on the earth and ultimately reestablish his creation in accordance with his intentions. As interesting and edifying as the stories about Joseph are, we must never forget to ask the vital hermeneutical questions, "Why did the author include this?" and "How does this story help us understand the author's purposes?" Being aware of the co-text helps us begin to answer those questions, or at least to focus more readily on them.

Identify and Label the Scenes in the Narrative

Next, we must identify the scenes in the narrative. Narratives usually consist of at least a couple of scenes that break them down into smaller units. Identifying these scenes helps to focus attention on what the author wanted to emphasize since the choice of what to include was made based on consideration of his overall purpose. Scenes are identified by looking for changes in setting, the nature of the action, and the major characters.

This text consists of six scenes. It is helpful to label each scene in terms of the main character(s) in order to more readily see the thrust of the passage. The six scenes are:

Scene One: Yahweh is with Joseph in Egypt (vv. 1–2).

---

28. In the flood narrative, for example, the account of Noah begins in Genesis 6:9 and continues through 9:17. There is no major break at chapters 7 and 9, though there is a section break at chapter 8.

Scene Two: Yahweh prospers Joseph and Potiphar's house (vv. 3–6a).

Scene Three: Joseph is faithful in the face of temptation by Potiphar's wife (vv. 6b–10).

Scene Four: Joseph is falsely accused and convicted (vv. 11–19).

Scene Five: Joseph is sent to prison (v. 20).

Scene Six: Yahweh is with Joseph in prison and prospers him there (vv. 21–23).

Note that this scene structure corresponds to the major sections in Genesis 39 that were identified above. If you determined that a scene crosses the boundaries of what were seen as the major section markers, you would probably need to reevaluate the scenes or section boundaries.[29]

While scene analysis is not the main criterion by which the meaning is ascertained, it is nevertheless a useful tool. In this instance, we can see already the emphasis on Yahweh's presence with Joseph and his role in prospering Joseph in the midst of his circumstances.

Analyze the Plot

Once scenes have been identified, we then must analyze the plot of the narrative. This can be done in a number of ways. It is most helpful to analyze plot in terms of tension, focusing on where and how the tension is built up and ultimately released (the **climax** of the narrative).

While it is possible to graph all sorts of subtle or minor changes to the tension, this really isn't necessary. Rather, a simple graph showing how each scene develops or resolves tension is all you need. Does the tension rise or fall in the scene? Remember that the determining factor is how the implied reader would have evaluated the scene, not our assessment as modern readers. Look for instances in which the implied reader has more and more questions, which are then relieved through or after the climax of the narrative.

---

29. It is possible, and even likely, that you will rethink certain elements of structure, scene, plot, etc., as you further analyze the text. As you get more into the details, you will discover new aspects of the author's intention that you may not have recognized at first glance. So, you should not think of your conception of structure or scene as "set in stone." Rather, you must be willing to adjust your thinking in light of new information about the intentions of the author. As we have noted previously, interpretation is a dynamic, not a mechanical or even necessarily linear, process.

Figure 6 illustrates the tension for the six scenes identified in the previous section. At the start of the narrative, the tension line is fairly flat, as the reader learns that Joseph has been sold to Potiphar and that Yahweh is with Joseph (vv. 1–2). The tension begins to rise slightly in the second scene, as Joseph, a foreign slave, is granted greater and greater responsibility (vv. 3–6a). In the third scene, the tension mounts considerably as Joseph is tempted by Potiphar's wife (vv. 6b–10). The implied reader is unaware of how the situation will be resolved and must therefore consider that Joseph actually might commit the adultery with which he is being tempted. Furthermore, when we note that Joseph is portrayed in Genesis 37 as a fairly spoiled boy—rebuked even by his father, who has shown tremendous favoritism toward him—who uses deceit to exacerbate the tension in his family and consolidate his position as the favored son (cf. Gen. 37:2–10), he appears to be a fairly unlikely candidate for success. In short, nothing in Genesis 37 would cause the implied reader to expect that Joseph would necessarily respond faithfully in the face of temptation.

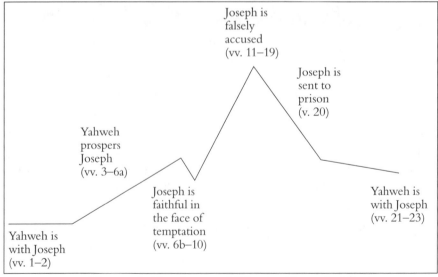

Figure 6: Tension and Plot in Genesis 39

Joseph's somewhat surprising faithfulness causes the tension line to drop slightly, as he has responded well to the temptation and, in terms of his choices at least, is out of danger. However, the tension rises starkly in the face of the false accusations of Potiphar's wife, first to the men of the household and finally to Potiphar himself (vv. 11–19). The point of highest tension comes in verse 19, when the **narrator** notes that Potiphar's anger is kindled. Presumably the question in the reader's mind now is, "If God is with Joseph (as the text says he is), what will happen to him now?" The reader—living in Moses' day or later—might expect Joseph to be executed, since according to Deuteronomy 22 execution is the punishment for free citizens in Israel guilty of rape. The fact that he is a slave makes this all the more likely. Though this is taking place in Egypt prior to the giving of the law, such laws were known throughout the ancient Near Eastern world, and the implied reader would have been prepared for such a punishment. At this point in the narrative, the reader has only questions, but no answers.

The tension is relieved when the reader learns that Joseph is thrown into prison (v. 20). His life will be spared, even if he is to experience suffering despite his innocence. Finally, the tension line flattens out as the text notes that Yahweh was once again with Joseph and causes him to prosper in prison (vv. 21–23). Despite this leveling, the tension is not at the same level it was at the beginning, since the reader is now aware that Yahweh's presence does not guarantee freedom from difficulty. The reader doesn't know what situations will arise next to challenge Joseph or how they will affect the promises Yahweh made to Abraham. Those questions are worked out in subsequent narratives in Genesis 37–50.

By constructing a graph of the tension in this way, we can more easily see what the author is seeking to emphasize. Given the turning point in this narrative, we would not look for the author's primary emphasis to be in those areas where he raises questions. Many people maintain that the communicative intention of the passage is a call to protect one's boundaries so as to avoid sexually tempting situations. But if we note where the climax of the story is from the perspective of the implied reader, we begin to see that the author is more concerned with highlighting Yahweh's faithfulness to Joseph (by virtue of his presence with him, no matter what the circumstances) than with establishing boundaries in sexually "dangerous" situations. Analysis of the plot by means of examining tension helps us to identify that fact more readily.

I am not suggesting that it is illegitimate to use a text such as Genesis 39 to discuss appropriate sexual boundaries. Indeed, Joseph's surprising faithfulness to Yahweh is found precisely in an area where we might expect a young, lonely man to falter. That is a valid point to make in communicating the text. But we must remember that the author uses this specific example of faithfulness to communicate a larger point. Communicators of the text must be able to differentiate between the meaning of the text (what the author intended to communicate to the audience) and elements used to develop that meaning. Both can be legitimate to convey in a sermon or lesson, as long as it is clear which is which.

Examine the Details of the Scenes

Once we have examined the scenes and the plot, we can begin to examine the details of the scenes. Here we are concerned with the literary devices that are used, as well as other subtle indications of the author's intention.

One of the major features of this narrative is the repetition of the idea that Yahweh was with Joseph in the midst of his dire circumstances (vv. 2, 3, 21, 23). Clearly, this idea is part of the communicative intention of the author. Coupled with this is the related idea of the prospering of Joseph and his masters (vv. 2, 3, 5, 21–23). The repetition of this related idea, as well as its close relationship to the idea of Yahweh's presence, points to the author's desire for the reader to understand that God's presence matters and that, unlike the gods of the ancient Near Eastern world, Yahweh is a God who can accomplish whatever he desires. Moreover, Yahweh's presence with and prospering of Joseph does not have anything to do with Joseph's behavior. Yahweh is said to be with Joseph and to prosper him *before* he does anything praiseworthy! This suggests that the author wanted to communicate the sovereignty of Yahweh rather than focus primarily on Joseph's righteousness.

Note, too, that the blessing is not only to Joseph but also to Potiphar and, later, to those in charge of the prison. That the foreigners would be blessed is in keeping with the idea prevalent in Genesis that Abraham's election (represented here in Joseph, a great-grandson of Abraham) was for the purpose of blessing the nations. Though obviously not completely fulfilled here, the presence of a descendant of Abraham is nevertheless a blessing to the Egyptians and helps demonstrate the importance of Israel being a vehicle through whom the nations would be blessed (Gen. 12:1–3).

We also want to note the presence of **characterization** in this pericope. Verse 6 contains **explicit characterization**, noting that Joseph was "handsome in form and appearance" (ESV). We know nothing else about Joseph's appearance (e.g., how tall he was, the length of his hair or beard, the kind of clothing he wore), so it is telling that the author included this detail, especially so since explicit characterization is relatively rare in Hebrew narratives. Why was this detail included, then? Undoubtedly it was because it helps explain why Potiphar's wife sought him, despite the inequality in status between them.[30]

Implicit characterization is found through the actions and speeches of the characters. Potiphar's wife is shown to be a woman without integrity, as she seeks to seduce Joseph, despite his protests and her status as a married woman (vv. 7, 10). Her speech to the men of the household puts blame on Potiphar for bringing Joseph into the house and is reminiscent of Adam's accusations following the Fall, when he ascribed blame to Yahweh for giving Eve to him (Gen. 3:12).[31] In contrast, Joseph's speech to her demonstrates a marked development in his character, as he has grown from an arrogant boy in Genesis 37 to a man of integrity even in the face of such temptation. Most importantly, he notes (v. 9) that God would be the offended party, which shows his awareness of Yahweh's character and role in his life. This helps set the stage for his later acknowledgement of Yahweh's sovereignty in every aspect of his life (Gen. 50:20).

In addition, there is a rich use of literary devices in this chapter. First, we should note that the garment left by Joseph when he fled Potiphar's wife ties in chapter 39 with the preceding one, where a widowed Judah unknowingly impregnates his daughter-in-law, whose needs he had been ignoring. In both instances, personal articles are used to convict a patriarch of sin, though in Joseph's case he is actually innocent. Moreover, Joseph's garment in chapter 39 represents the second time a garment of his has represented trouble for him, as Jacob's gift of a coat for Joseph caused jealousy among his brothers (Gen. 37:3–4). Moreover, there is irony in that each time Joseph is defrocked by someone acting with evil intentions (the brothers in Gen. 37 and Potiphar's wife in Gen. 39) and the situation seems hopeless, Joseph rises to greater power and influence because of Yahweh's presence with him.

---

30. Mathews, *Genesis 11:27–50:26*, 734, notes that the language used to describe the attraction of Potiphar's wife for Joseph is the same language used to describe Rebekah's attraction to Isaac in Genesis 24:64.

31. In both instances the complaint is ironic, given that the presence of both Eve and Joseph was previously seen as a blessing to Adam and Potiphar's wife, respectively.

We can also see foreshadowing in this text. Joseph's experience of bondage and deliverance, as well as the temptation to give in to the demands of the nations (represented here by Potiphar's wife), all foreshadow Israel's experience as a nation.[32] Genesis 39 shows Yahweh at work in Joseph's life, which prefigures his actions on behalf of the nation as a whole, carried out because of Yahweh's faithfulness to his covenant and "solemn oath" (Gen. 22:16) given to Abraham.

Finally, we should note the careful use of words in this chapter. Potiphar is frequently referred to as Joseph's "master" (אָדוֹן) in verses 2, 3, 7, 8, 16, 19, and 20, and Potiphar's wife refers to Joseph as a "slave" (עֶבֶד) in verses 17 and 19. This stands in contrast to the reality of Joseph's position, which is granted him by Yahweh. Despite his status as a slave, he declares in verse 9, "No one is greater in this house than I am" (NIV). This juxtaposition shows how important the hand of Yahweh was to Joseph.

None of these literary devices is present by accident. Rather, the author deliberately chose them in order to convey his intentions to the reader. It is important that we notice such things and seek to determine how they help communicate the author's intentions.

Identify the Communicative Intention of the Author

Having examined the details of the scenes and carefully examined the text, we can now identify the communicative intention of the author. At this point, we are seeking to address the question of *why* the author included the text. What did the author want the reader to understand from this text? What is the text seeking to do?

Consideration of the analysis carried out previously will answer these questions. For example, though Genesis 39 often is presented as being primarily about the importance of avoiding situations in which one might be tempted sexually, it is rather unlikely that this is the author's primary intention.[33] We can see this by examining the repeated words and ideas, the emphasis on Yahweh's sovereignty, and the importance of his presence in the chapter. We determine the communicative intention in light of the context of the original author and audience; how would *they* have seen the text?

In this case, the emphasis is on Yahweh's sovereignty. The repetition

---

32. Wenham, *Genesis 16–50*, 378.
33. That is not to say that the topic is unimportant, or unaddressed in the chapter. Rather, it is not the primary intention of the author.

of the statement that Yahweh was with Joseph (vv. 2, 3, 21, 23), and the prosperity that resulted (vv. 2, 3, 5, 21-23), points to this as a central idea of the text. Moreover, the climax of the narrative, as we have seen, comes when Joseph is thrown into prison and Yahweh is said to be with Joseph even there (v. 23). This suggests that the author wanted to highlight the faithfulness of Yahweh, who is with his people in the midst of difficult, even catastrophic, situations.

Rather than being primarily about avoiding sexual temptation, then, this text is present to highlight the faithfulness and sovereignty of Yahweh. An important theme of the Pentateuch is Yahweh's acting to reverse the effects of the Fall and restore creation to its intended glory. Part of Yahweh's plan involved the election of Abraham and the elevation of Israel as a paradigmatic nation. This account of Joseph's life communicated to Moses' audience the idea that Yahweh is faithful to his promises. Accordingly, they could trust in Yahweh even as they faced difficult situations. Genesis 39 reminded and encouraged the Israelites as they faced adversities and the temptation to be like the nations around them. It contributed to the shaping of the Israelites' worldview by highlighting Yahweh's faithfulness to Joseph, who represented the nation's experience in later years.

At the same time, Joseph is shown to be a man of character. We have noted his development from the unlikely candidate for success in Genesis 37 to a man of character in chapter 39. This highlights for the audience the importance of being loyal to Yahweh in their actions. As we have seen, Israel was called to show loyalty to Yahweh in every aspect of life, big and small. Joseph's faithfulness was intended as an example of what it means to be loyal to Yahweh in challenging situations. Given that Joseph presumably could have had sex with Potiphar's wife without being caught, his faithfulness to Yahweh is all the more striking and noteworthy as an example to the Israelites.

It should be readily apparent that this understanding of the author's communicative intention is, first of all, based on the data of the text. It is a result of a careful consideration of the details of the text as well as an understanding of the themes and priorities of the book as a whole. Second, it is more than simply a tale with a "moral." It is simply not the case that the "moral" of this story is something like, "People of God should avoid situations where they could be sexually compromised." While this is undoubtedly true, it is too simplistic and does not do justice to the deeply theological intentions of the author.

Recontextualize the Text for a Contemporary Setting

Finally, we are in a position to ask how the text is relevant for a contemporary audience. That is, the communicative intention of the author must be recontextualized for a different setting.

In the case of Genesis 39, I have suggested that the author's communicative intention was primarily to highlight Yahweh's sovereignty and his faithfulness to his promise and covenant with Abraham. A secondary aspect was Joseph's faithfulness to Yahweh, as that demonstrated the importance of showing loyalty to Yahweh in every circumstance.

As we seek to recontextualize this intention for a contemporary setting, it is apparent that much of that intention is relevant for the people of God today. There is little or nothing here that is limited to the particular ethnic or national elements of ancient Israel, so the Christocentric redefinition of the people of God does not significantly alter the relevance or applicability of the text for a contemporary audience.

In light of that, the text functions today much as it did for the original audience. It reminds the contemporary believer of God's faithfulness to his promises to Abraham. Indeed, as most contemporary Christians are themselves the fruit of God's faithfulness to that promise (in that most contemporary Christians are ethnically Gentile and thus are blessed through the ministry of Israel as fulfilled in Christ), the account in Genesis 39 perhaps has even more poignancy. As with ancient Israel, the modern people of God are called to trust in and know Yahweh and the things he has promised and done for his people.

Moreover, the call to be a blessing to the nations has not ended with the Christocentric redefinition of God's people. So, the contemporary people of God must seek to be a witness to those not yet identified with Christ. Just as Joseph's faithfulness in Genesis 39 showed the original audience the importance of being faithful to Yahweh, it functions in much the same way for the contemporary people of God. We, no less than the ancient Israelites, are called to model faithfulness to God to a watching world.

Communicating the Text

We can now turn our attention to some strategies for effectively communicating the message of this text. Here, we will seek to apply the principles introduced in chapter 5.

Let the Story Speak for Itself

An important strategy for communicating narratives is to allow the story to speak for itself. As we saw in chapter 5, narratives are uniquely suited to *showing* rather than *telling*. The story can convey truth powerfully, and it is not necessary for the communicator to always draw explicit conclusions for the listener.

In seeking to communicate the meaning of Genesis 39, one could simply state the communicative intention, much as I have done in the previous section. But it might be more effective to allow the listeners to draw their own conclusions about the intention of the author.

One way to do this is to raise questions that point to the author's communicative intention. You may leave these questions unanswered, but they are addressed by the text itself. For example, in looking at Genesis 39, I might recount the story in a dramatic fashion (ensuring that details are not made up for dramatic purposes but are part of the biblical text). I could then say something like, "What could possibly account for Joseph's success in such dire circumstances? His years of experience in management? His extensive education? Or is there some other factor that might explain this unlikely success story?" I would hope that the listeners would note the repetition of the statement that Yahweh was with Joseph and correctly conclude that this is the reason for Joseph's success.

Similarly, to help the listener understand why this account is present in the text at this point and how it contributes to the development of the **metanarrative** of the Old Testament, I might raise questions like, "Why did Yahweh choose to protect and preserve Joseph in the midst of these situations? Was it because of his consistent, demonstrated righteousness? Or was there another reason?" If I have set the stage with a depiction or discussion of Genesis 37 (either in another lesson or sermon or earlier in the same one), the listener should be able to conclude that the preservation of Joseph was *not* because of Joseph's righteousness but because of Yahweh's faithfulness. This is particularly effective if the thematic elements of the book have been dealt with consistently, allowing the listener to draw on that knowledge in coming to conclusions about this text.

Another strategy is to be explicit about what the text is *not* about in order to direct the listener to a different conclusion. This is especially valuable if there is a widespread or popular misconception of what the text is about, as I believe is often the case with this text. As noted, many people associate this text primarily with avoidance of dangerously tempting sexual situations, a view that is not really supported by the data of the text. To communicate this idea and help listeners begin to think about the text differently, I might say, "To many, this text is about how to avoid sexual sin. That is an important and vital concept in our overly sexualized culture. But that doesn't really take into consideration the original setting of this text and the issues faced by the original listeners." I could follow this with a discussion of the text that points to an alternative conclusion. I might then say, "If it's not about avoiding sexual sin, why did Moses include this? What might he have wanted the original audience to know, and why would that be important to them?" This allows the listeners to draw their own conclusions.

These are merely suggestions as to how you might allow the story to speak for itself. Effective communication of Genesis 39 (or any text, for that matter) will require sensitive awareness of the audience's knowledge of the text and its context, and careful, intentional efforts to point in the direction the author intended. This can be a very powerful means of communicating the meaning of the text in a contemporary setting.

Tie in Contemporary Parallels to the Biblical Story

A second strategy is to look for contemporary parallels to the biblical story. This helps the listener see the relevance of an ancient text for the radically different circumstances faced by God's people today.

In looking for contemporary parallels, it is important that you be aware of the significance of Jesus' redefinition of the people of God around himself. This ensures that parallels raised are in fact truly parallel and not off base due to the implications of that redefinition. It is also important to concentrate on looking for parallels that illustrate/illuminate the author's primary intention, not simply some minor aspect of the story.

For Genesis 39, you would need to look for instances in contemporary society in which someone was experiencing misfortune or difficulty that was used by God to further his purposes. The parallel need not be exact, of course (since neither you nor I are likely to know many people sold into slavery!), but it should be illustrative of the author's intentionality. In this case, I might use an example like this:

I know a man who was severely injured after being kicked in the head by a horse. I'll call him "Bob." Bob nearly died as a result of his injuries, and he spent a significant amount of time in the hospital recovering from those injuries and the many operations that were necessary to repair his skull and face. He was assigned a room in the hospital with another severely sick or injured patient, who was extremely disagreeable. I'll call him "Joe." Joe had no friends or family who visited him, except for one work colleague who visited once at the end of his time in the hospital. Even the doctors and nurses grew exasperated with him and, out of frustration with him, would ignore his petty complaints and requests.

One night Bob had an opportunity to share the gospel with Joe. He was able to point out that even though Joe was friendless in the world, there was someone who loved him deeply and perfectly and was longing to be with him always. Jesus, Bob explained, will never leave or abandon those who have entered into relationship with him. Joe came to know the Lord that night.

Bob spent much of his time in the hospital wondering about why he was suffering and, more importantly, marveling at the care he was receiving. He came to see that in that experience, the Lord was with him. And because of that, a person dearly loved by God and created in his image came to know Jesus. Bob will readily testify that his suffering was worth it if it allowed Joe to come to know Jesus and experience the abundant life Jesus offered. Bob said to me once, "If I had to get kicked in the head by a horse so that [Joe] could know Jesus, it was worth it."

Obviously this is not a replica of the situation faced by Joseph in Genesis 39. But it is a parallel that helps illustrate the author's communicative intention. Note especially how the illustration highlights the missional or witness aspect of the story. Joseph was preserved and protected in order to carry out Yahweh's plan to bless all nations. The illustration above captures this important aspect of the message of the text.

Note too that the illustration works even in light of Jesus' redefinition of the people of God. That is, even though Jesus has redefined the people of God around himself, they are still called to be witnesses to a watching world, and God is still sovereign and at work in the lives of his people to accomplish his plans for all creation.

Communicate Literary Artistry

The artistry of the text is important to communicate to the contemporary listener. This is particularly true since many people are unaccustomed to seeing the biblical text as being especially artfully written.

Here, I might note the use of the word *garment* and how the word and the thematic element—since the garment in question in 37:3 is specifically a coat (כְּתֹנֶת) and not the more general word *garment* (בֶּגֶד), which appears in 39:13—tie chapters 37 to 39 together. Perhaps this would help the contemporary audience to see the coherence of the biblical narratives and that they are not just random stories to be plucked out of their literary settings.

Foreshadowing is another aspect of the literary artistry that should be highlighted here. The fact that Joseph's situation anticipates the experience of the nation as a whole helps communicate important truths about God and his relationship with his people. For the Israelites, the knowledge of Yahweh's presence and power was necessary as they faced challenging or dangerous circumstances. Noting this literary element helps the contemporary listener understand better how to interpret the text[34] and how to use the data of the text to draw conclusions. It also helps demonstrate the relevance of the text for today.

Allow for Ambiguity

The final consideration in communicating the message of the text is to allow for ambiguity. We must ask if the author intended to leave questions unanswered. He may not have, but if ambiguity is intended by the author, then our efforts at communicating the author's intention should not eliminate that ambiguity.

Only one place in Genesis 39 represents a possible case of intentional ambiguity on the author's part. When Potiphar heard the false allegations of his wife against Joseph, verse 19 recounts that "his anger began to burn."

---

34. As noted in chapter 5, an important aspect of communicating biblical texts is teaching others how to interpret the texts for themselves. If we who are called to ministry of the Word fail to do this, we will either teach people that biblical interpretation is only for the "initiated," which may cause them to give up attempting to interpret on their own, or we will imply that interpreters can do anything with the text that they want, as long as the conclusions they come to are orthodox. Both conclusions are dangerous.

What is unclear is the object of his anger. One obvious possibility is that his anger burned against Joseph. He was, after all, the one accused. But the fact that Joseph was not executed for this violation (particularly since the statement בָּא־אֵלַי, "he came into me," also could be taken as a euphemism for sexual intercourse,[35] implying that Joseph raped Potiphar's wife) may suggest that Potiphar's anger also was directed at his wife. The author may have deliberately left the door open to this possibility and didn't intend for certainty on this point.[36]

Here, again, the key is what the author intended. If the author intended ambiguity, that intentionality must be respected and communicated. On the other hand, if the author intended certainty, then our attempts to communicate the author's intentions must reflect that as well. It is important not to override the author's intentions in an effort to be engaging or provocative, no matter how well-intentioned that desire may be.

In this instance, I think it is most likely that Moses is intentionally ambiguous as to whom Potiphar was most angry at. He may have been angry at both or the situation in general.[37] Because the text doesn't specify, and good reasons exist for thinking that he was angry at his wife (primarily because Joseph wasn't executed), this is a reasonable conclusion. Accordingly, I would attempt to convey that ambiguity.

In this way, the message of Genesis 39, though part of an ancient text addressed to a vastly different audience, may be seen as relevant for a contemporary audience. Effective communication of the meaning of the biblical texts is vital to the health and vitality of the church today, no less than it was for Moses' original audience.

---

35. Wenham, *Genesis 16–50*, 376.
36. Ibid., 377.
37. John E. Hartley, *Genesis*, NIBC (Peabody, MA: Hendrickson, 2000), 321. See also Nahum Sarna, *Genesis* בראשית: *The Traditional Hebrew Text with the New JPS Translation* (Philadelphia: JPS, 1989), 275.

GLOSSARY

Akkadian. An Old Babylonian language, written in cuneiform script. Many ancient Near Eastern parallel texts are written in this language.

allegorical. An approach to interpretation in which spiritual or moral truths are taught through textual images and events, such that there is a one-to-one correspondence between the textual details and the real world.

apodictic law. Law presented as commands, without reference to specific cases ("thou shalt . . ." or "thou shalt not . . .").

Biblia Hebraica Stuttgartensia (*BHS*). The primary Hebrew text that is the basis for most English (and other modern language) translations. *BHS* is based on the Leningrad Codex, a manuscript dating to A.D. 1008.

casuistic law. Case law; laws presented in the form of a specific case ("if . . . , then . . .").

catechetical. Instruction in religious doctrine, often presented in a question-and-answer format.

characterization. The kind of information provided about a character in a text. (See also *implicit characterization* and *explicit characterization*.)

chiastic. Term applied to a text demonstrating a structure in which the second half is symmetrical with the first half (known as a chiasm or chiasmus), such as A-B-C-D paralleled by D'-C'-B'-A'.

Christian reconstructionist. See *theonomist*.

Christocentric. Christ-centered.

climax. The turning point in a narrative; the point at which the implied reader's questions begin to be resolved.

contextualization. The task of applying an author's intended meaning in a different setting. It also can refer to the fact that the original meaning is communicated in a particular setting with its unique norms, values, etc.

co-text. The literary placement or setting of a text. Sometimes referred to as "literary context."

Dead Sea Scrolls. A collection of scrolls dating from the mid-third century B.C. to A.D. 135 that includes all or part of every book of the Old Testament except Esther. Found in caves near Qumran.

Decalogue. Ten Commandments.

documentary hypothesis. A theory as to the origin of the Pentateuch that was dominant from the mid-nineteenth century until the late twentieth century. It maintains that the Pentateuch is the result of a combination of several hypothetical sources, usually identified as J, E, D, and P.

explicit characterization. Specific information provided about a character, such as appearance, height, or manner of dress. (See also *characterization* and *implicit characterization*.)

genre. Type or class of literature. The two main genres in the Pentateuch are narrative and law.

Holiness Code. A hypothetical source some scholars see in Leviticus. Found in Leviticus 17–26 and referred to as H.

Horeb. Another name for Mount Sinai that is used frequently in Deuteronomy.

implicit characterization. What is conveyed about characters through what they do, say, or think. (See also *characterization* and *explicit characterization*.)

implied author. A literary presentation of the real-life, empirical author. What the empirical author presents about himself or herself in the text. What the implied author reveals in his/her text is usually less than the totality of what he or she thinks or knows about a particular subject.

implied reader. The ideal reader envisioned by the author of a text. The implied reader knows the conventions, language, and context well enough to properly understand the author's communicative intention.

LXX. See *Septuagint (LXX)*.

Masoretes. Jewish scribes who sought to preserve the consonantal text of the Hebrew Old Testament, resulting in the Masoretic Text.

Masoretic Text. A Hebrew version of the Old Testament that is the product of a "school" of Jewish scribes who worked from about the sixth to tenth centuries A.D.

metanarrative. An overarching story or concept that illustrates how the world is understood.

narrative. A selective record of a series of events that uses shared conventions to convey the author's communicative intention in an engaging manner.

narrator. The representation of the implied author in a narrative. The narrator conveys the "voice" of the implied author. In most biblical narratives, the narrator is omniscient, knowing the thoughts, emotions, and private actions of the characters.

orthography. The study of writing and spelling of a language.

paradigm. A typical or especially clear example of something that can be applied in other analogous situations.

patristic. Dealing with the era of the early church (the era of the church "fathers"), usually considered to be from the end of the first century to the end of the eighth century.

pericope. A self-contained story from a larger book/narrative.

primeval history. The earliest history of humanity; often used in reference to Genesis 1–11.

recontextualization. The application of the meaning of a text into a situation different from its original context.

Reformed. A term applied to ideas, beliefs, or people associated with a Calvinistic Protestant theological system.

Samaritan Pentateuch (SP). A version of the Pentateuch dating to the second century B.C. used by the residents of Samaria. These part-Jewish, part-Gentile people rejected the rest of the Old Testament and used this expanded form of the Pentateuch in worship.

Septuagint (LXX). A Greek translation of the Old Testament dating to the third century B.C. It differs in many instances from the Masoretic Text.

suzerain. The superior party in a feudal system. The one to whom loyalty is due. Often referred to as the "Great King" in ancient Near Eastern studies. (Cf. *vassal*.)

theocratic. Term referring to a system in which God rules a nation or people directly.

theonomist. A person who adheres to the belief system of theonomy, which is the belief that the whole of the Old Testament law—including its penalties—should be applied to civil society today. Theonomy is also known as Christian reconstructionism.

Transjordanian. A term referring to "across the Jordan," from the perspective of the land of Israel.

Ugarit. Capital of an empire of the same name that existed in the late second millennium B.C., located in northern Syria.

vassal. The inferior party in a feudal system or in ancient Near Eastern political treaties. This is the party expected to show loyalty to the suzerain ("Great King").

vowel letters. Hebrew consonants (א, ה, י, and ו) that can at points function as vowels. The practice of using vowel letters emerged in about the tenth century B.C. to assist in pronouncing the unpointed consonantal text.

Yahweh. Personal name of the God of Israel, related to the Hebrew word הָיָה ("he was"). See Exodus 3:14–15.

OTHER BOOKS IN THIS SERIES

Interpreting the Historical Books

An Exegetical Handbook
Handbooks for Old Testament Exegesis
Robert B. Chisholm Jr.
Series Editor, David M. Howard Jr.

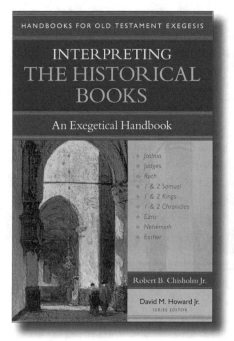

A VALUABLE REFERENCE TOOL FOR STUDENTS AND PASTORS, the Handbooks for Old Testament Exegesis (HOTE) series gives readers an enhanced understanding of different Old Testament genres and strategies for interpretation. *Interpreting the Historical Books* begins by exploring the components of narrative-setting, characterization, and plot, and then develops the major theological themes in each of the Old Testament historical books. A glossary is included, along with samples of moving from exegesis to proclamation.

Robert B. Chisholm Jr., Th.D., Dallas Theological Seminary, is chair of the Old Testament department and professor of Old Testament studies at Dallas Theological Seminary. His books include *Handbook on the Prophets*, *A Workbook for Intermediate Hebrew*, and *From Exegesis to Exposition: A Practical Guide to Using Biblical Hebrew*.

978-0-8254-2764-0 | 232 pages | Paperback

Interpreting the Psalms
An Exegetical Handbook
Handbooks for Old Testament Exegesis
Mark D. Futato
Series Editor, David M. Howard Jr.

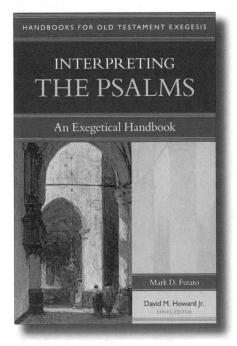

A HELPFUL RESOURCE FOR PASTORS AND STUDENTS, *Interpreting the Psalms* begins by explaining the nature of Hebrew poetry and the purpose of the Psalms. An accomplished scholar of the Psalms, Mark Futato next explores issues related to properly interpreting Israel's songbook and concludes with a sample of moving from interpretation to proclamation. A glossary is included. As readers work through *Interpreting the Psalms*, they will begin to see and interpret the poetic texts as the writings were intended to be understood.

Mark D. Futato, Ph.D., The Catholic University of America, is the Robert L. Maclellan Professor of Old Testament at Reformed Theological Seminary in Orlando. He is the author of several volumes on the Psalms, including *Transformed by Praise* and *Joy Comes in the Morning*, as well as the grammar *Beginning Biblical Hebrew*.

978-0-8254-2765-7 | 240 pages | Paperback

OTHER ACADEMIC &
PROFESSIONAL BOOKS

Ancient Near Eastern Themes
in Biblical Theology
Jeffrey J. Niehaus

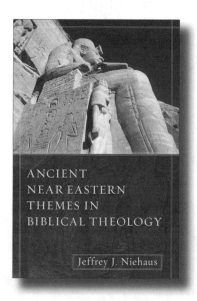

ANCIENT
NEAR EASTERN
THEMES IN
BIBLICAL THEOLOGY

Jeffrey J. Niehaus

A N EXPLANATION OF THE MANY PARALLELS between the Old Testament (and Bible as a whole) and the ancient Near East, this work includes creation and flood narratives, common literary and legal forms, supposed acts of deities and the God of the Bible, and more. Niehaus shows that these parallels cannot be identified as cases of biblical dependence on ancient Near Eastern theology. Instead he proposes that they represent "a shared theological structure of ideas in the ancient Near East, a structure that finds its most complete and true form in the Old and New Testaments." This comprehensive and enlightening resource promises to help students and discerning Bible readers to intellectually grasp and appreciate the overarching story of the Bible within its cultural development.

Jeffrey J. Niehaus, Ph.D., Harvard University, is professor of Old Testament at Gordon-Conwell Theological Seminary. He is the author of *God at Sinai: Covenant and Theophany in the Bible and the Ancient Near East* as well as commentaries on Amos and Obadiah. He has also written articles for *JETS*, *JBL*, *Tyndale Bulletin*, and *Vetus Testamentum*.

978-0-8254-3360-3 | 208 pages | Paperback

Available wherever books are sold
■■■■■ **www.kregel.com** ■■■

Giving the Sense
Understanding and Using Old Testament Historical Texts
Editors, David M. Howard Jr. and Michael A. Grisanti

A UNIQUE COLLECTION OF OLD TESTAMENT ESSAYS, this work is designed to supplement courses on the history of Israel. These essays survey the four major periods of Israel's history and explore the theological, literary, historical, and archaeological dimensions of each era. The last two essays discuss how to preach from the Old Testament historical narratives. Almost all of the essays are original to this project. This book moves from methodological issues to an overview of Israel's history, and finally to many diverse topics, all relating to ancient Israel.

David M. Howard Jr., Ph.D., The University of Michigan, is professor of Old Testament at Bethel Theological Seminary, St. Paul, MN. He is the author of four books, including *An Introduction to the Old Testament Historical Books* and *Joshua* in the New American Commentary Series.

Michael A. Grisanti, Ph.D., Dallas Theological Seminary, is associate professor of Old Testament at The Master's Seminary in Sun Valley, CA, and is a contributor to the *New International Dictionary of Old Testament Theology and Exegesis* and *Missions in a New Millennium: Change and Challenges in World Missions*.

978-0-8254-2892-0 | 482 pages | Paperback

Using Old Testament Hebrew in Preaching
A Guide for Students and Pastors
Paul D. Wegner

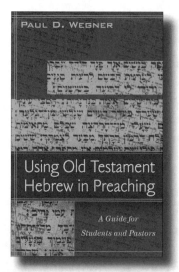

A WORKABLE GUIDE FOR PREACHING, this book unearths the treasures of the Old Testament. Wegner emphasizes the importance of using Hebrew in preparation for preaching and offers a detailed process for moving from text to exegesis to proclamation. Students and ministers will profit from the bibliographies and illustrations. *Using Old Testament Hebrew in Preaching* will motivate any serious Bible student to delve into the richness of the Hebrew Old Testament and to proclaim its truths with confidence.

Paul D. Wegner is professor of Old Testament at Phoenix Seminary and is the author of three books, *Bible Introduction: The Journey from Texts to Translations*, *A Student's Guide to Textual Criticism of the Bible*, and *An Examination of Kingship and Messianic Expectation in Isaiah 1–35*.

978-0-8254-3936-0 | 176 pages | Paperback